SECOND EDITION

THE EXPANDED DIALECTICAL BEHAVIOR THERAPY SKILLS TRAINING MANUAL

DBT for Self-Help, and Individual and Group Treatment Settings

Lane Pederson, PsyD, LP, DBTC
with Cortney Sidwell Pederson, MSW, LICSW, DBTC

"There are many books and resources about DBT, but Pederson's second edition rises above as an essential. His strategies have been proven in more than a decade of successful clinical practice, and this new book makes his important work accessible to all."

-Cathy Moonshine, PhD, MSCP, MAC, CADC III
Author of *Acquiring Competency and Achieving Proficiency with DBT, Volume I & II*

"Dr. Pederson's second edition is a must-have book for both clinicians and clients. As a leader in "Second-wave DBT," Dr. Pederson continues to generate amazing and accessible content. This book provides new perspectives on the classic skill modules by expanding explanations and introducing new examples and handouts. One of the most exciting aspects of this book is the expansion of six other skill modules: Dialectics, Cognitive Modification, Problem-Solving, Addictions, Building a Satisfying Life, and Social Media. The new modules help clinicians and clients address their real world struggles by providing meaningful content and fresh ideas. I strongly encourage you to add this book to your desktop collection of works. I have been working with DBT theory, skills, and concepts since the 1990's with thousands of clients and this work will be immediately integrated into my training and practice."

-Mark Carlson, PsyD, LP
Founder & CEO of Mental Health Systems, specializing in DBT treatment

"An abundance of fresh, practical and reproducible tools for healthier emotions and stronger resilience. The second edition updates and expands the knowledge, research and skills so greatly needed by mental health professionals and those who depend upon us to deliver the most accessible, effective and well-proven treatments possible."

-Henry Emmons, MD
Author of *The Chemistry of Joy and The Chemistry of Calm*

Published by
PESI Publishing & Media
PESI, Inc
3839 White Ave
Eau Claire, WI 54703

Cover: Amy Rubenzer
Editing: Hazel Bird
Layout: Amy Rubenzer

Printed in the United States of America

ISBN: 9781683730460

Lane Pederson, PsyD, LP, DBTC is not affiliated or associated with Marsha M. Linehan, PhD, ABPP, or her organizations

PESI Publishing
& Media
www.pesipublishing.com

To Sophie and Sawyer, awesome in their strong minds, pure hearts, and creative undertakings.

Table of Contents

DBT Programs and Therapists: A Brief Introduction
DBT Skills: An Orientation for Clients
Your Life Vision (LV)
Worksheet: Life Vision: Big Picture
DBT Beliefs About Skills Training
Common DBT Program Expectations
The Diary Card: Monitoring What Is Important
Diary Card Instructions
Worksheet: Standard Diary Card
Worksheet: Blank Diary Card
The Basics of Behavior
Using Behavior and Solution Analysis to Create Change
Visual Behavior and Solution Analysis
Worksheet: Visual Behavior and Solution Analysis
Worksheet: Behavior and Solution Analysis: Short Form
Worksheet: Behavior and Solution Analysis: Long Form

Introduction to Dialectics
Dialectical Principles
Dialectics Worksheet 1: Conflicts 1
Dialectics Worksheet 2: Conflicts 2
Dialectics Worksheet 3: Exercises
Dialectics Applied to Other Skills

Introduction to Mindfulness
Myths About Mindfulness
States of Mind
The Path to Wise Mind (WM)
Focus on Nonjudgmental Stance (NJS)
Focus on One-Mindfulness (OM)
Mindfulness Worksheet 1: Sticky Judgments
Mindfulness Exercises
Mindfulness Worksheet 2: Daily Practice
Mindfulness Worksheet 3: 10 Days to a 10-Minute Meditation Practice
Mindfulness Worksheet 4: Maintain Your Meditation Practice

Two Steps to Wise Mind/Clear Mind
Nonjudgmental Stance (NJS), Self-Acceptance, and Change
One Moment at a Time
Bridge-Burning (BB)
Building New Bridges
Additions Worksheet 3: Bridge-Burning
Urge-Surfing (US): Ride the Wave
Emotions, Thoughts, and Situations That Trigger Addictive Behavior
Observing and Describing the Effects of Addictive Behavior
Additions Worksheet 4: Describing the Consequences of Addictive Behaviors
Cycle of Emotions and Ineffective/Addictive Behaviors
Mental Illness and the Ineffective/Addictive Behavior Cycle
Observing and Describing a Process of Relapse
Opposite to Emotion With Urges for Addictive Behavior: U-Turn
Addictions Worksheet 5: Opposite to Emotion and the U-Turn
Using DEAR MAN to Refuse Addictive Behaviors
Using Interpersonal Effectiveness to Address Resentments
Addictions Worksheet 6: Resentments
Using Interpersonal Effectiveness to Make Amends
Addictions Worksheet 7: Making Amends

Introduction to Building a Satisfying Life
Using ROUTINE (RO)
Everyday Care
Building a Satisfying Life Worksheet 1: Activities List
Building a Satisfying Life Worksheet 2: My Routines and Schedule
Building a Satisfying Life Worksheet 3: Small Routines

Introduction to Social Media
MEDIA (ME)
Other Suggestions

Teaching DBT Skills: Methods and Styles
Developing Skills in the Face of Barriers
Other Skills Training Tips
Clinical Policies, Contingencies, and Related Forms

Master Skills List
Source Citations for Modules and Skills
Other Resources
Bibliography

About the Authors

Dr. Lane Pederson has provided dialectical behavior therapy (DBT) training and consultation to over 10,000 professionals in the United States, Australia, South Africa, Canada, and Mexico through his company Lane Pederson and Associates, LLC (www.DrLanePederson.com). Notable organizations for which he has provided training include Walter Reed National Military Hospital, the United States Navy, the Federal Bureau of Prisons, the Ontario Psychological Association, and Psychotherapy Networker. He has provided DBT training for community mental health agencies, chemical dependency treatment centers, hospital and residential care settings, and therapists in forensic settings. Dr. Pederson also co-owns Acacia Therapy and Health Training in South Africa.

Dr. Pederson's DBT publications include *The Expanded Dialectical Behavior Therapy Skills Training Manual* (2nd ed., PESI, 2017), *Dialectical Behavior Therapy: A Contemporary Guide for Practitioners* (Wiley-Blackwell, 2015), and *Dialectical Behavior Therapy Skills Training in Integrated Dual Disorder Treatment Settings* (PESI, 2013).

A real-world practitioner, Dr. Pederson co-owns Mental Health Systems, PC (MHS), one of the largest DBT-specialized practices in the United States (www.mhs-dbt.com). At MHS Dr. Pederson has developed DBT programs for adolescents, adults, people with dual disorders, and people with developmental disabilities. He has served in clinical and training directorships, has directed practice-based clinical outcome studies, and has overseen the care of thousands of clients in need of intensive outpatient services.

Dr. Pederson also founded the Dialectical Behavior Therapy National Certification and Accreditation Association, the first active organization to certify DBT providers and accredit DBT programs (www. dbtncaa.com).

Dr. Pederson currently serves on the advisory board for the doctoral counseling program at Saint Mary's University of Minnesota and is a peer reviewer for *Forensic Scholars Today*.

Cortney Sidwell Pederson, MSW, LICSW, DBTC, is a DBT therapist who has designed and implemented customized DBT programs. She has worked with adolescents and adults in multiple settings across various levels of care. She also participates in the ongoing training and supervision of DBT therapists at MHS.

The authors live in Minnesota with their children and dogs.

Preface

Our work with dialectical behavior therapy (DBT) began in 1999 at a nonprofit community mental health center. Back then, DBT was just starting to disseminate into the mental health field as an exciting and promising treatment for clients with borderline personality disorder.

The DBT program developed in that setting had a group format based on a day-treatment model and level of care. This program treated some of the highest-risk clients in Minneapolis, Saint Paul, and the surrounding areas and developed a reputation for effective work with difficult client problems.

Our DBT team was active, involved, motivated, and idealistic. We studied and discussed the foundations of DBT and made it our own, always looking to our clients for information on how to improve the program. We wanted to provide the best possible service, and we cared passionately about the program and our clients.

As our DBT program developed, we consulted constantly, pushed each other to be more effective therapists, and looked to our clients to inform the treatment. Our approach embodied evidence-based practice as defined by the American Psychological Association many years later. Many of the therapists from this DBT day-treatment program went on to develop successful DBT programs in other clinics or in their own practices over the next decade.

Today DBT continues to be at a critical crossroads. The direction promoted by the original developer of DBT, Marsha M. Linehan, is strict adherence to the model as she researched it, called standard DBT. Often falsely framed as a mandate that DBT therapists need to follow, this direction has and will continue to lead to an ossification of the approach. The other direction is applying DBT guided by contemporary evidence-based practices. This direction recognizes that the service delivery framework and protocols of standard DBT are effective for many clients, but that they also fail to address the needs of many other clients across settings and levels of care. One size does not fit all.

Rhetoric aside, what does the evidence say? The jury has been in for some time, and the evidence is clear that adherence to particular treatment manuals and the use of "specific ingredients" in therapy accounts for little change, whereas the application of a credible approach in the context of therapeutic factors (i.e., common factors) results in robust change (Duncan, 2015; Duncan, Miller, Wampold, & Hubble, 2010; Wampold, 2001). Moreover, the amount of research on adapted DBT has far outpaced the research on the original model, and a recent randomized clinical trial component study comparing standard DBT to two dismantled conditions—DBT skills training and individual DBT therapy respectively—found no significant differences between the DBT applications in terms of the major variables of interest and no reliable differences in terms of the minor variables of interest (Linehan et al., 2015). This finding is especially interesting considering that the study had methodological flaws that favored standard DBT.

Bluntly, for those who can separate ego, money, politics, and blind allegiance from DBT practice, employing varied applications across settings fits best with the research evidence and provides much-needed diversity in DBT services for clients. For a full discussion of applications of DBT and the accompanying research, the reader is referred to Pederson (2015).

We therefore encourage DBT providers and programs to follow the evidence, *especially the clinical outcomes you monitor in your own settings with your own clients*. The theory and interventions that comprise DBT reside in the public domain and are owned by *no one*. DBT has already transcended its original developer to reach many diverse clients and settings, in many adapted service delivery frameworks, creating a "second wave" in DBT.

Whichever wave you ride, we wish you the best in your application of the skills in this book to your clients in your setting, DBT or otherwise!

Acknowledgments

Thank you to Mike Conner, Mike Olson, Linda Jackson, Claire Zelasko, Teresa Fisher, Shannon Becker, and all our friends at PESI. PESI operates with high integrity, and we appreciate their support.

Many thanks to Hazel Bird, an outstanding editor whose skill and judgment are second to none. Her contributions improved this book beyond measure. And thanks to Julia Fox, who complied a long list of mindfulness exercises for the book.

A special acknowledgment goes to everyone at Mental Health Systems, PC (MHS). The staff and therapists at MHS are first rate, and we appreciate working alongside talented, committed, and fun people.

Next, we thank the thousands of people we have trained in DBT, who have continuously stimulated our curiosity and passion with their questions and comments. Many of the improvements in this edition come from our experiences together.

Finally, much gratitude goes to past, current, and future clients, who constitute the best teachers and the greatest inspiration. Thank you for your willingness to practice skills in the toughest of situations.

About This Book:
An Orientation for Therapists

Skills training is essential to dialectical behavior therapy (DBT), and the focus of this book is almost exclusively on teaching DBT skills to clients. We refer readers interested in full explanations of DBT theory, philosophy, and interventions to practitioner books such as *Dialectical Behavior Therapy: A Contemporary Guide for Practitioners* (Pederson, 2015) or *Dialectical Behavior Therapy in Private Practice: A Practical and Comprehensive Guide* (Marra, 2005).

Most DBT manuals focus on four main skills modules: Mindfulness, Distress Tolerance, Emotion Regulation, and Interpersonal Effectiveness. This book approaches the skills in these classic modules with fresh perspectives, expanded explanations, and new examples and worksheets. New skills have also been added to these modules on occasion, and a couple of original acronyms have been changed to improve their use. Readers who use a variety of skills manuals will notice these differences and can choose what to teach or apply based on what works best for their clients.

Building on the four original modules, this book expands into six other skills modules:

- **Dialectics:** The Dialectics module teaches clients how to find the middle path with thinking and behaviors. As with mindfulness, learning dialectics can be complicated, but the concepts are enormously helpful when understood and applied.

- **Cognitive Modification:** Cognitive skills have largely been absent from DBT. This manual takes a dialectical view of cognitive interventions and adapts them to fit DBT philosophies, teaching clients how to observe and shift thinking without invalidating feelings.

- **Problem-Solving:** Clients often try to solve problems through Emotion Mind or through haphazard, trial-and-error approaches that are not grounded in values. The Problem-Solving module teaches clients how to define problems and options and how to take action guided by their priorities, goals, and values.

- **Addictions:** This module explains the basics of addictions and assists with pattern recognition, decreasing vulnerability, managing triggers, and applying specialized skills to overcoming addictive behaviors of all types.

- **Building a Satisfying Life:** Research shows the importance of structure, and this module teaches clients how to structure a satisfying life with ongoing and balanced routines.

- **Social Media:** Sorely needed in this age, the Social Media module teaches clients the essentials of using media responsibility to both harness its resources and avoid its pitfalls.

To be manageable to therapists and clients, each module and its component skills are made up of enough text to explain the concepts but not so much as to overwhelm the reader or compromise the book's direct usefulness in therapy. To an extent, the amount of text on each skill has been designed to make bibliotherapy a doable assignment for the majority of clients. In addition, as you or your clients study the skills in this book, you will notice a fair amount of repetition of concepts. The repetition and overlap are by design so that central ideas can be overlearned. Effective ideas can take on a mantra-like presence in time, orienting clients toward skill use.

Clients can typically start with the Getting Started section for a basic orientation to DBT and then work systematically through the book. An overview module on dialectics comes first and is followed by modules focusing on the original four skill sets. At the end of the book there is an additional section for therapists that covers skills training strategies, practical information about facilitating skills groups, and common clinical policies and related forms. Although this section is intended for therapists, clients can read these sections if interested to further demystify the approach.

What's New in This Edition?

The second edition of this book contains several changes and additions to improve its use. First, the original text underwent extensive rewrites and editing. This included reordering the skills to feature dialectics and the original four modules first followed by the supplemental modules, as well as putting all of the content that primarily addresses therapists at the back of the book. These changes maximize flow and readability.

Second, the binding was changed from a traditional format to a spiral-bound presentation. Seasoned skills trainers who want the book to lay flat during sessions and at the copy machine will appreciate this change. In another format change, this edition adds online access to worksheets and exercises.

Next, in terms of content, this edition elaborates on important concepts such as nutrition and exercise in the Emotion Regulation module and adds guidelines on making friends in the Interpersonal Effectiveness module. It also rolls the previously standalone module on boundaries into Interpersonal Effectiveness. Further, special attention was paid to the Dialectics and Mindfulness modules, with explanations that increase their understandability along with new exercises and practice for both modules. Moreover, and following the spirit of the first edition, completely new DBT skills and skills modules were added, including much-needed modules that address social media use and addictions. While the new skills and modules along with the supplemental skills and modules from the first edition should be considered "add-ons" to the original four DBT modules, there are certainly clients who will benefit from learning them.

Other add-ons to the original edition for the therapist section include suggestions and guidelines for training skills, establishing a curriculum, and developing a timeline for getting through skills curriculums.

Whereas additions were made to improve the manual, there were also a couple of instances of addition by subtraction. Although the Dialectics module was greatly expanded, the acronym MIDDLE Cs from the original edition was dropped based on feedback from therapists and clients who found it to be confusing. Other text or exercises found to be cumbersome or of limited usefulness were also deleted. Sometimes less is more.

Getting Started

Learning the Foundations of DBT Skills Training and Programs

DBT Programs and Therapists: A Brief Introduction

DBT stands for dialectical behavior therapy. It was developed at the University of Washington, Seattle, to treat people who have chronic suicidal thinking and behaviors as well as other behaviors that disrupt their lives. The first population studied with DBT was women with borderline personality disorder (BPD).

Today, we know that DBT can be used across clinical settings for a variety of problems (Dimeff & Koerner, 2007; Marra, 2005; Moonshine, 2008a, 2008b; Pederson, 2015) and that the skills and approach can be used proactively in health and growth models, too.

DBT is an approach that is both highly innovative and highly derivative (dialectically speaking). The developer of DBT largely borrowed and repackaged ideas and interventions that already had substantial research and practice to support their use. In *Cognitive-Behavioral Treatment of Borderline Personality Disorder*, the original book on DBT, the developer wrote:

> *The strategies used in this and the following chapters no doubt have many things in common with aspects of the other varieties of psychotherapy currently in use . . . In writing the original draft of this volume, I read every other treatment manual I could find, both behavioral and nonbehavioral. I also read books that tell new therapists how they are supposed to behave in therapy. Whenever I found a treatment component or strategy that was the same or similar to one used in DBT, I tried to use similar language to describe it. Thus, in a sense, much of this manual has been "stolen" from preceding manuals. (Linehan, 1993a, p. 200)*

In therapy, few ideas are completely new and novel, but really committing to and emphasizing helpful concepts can be hugely effective. One established concept that DBT commits to and emphasizes is that we need to learn skills to replace behaviors that do not work and to address problems that cause difficulties in how we function in life.

Teaching skills is essential to DBT. Skills can be taught in either individual or group settings (or both), and they are the central focus of this book. In addition to skills training, DBT emphasizes an accepting, nonjudgmental, and validating approach to clients. This approach means that DBT therapists work hard to understand their clients' world and acknowledge how their clients' feelings, thoughts, and behaviors make sense given the context of their unique situation.

This validating approach is dialectically balanced with change strategies. Often, therapists will use validation to demonstrate that they understand the client's emotions and perspectives, which then opens the client to try something different with skills and behaviors. The DBT change strategies used by therapists follow traditional behaviorism but also borrow from cognitive, psychodynamic, strategic, and gestalt orientations, among others. DBT approximates a technically eclectic approach, yet it is a standalone therapy in that it has its own guiding theory, called the biosocial theory. This guiding theory postulates that people struggle with emotion dysregulation, which has a reciprocal relationship with invalidating environments. In other words, many people have sensitive and intense emotions, and important people in their lives can have difficulty understanding and supporting them.

Supplementing this great variety of change strategies, DBT incorporates the concepts of mindfulness and the philosophical underpinnings of dialectics, as explained in the Dialectics module.

DBT therapists use specialized tools in therapy such as diary cards and behavior and solution analysis. Diary cards are forms on which clients track symptoms, feelings, and skills; they also help therapists to determine the priorities for treatment and to monitor their clients' progress. Behavior and solution analysis is used to understand behaviors and highlight options to help clients use their skills. In addition to these tools, therapists address safety issues and anything that interferes with treatment (e.g., lateness, absences, nonparticipation) before any other issues.

DBT therapists are sometimes available by phone to coach clients between appointments, and they actively seek consultation from other therapists to stay motivated and effective.

Note that some therapists may not be DBT oriented but may follow another approach and/or integrate approaches along with teaching skills from DBT and other sources. It is fine for therapists to use different approaches; the key is whether the approach works for their clients. Therapists and clients can address the therapist's approach during a discussion on informed consent prior to treatment.

Some DBT therapists treat clients only in individual sessions whereas other DBT therapists treat groups of clients in DBT programs. DBT programs vary in their design based on differing treatment settings. "How much" DBT clients require depends on their unique needs and the level of care indicated. As a general rule, if clients have ongoing safety issues or are chronically unstable, they will probably do best in a structured, comprehensive DBT program.

Professional opinions vary about whether structured DBT programs should follow the original researched treatment model—called standard DBT—but research is clear that high adherence to treatment models (i.e., therapists' close application of the therapy manual as it was originally researched) has no meaningful effect on clinical outcomes (Webb, DeRubeis, & Barber, 2010), so not all programs have to follow the standard model exactly. Be wary of therapists who talk of "real" DBT and who denigrate other therapists or programs. Effective therapists are backed up by their own clinical outcomes and need not talk down others.

The evidence-based practice of psychology, as defined by the American Psychological Association (2005), recognizes that researched models are not directly applicable to all real-world clients, so changes based on therapists' expertise guided by clients' culture, characteristics, and preferences are frequently indicated. Just as different treatment models may be equally beneficial, a variety of established DBT models are too. In other words, one size does not fit all. Monitoring clinical outcomes and adjusting treatment based on that information are also essential parts of evidence-based practice.

In the real world, DBT programs are developed to meet the needs of unique clients seen in unique settings because clients can be different in important ways from research subjects (e.g., differences in gender, ethnicity, diagnosis, and level of care needed). The approach should be customized to the client. The standard model and other applications of DBT are both valid, and the effectiveness of one over another depends on the needs of the client.

That said, clients choosing a DBT program or therapist should be sure to ask about how clinical outcomes (data showing how effective the treatment is) are monitored and used to adjust the therapy approach for clients and to make overall program improvements.

Overall, the therapeutic factors of "good" DBT (and other treatments for BPD) will include clear structure, rules, and expectations; a dialectical balance of validation and change; and an accepting, respectful, and active therapist who supports *and* challenges clients (Weinberg, Ronningstam, Goldblatt, Schechter, & Maltsberger, 2011). These factors, applied through active and collaborative alliances between clients and therapists with agreed-upon goals, will strongly predict positive change (Duncan, 2015; Wampold, 2001).

DBT Skills: An Orientation for Clients

DBT skills are life skills. Many people have said they wish these skills had been taught to them in school. A lot of people never had the opportunity to learn skills and perhaps did not have parents or anyone else model a skillful approach to life.

If we do not see examples of skills being used, it is more difficult to learn them. As you study these skills, be on the lookout for instances in which you might see skill use by others around you. Actively learn through seeking connections and through practice. Practice makes you prepared to use skills successfully in your life.

Learning DBT skills is like learning a new language. Try to encourage yourself to minimize frustration. Skills you might not have learned yet will be referenced as you study other skills. This cross-referencing is deliberate, so over time you can see the connections between skills and how they work together.

When we learn languages, words have limited meaning until they are put into sentences and then into conversations. Skills work the same way. Keep connecting skills to other skills until they form chains of new behaviors, creating a more satisfying life. We learn a language through speaking it, and we need to practice skill use every day until it is fluent.

Many of the skills' names are referred to by their abbreviations (e.g., Opposite to Emotion is often called "O2E"). The relevant abbreviation is included after the name of the skill in the main headings, so you will associate the names with the abbreviations. For example, Wise Mind is abbreviated as WM, so it will appear as Wise Mind (WM) in the heading for the section about this skill. You can also reference the Master Skills List (Appendix 1) to see the skills' names and abbreviations along with brief explanations.

All of the teachings and applications have a "core concept" identified. This idea orients you to a primary function or purpose of the skill. As you study and practice each skill, try to see how the core concept might relate to your priorities, goals, and values. If you can make a connection, it will help to motivate you to continue refining that skill until it is a part of your life. Again, remember that learning skills requires daily review and practice.

Work on creating your satisfying life one step at a time, one day at a time. We all have setbacks. These setbacks and problems can be opportunities to learn and grow. Do not give up. There are many people like you on similar journeys. Keep moving and stay open to influencing and being influenced by your world.

Before jumping in, it helps to outline your Life Vision, which you can do using the information in the following section. Your Life Vision will help to guide you through the skills and keep your journey on track.

Your Life Vision (LV)

■ *CORE CONCEPT*: Knowing why you want change motivates you to change.

A vision for your life helps to define your priorities, goals, and values and the roads you want to explore on your journey. Fill in each section of this worksheet and refer to it often. Do not judge what you write down: It is your vision based on your wants, needs, and dreams. You will start with a big picture and then fill in details. Imagine you are painting a picture of a life you can work toward.

Look to revise the picture every few months as you grow and improve. We are all works in progress, so changes will happen. Use the information from this exercise for treatment planning with your therapist.

It is difficult for some people to imagine a satisfying life, especially when they feel hopeless and out of options. If this is your situation, fill in what you can today and do not judge yourself for struggling with this exercise. As you learn skills over time, your Life Vision will come into focus.

Life Vision: Big Picture

Describe your priorities, goals, and values in life. What is important to you? What is your motivation to improve? How would you like life to be different? What would/will you be doing if you managed life more effectively? What are your dreams in life?

Describe what you do effectively and what you want to improve on in each of the following areas. See how what you do and what you want to improve on will be part of the big picture. Remember that even small details can impact your Life Vision in important ways. Create one manageable goal for each area that builds on what you do effectively or that addresses a desired improvement. Keep in mind that your goals may change each time you review and revise this section.

Mental health:

_____

Physical health:

_____

Chemical health (avoiding drugs and alcohol):

_____

Education (school or self-education):

_____

Productivity (work or projects):

_____

Volunteering or contributions:

_____

Finances:

_____

Home environment:

_____

Leisure:

_____

Family:

_____

Friends:

_____

Spirituality (religion or other connection):

_____

Choose one to three of your goals in these areas to get started on, and refer to them often.

Describe your strengths and other resources that will help you move toward your goal(s):

_____

_____

_____

_____

Describe how your life will be different when you accomplish your goal(s):

_____

_____

_____

_____

DBT Beliefs About Skills Training

■ *CORE CONCEPT:* How we think about ourselves and skills training influences the success of our efforts.

The following beliefs provide a foundation for DBT and skills training. Consider these beliefs and use them to guide your approach to learning and practicing skills.

You are Doing Your Best

Everyone, yourself included, is doing their best in any given moment. None of us want to make mistakes, offend or put off others, or fall into behaviors that do not work. When you or someone else is struggling, remember this belief and dialectically balance it with the next belief.

Skills Help You to Do Better

Even though we are all doing our best, sometimes our best is not enough to be effective. We all have room for improvement, and skills help us to be better.

Skills Apply to All Areas of Your Life

Most of us are skillful sometimes, with some people, in some situations. The trick is to learn how to use skills in our trouble spots: with those people and situations in which we struggle to be effective. Practice your skills across all areas of your life.

No Matter How a Problem Happened or Who Caused it to Happen, You are Responsible for a Skillful Response

Sometimes we cause our own problems and sometimes other people cause them. Sometimes stuff just happens. Blaming others and getting into behaviors that make situations worse tends to be self-defeating. Focus less on how something happened or who should be accountable, and focus more on how you can be skillful in the face of difficulties.

Skills Work When You Work the Skills

Merriam-Webster's Dictionary defines a skill as "the ability to do something that comes from training, experience, or practice." You have to work the skills for the skills to work. It's that simple. Do not give up. Again, practice your skills to be more skillful.

Common DBT Program Expectations

■ *CORE CONCEPT:* Program expectations create a safe and effective environment.

The following guidelines are intended to build and maintain a healthy and effective skills training program for you and others. Note that your particular therapist or program may have different or additional expectations. Whatever the expectations, they are intended to maximize benefit for all.

Be an active participant

Research is clear that the active participation of clients is essential to achieving a successful outcome (for any therapy). You will get out of treatment what you put into it. Commit yourself to throwing your whole self into the process!

Be on time, stay the whole time, and attend all scheduled sessions

Not only is following this tip respectful but it is also essential for the treatment to work for you. You cannot participate and benefit if you miss sessions. Prioritize your attendance and address barriers with your therapist and/or program group. If you have to miss a session or be late, be sure to call ahead.

Offer support, validation, and suggestions to others

Research shows that group cohesion, simply defined as how connected members are to one another, has a major effect on treatment outcomes. Building relationships between members happens through active involvement with one another, which is also a great way to develop your interpersonal effectiveness skills.

See and encourage the best in others (and yourself)

Give others the benefit of the doubt. People are in skills programs because they need to learn and practice new behaviors, including new skills for relating to other people. Remember that we are all doing our best, and continue to help those who are struggling with support, validation, and suggestions.

Never glamorize or promote harmful behaviors to others

Some programs strictly forbid discussing behaviors that could be "contagious" to others. Other programs allow members to discuss harmful behaviors such as self-injury or drug use in general, and not specific, detail. When this is allowed, the goal is to understand the behavior and provide alternatives and solutions in the form of skills. Research shows that behavior contagion can happen for better or worse; in other words, contagious behavior can be harmful or helpful. Never talk about harmful behaviors in ways that might tempt other people to try them out. In all skills programs, we want to promote skillful behavior. Make skill use contagious in your program.

Keep relationships skillful

Romantic and other private relationships are not allowed between members of the same skills program. Any time members spend time together outside the program, those members must commit to not engage in any problem or potentially problematic behaviors together (e.g., drinking alcohol, doing drugs, gambling, and self-injury are strictly forbidden). When relationships negatively affect the treatment process, the relevant therapy-interfering behavior issues will be addressed.

Be willing to ask for, and accept, help

If you allow yourself to be a little vulnerable to others and a lot willing to accept their feedback, other people will too, and you will have an effective program group.

Keep others' information confidential

Confidentiality is vital for therapy to be a safe place to share. Do not disclose who else is in your DBT program or any information that other people discuss in the program. What is discussed in the program room stays in the program room.

Complete your diary card, homework, and behavioral and solution analysis as assigned

Your therapist(s) and the program have your best interests in mind, and they want to see you do well. Assignments are given for your benefit. If you are struggling with an assignment and need help, or otherwise wish to negotiate what is assigned, then you must use your interpersonal effectiveness skills. As a rule, DBT therapists will not change expectations and assignments if clients are not skillful in negotiating because they do not want to reinforce unskillful behavior. Further, even when a client is skillful, the expectation or assignment sometimes cannot be changed.

The Diary Card: Monitoring What Is Important

■ *CORE CONCEPT:* The diary card is an essential tool to build awareness and skill use.

DBT uses diary cards to track anything that is important to your well-being, treatment, and/or process of change as well as the skills you practice. In many ways the diary card is like an abbreviated journal that guides your progress, and it provides a wealth of information that allows your therapist to support you and set priorities for your time in session together.

Some DBT therapists and programs use a standard diary card that monitors issues common to DBT clients, and other therapists and programs create specialized diary cards for particular client populations (e.g., children, adolescents, people with chronic pain) or even for each individual client. Examples of a standard diary card and a blank one for you to customize are included in this section.

Standard diary cards usually track three key areas of concern for many DBT clients: urges to act on suicide (called "SI," for suicide ideation), urges to act on self-injury (called "SIB," for self-injurious behavior), and urges to act on therapy-interfering behaviors (called "TIB," for therapy-interfering behavior). Urges toward suicidal behavior relate to any action that could or would result in your death; urges toward self-injury relate to any nonlethal action that causes harm and/or tissue damage; and urges toward therapy-interfering behavior relate to any action that would interrupt or otherwise interfere with having an effective course of treatment. Common therapy-interfering behavior includes being late to or absent from appointments, avoiding talking about relevant issues, violating boundaries in relationships, and not following skill plans.

In addition to tracking SI, SIB, and TIB, people with substance abuse and/or other addictions will typically track urges to engage in those addictive behaviors, and people with eating disorders will track urges to engage in overeating, binging, purging, and/or restriction and over-exercising, depending on the particular areas of concern.

To round out the diary card, there is space to list the skills you practiced, space to write down feelings, and space to record gratefulness. Some therapists and programs will also have clients monitor their treatment goals and objectives on the diary card.

Diary cards are typically completed every day, preferably at the same time, with information from the previous 24 hours from time it is filled out. Most people spend 5 to 15 minutes to thoughtfully complete the card. Forgetting to fill it out or choosing not to fill it out can be considered TIBs.

Some people feel overwhelmed when they first learn about the diary card, and they may initially struggle to complete it. If that happens for you, stick with it. It will get easier and will be a great aid to you reaching your goals. If you are not sure whether a diary card is worthwhile for you, consider these benefits of completing one consistently:

- What you track and monitor on the diary card is what changes. Observing and describing what you experience and being accountable to yourself to practice skills keep you moving forward.

- You will notice patterns in your emotions, urges, and symptoms over time, and this awareness will make you more effective in using your skills.

- You will be able to validate your emotions and reinforce your efforts and effective skill use, eventually seeing positive changes over time.

- When something is not improving, or even getting worse, you can rally your resources and skills around addressing it.

- You and/or your therapist can quickly see what is happening and determine your priorities, which will better guide your sessions and make better use of your time together.

To get started, you can either use the standard diary card provided or customize your own.

Diary Card Instructions

■ *CORE CONCEPT:* The diary card develops awareness and accountability to help you build a satisfying life.

Follow these directions:

- Fill out your diary card *every* day. Do it thoughtfully and bring the card to all sessions.

- For the Medications (RX) section, use Y (yes) if you took all medications as prescribed. If you missed any medications, or if you did not take them as prescribed, use N (no).

- For the Depression (DEP), Anxiety (ANX), and Anger (ANG) sections, use a scale of 10 to 0 and rate the *range* of your feelings by noting the highest and lowest levels (e.g., 8–4 for ANX) or, alternatively, rate your average levels (e.g., 7 for DEP).

- For the Suicidal Ideation (SI), Self-Injurious Behavior (SIB), and Therapy-Interfering Behavior (TIB) sections, use a scale of 10 to 0 and rate the *range* of your urges by noting the highest and lowest levels or, alternatively, rate your average levels. Additionally, use a Y (yes) or N (no) to note whether you *acted* on SI, SIB, or TIB urges or if you took any planning steps toward acting on them (e.g., 9–3/N or, alternatively, 6/N for SIB urges). (Note: People with substance abuse, other addictions, or eating disorder behaviors can record urges and action under either SIB or TIB or under one of the "Other" columns on this diary card.)

- For the Energy section, use a scale of 10 to 0 and rate the *range* of your energy level or, alternatively, rate your average level or energy.

- For the Sleep section, note the total number of hours of sleep. Make a slash mark (/) through the number if the sleep was not restful or was broken.

- For the Eat section, use Y (yes) for *any* efforts to eat healthy foods in a balanced manner. If you did not make any efforts, use N (no).

- For the EX (Exercise) section, use Y for *any* efforts to get movement into your day in a balanced manner. If you did not make any efforts, use N (no).

- For the Other sections, track any other symptoms, urges, behaviors, or issues important to your treatment.

- Under each category list the skills (see Appendix 1: Master Skills List) you used to address and manage what you recorded in that area (e.g., for DEP, you might list PL, O2E, and DM).

- On the back side of the diary card, write down your feelings, positive events, and what you are grateful for each day.

- Keep your diary cards. They are for you to track and monitor your progress.

If you use the blank diary card:

- Determine, perhaps with the help of your therapist, what you need to and want to monitor on the diary card. You will probably borrow from the categories above as well as develop your own customized areas.

- It is recommended that you follow the same principles and guidelines listed above even if the content of your diary card is different.

Standard Diary Card (Front)

	RX	DEP	ANX	ANG	SI	SIB	TIB	Energy	Sleep	Eat	EX	Other	Other
MON													
Skills													
TUE													
Skills													
WED													
Skills													
THU													
Skills													
FRI													
Skills													
SAT													
Skills													
SUN													
Skills													

Standard Diary Card (Back)

	Feelings	Positive Experiences	Gratefulness
Monday			
Tuesday			
Wednesday			
Thursday			
Friday			
Saturday			
Sunday			

Blank Diary Card (Front)

MON													
Skills													
TUE													
Skills													
WED													
Skills													
THU													
Skills													
FRI													
Skills													
SAT													
Skills													
SUN													
Skills													

Blank Diary Card (Back)

	Feelings	Positive Experiences	Gratefulness
Monday			
Tuesday			
Wednesday			
Thursday			
Friday			
Saturday			
Sunday			

The Basics of Behavior

■ *CORE CONCEPT*: The basics of behavior help you to understand why you choose certain behaviors and how you can change ineffective ones.

The principles of behaviorism are always happening around us, shaping our and others' behaviors. When we understand some basics about behaviors and how they work, then we are better able to change unhelpful behaviors and to replace them with skills. This section will get you started, but, because understanding behaviors can be complicated, you might want to do some of your own research and explore these concepts further with your therapist or program group.

Reinforcement

Reinforcement means rewarding a behavior so that it happens more often. There are two types of reinforcement, positive and negative. Related to reinforcement, positive does not mean "good" and negative "bad." Instead, positive means that something desirable is *added* following a behavior, and negative means that something aversive is *removed* following a behavior. Another way to think about it is that there are reinforcements that reward (positive) and reinforcements that relieve (negative). Here are some examples.

Positive reinforcement:

- A child is praised and taken to the park after cleaning his room (the praise and park are both rewards).

- You feel accomplishment after doing your workout (the sense of accomplishment rewards your workout efforts).

- You are paid for completing work (money is a powerful reinforcer because it can be used for a variety of rewards).

Negative reinforcement:

- A person completes a task to stop another person from nagging him or her (the removal of the nagging is a relief and reinforces completing the task).

- You buckle your seatbelt to stop the car from beeping at you (removing the annoying beep is a relief and promotes seatbelt buckling).

- You practice your skills instead of acting on a problem behavior so you do not have to complete a behavior and solution analysis (the removal of behavior and solution analysis is a relief and reinforces working on your skills).

Of course, behaviors can receive both positive and negative reinforcement at the same time:

- A person abuses drugs because taking a drug feels good (positive reinforcement-reward), and it removes painful feelings (negative reinforcement-relief) and withdrawal symptoms (negative reinforcement-relief). Alternatively, a person avoids drug use and (in time) feels clear-headed (positive reinforcement-reward) and does not suffer hangovers (negative reinforcement-relief).

- You practice your skills and receive recognition from the peers in your program (positive reinforcement-reward) and notice that painful emotions are becoming less intense (negative reinforcement-relief).

Punishment

Punishment is intended to decrease behaviors, and, similar to how reinforcement works, punishment can be positive or negative. With positive punishment, something aversive is added following a behavior, and with negative punishment something desirable is removed following a behavior. Here are some examples.

Positive punishment:

- You break a dish and then are scolded by your parent (the scolding is a punishment).

- You show up late for work and get written up by your boss (the write-up is a punishment).

- A person breaks the law and goes to jail (being locked up is a punishment).

Negative punishment:

- You mistreat a friend and lose the friendship (losing a desired relationship is a punishment).

- Your partner gives you the silent treatment after an argument (losing desired company or companionship is a punishment).

- A child cannot stay overnight with a friend after speaking disrespectfully to his or her parent (losing the desired activity is a punishment).

Although punishment is a common response to unwanted behaviors (note that unfortunately effective behaviors can sometimes be punished too), punishment does come with three complicating problems:

- It does not teach something new and more effective in terms of behavior. Without replacement behaviors, people go back to doing the punished behavior in the absence of the punisher.

- It causes hostility in relationships, especially between the person being punished and the person doing the punishing.

- It causes emotional intensity that gets in the way of more effective behavior.

For these reasons it is best to minimize punishing others and maximize teaching and reinforcing positive behaviors to replace and crowd out ineffective ones.

How to reinforce behaviors

The best way to get a new behavior to "stick" is to continuously reinforce it until it is established. That means reinforcing it every time it is performed. For example:

- You receive recognition and praise each time you practice a new skill (or praise yourself!).

- A child gets a star every time he or she completes a homework assignment. The star itself may be sufficient reinforcement, or the child may be able to save up a certain number of stars to cash in on a bigger reinforcement, such as a play date with a friend or a special outing with a parent.

Continuous reinforcement is not necessary once the behavior is established, but periodic reinforcement remains important to maintain the behavior. A powerful reinforcement schedule called "intermittent reinforcement" is often used to maintain desirable behaviors. With intermittent reinforcement, a behavior is rewarded only occasionally in an unpredictable manner (at least to the person receiving the reinforcement). Intermittent reinforcement is how slot machines work; the unpredictable payoffs keep people feeding money into these machines!

It is important to remember that sometimes ineffective behavior remains because others unwittingly reinforce it on an intermittent schedule. For example:

- A parent gives in to tantrum behavior every so often, so the child continues to use tantrums.

- A person intimidates others, and some people acquiesce to the behavior.

Always be careful what you reinforce!

Shaping behaviors

Shaping means reinforcing steps toward a goal behavior. This behavioral technique is especially helpful when a goal behavior is too big of a jump and needs to be developed gradually. For example:

- Someone is afraid to complete a shopping trip at the grocery store. First the person goes to the store to get one easily found item. Next the person goes to the store to purchase three items. Through successive steps the person is eventually able to complete an entire shopping trip successfully. Reinforcement is provided at each successful step.

- A person who is inactive goes for a 5-minute walk, then a 10-minute walk, and so on until the person can walk continuously for an hour. Again, each successful step is rewarded.

Generalizing behaviors

Many of us learn (or already have) effective behaviors in some areas or with some people, but we cannot yet do the behavior in another area or with another person. Generalizing happens when the behavior reliably transfers to the new area or person. For example:

- You practice assertiveness skills with your therapist in session and then generalize assertiveness to other people and situations (e.g., with your partner, with people at work)

- A person practices distress tolerance behaviors in hospital, and then transfers those skills to his or her home environment.

General behavior change strategies

Learning to be more effective and developing new behaviors takes effort, and remembering the basics of behavior can be tricky, especially when you are in the middle of it all. As you work through this book you will learn many new skills and strategies that will help you build a more satisfying life, and you will learn a lot more about effective behavior, perhaps becoming a bit of an expert yourself. Here are a few ideas to get you started:

- **Observe the skillful behaviors of an effective person:** What skills does he or she use? Act "as if" and see if you can emulate the behavior of this person.

- **Strive to become a model for others with your skillful behavior:** Think, "What do I want to show others?" and "Who can I model effective behavior to?" Practice your skills and start shaping more effective behaviors to demonstrate to others.

- **Understand your vulnerabilities that set up ineffective behavior:** Too little self-care and stress management set people up to act on problem behaviors. What are your vulnerabilities? Not enough quality sleep? Missing meals? Lack of exercise? Getting behind on work at home, school, or work? Identify your vulnerabilities and use skills to address them to short-circuit acting on ineffective behaviors.

- **Crowd out ineffective behaviors:** Resolve to practice at least five skills before engaging in a behavior you want (and need) to change (e.g., self-injury, overeating or binging, substance use behaviors). Better yet, practice dialectical abstinence with your harmful behavior(s) and commit to using your comprehensive skills plan (e.g., a safety plan or a relapse prevention plan). When you start meeting your needs and passing time through skillful behavior, eventually there is no "room" for self-defeating and harmful behaviors.

- **Give yourself credit:** Your environment may or may not reward you. Even if you do receive reinforcement from others for using skills, it is still important that you learn to praise yourself for efforts and accomplishments. You might even develop your own reward program for skillful behavior.

- **Practice your skills until they become self-reinforcing:** Some skills have immediate rewards and others have delayed benefits. The more time and consistency you put into skillful behaviors, the more rewarding they become in and of themselves. Being skillful feels good!

Using Behavior and Solution Analysis to Create Change

■ *CORE CONCEPT:* Behavior and solution analysis helps you to understand and change problem behaviors.

Behavior analysis (also called chain analysis or change analysis) is a tool used to understand what precedes and follows a behavior, usually called a "problem behavior" or "target behavior." The more we understand about our behaviors, the more options we have for changing ineffective ones. It should be noted, though, that behavior analysis can be used to understand more about effective behaviors too: what helps to prompt them, and how the results of performing those behaviors differ from the consequences of target behaviors. Understanding more about our effective behaviors can lead us to strengthen them.

Do not be intimidated by behavior analysis. Although it can get quite detailed, the simplest behavior analysis is "A-B-C." What are the **A**ntecedents leading to the **B**ehavior of interest, and what **C**onsequences follow it? When a sequential, step-by-step picture of the antecedents and consequences of any behavior is established, you can look at each step to problem-solve with skills or actions that will create positive change. These problem-solving steps are called "solution analysis."

Behavior analysis starts by identifying the specific target behavior. Examples might include drinking or getting high, self-injury, not participating in therapy, missing an appointment, not taking medications, or breaking a program rule. After the behavior is identified, the prompting event, or what triggered or set off the behavior, is described. Then, leading up to the prompting event, it is necessary to investigate what made you more vulnerable to acting on the target behavior in the first place. For example, did you experience poor sleep, miss medications, get into a fight, or leave open opportunities to engage in unskillful behavior?

Once the target behavior, vulnerabilities, and the prompting event are well defined, you can begin to establish the links that bridge the prompting event to the target behavior. Potential links include emotions, thoughts, physical sensations, and other behaviors leading up to the target behavior. This step slows down the action so that you can see everything that comes between a prompting event and a behavior, building awareness of what is often missed unless explored in detail.

The last part of the behavior analysis is identifying the consequences of the target behavior. Consequences involve the impacts of the behavior on you, on other people, and on the environment. Some consequences reinforce the target behavior while most other consequences are detrimental. It is also important to see whether certain consequences become vulnerabilities for future target behaviors. For example, if a consequence was feeling shame, that feeling could make one vulnerable to escaping that painful emotion through a target behavior such as self-injury.

With the sequence from vulnerabilities through consequences established, you can then develop the solution analysis for each step, starting with skills to reduce vulnerabilities and ending with skills for dealing effectively with the consequences, including making appropriate amends with others by repairing mistakes and correcting whatever harm was done.

As you complete a behavior and solution analysis, remember to be nonjudgmental and yet accountable to yourself. The goal of this tool is to help you apply your skills so you can be more effective next time.

The following pages contain sample behavior and solution analyses. Use the form or forms that work best for you. Also note that many of the worksheets in this manual follow the basics of behavior analysis: building awareness of what comes before and after particular behaviors in order to problem-solve with skills.

Visual Behavior and Solution Analysis

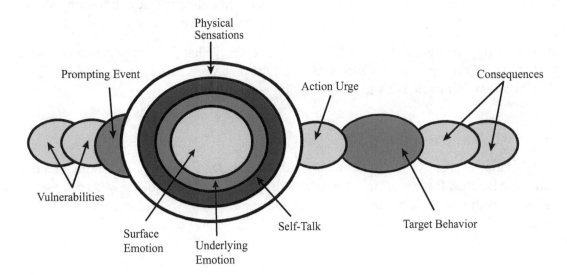

Directions

The more you understand about behaviors you want to change, the more you can be effective in the use of your skills to meet that goal. Start anywhere on the behavior and solution analysis and work forward and/or backward to figure out each link, then identify other skills you could use or choices you could make with your new awareness. Remember to be *nonjudgmental* with yourself, the situation, and others. The following explains each identified link, but remember that you can add as many links as you need to understand what happened and that *every link presents an opportunity for change*. Also, look for skills that you might already have been using but not have noticed or for which you need more practice. The chances are you have been using skills!

- **Vulnerabilities:** What made you vulnerable to acting on the prompting event with the target behavior? Examples might include not doing self-care, having a tough day, getting into a conflict, or other stressors. Be as specific as possible.

- **Prompting event:** What triggered or set off the target behavior? Describe in nonjudgmental, descriptive words.

- **Surface emotion:** What emotion(s) occurred after the prompting event that was/were most easily noticed?

- **Underlying emotion:** Was/were there an emotion or emotions further below the surface? Examples might include feeling hurt or embarrassed underneath anger or feeling guilty underneath depression.

- **Self-talk:** What automatic thoughts or beliefs were happening that fed your emotions and the following action urge?

- **Physical sensations:** What was happening in and with your body?

- **Action urge:** What did the emotions and other factors motivate or pull you to do? This link is a critical moment of choice in changing the behavior, knowing that we do not need to act on our urges.

- **Target behavior:** This is the behavior you want (and need) to change. You will want to develop skillful alternatives to this behavior, but remember that using skills at earlier links might effectively short-circuit the behavior too.

- **Consequences:** What happened after the behavior? What did you gain and/or lose, in both the short term and the long term? Did the outcomes cause a new vulnerability or stressor and/or cycle back to the beginning again?

Solutions

At each step, brainstorm skills or choices that could create behavior change and more effective consequences. Also plan for how you can deal skillfully with the consequences you are experiencing, *including how you may need to make amends with others.*

Visual Behavior and Solution Analysis

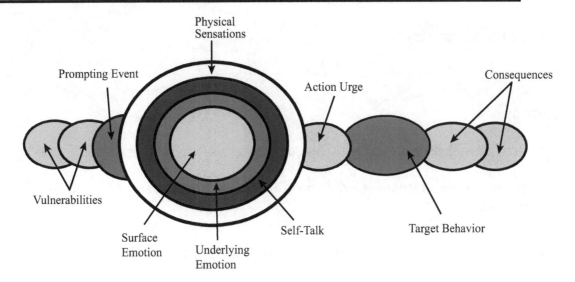

Describe your vulnerabilities:

_____

Describe the prompting event (what triggered or set off the target behaviors?):

_____

Describe your emotion on the surface (the one mostly easily noticed):

_____

Describe any underlying emotions (the ones hidden underneath):

_____

Describe your self-talk:

_____

Describe your physical sensations:

_____

Describe the action urge:

_____

Describe the behavior:

_____

Describe the consequences:

_____

Solutions:

Fill in alternative skills and choices that would be more effective at each step.

Consider how these alternatives would have altered the consequences for you and for other people.

Describe how you will use skills effectively to deal with the consequences that exist:

_____

_____

_____

Describe who else was affected by your choice(s):

_____

_____

_____

Describe how you will make amends with these people (if appropriate):

_____

_____

_____

Behavior and Solution Analysis: Short Form

Name:_____ Date:_____

PURPOSE: To get your needs met more effectively through problem-solving ineffective behaviors and planning for skillful behaviors.

What was the target behavior? Be specific.

_____

What led up to the target behavior? Give specifics of what made you vulnerable and each factor (e.g., emotions, thoughts, behaviors, sensations, situations) that came before the problem behavior.

_____

What did you gain or expect to gain by making the choice you did? How did you think it might help or benefit you? Did it meet your needs?

_____

What were the negative consequences of your choice for you and others?

_____

What skills could you use to meet your needs more effectively next time (in the short term and long term)?

_____

Short-term plan:

_____

Long-term plan:

_____

Behavior and Solution Analysis: Long Form

Name: _____ Date: _____

PURPOSE: To get your needs met more effectively through problem-solving ineffective behaviors and planning for skillful behaviors.

Step 1: Describe the target behavior

What did you do?

_____

How did you do it?

_____

Where did you do it?

_____

When did you do it?

_____

Who else was involved?

_____

Step 2: Identify what was going on in your life before the target behavior

What event set off the target behavior?

_____

_____

What were the events leading up to the event that set off the target behavior?

_____

_____

Which of the events leading up to the target behavior were the most important?

_____

_____

What were you feeling prior to and during the target behavior?

_____

_____

What were you thinking prior to and during the target behavior?

_____

_____

What need(s) were you trying to meet with the target behavior?

_____

_____

At what point did you make your decision to use the target behavior?

_____

_____

Step 3: Identify the consequences of the target behavior

How may you have benefited from the target behavior (in the short and long term)?

_____

_____

How may you have been hurt by the target behavior (in the short and long term)?

_____

_____

What changes happened with the following (in the short and long term):

_____

_____

Emotions:

_____

Thoughts:

_____

Physical sensations:

_____

Behaviors:

_____

Events around you:

_____

The way others treat you:

_____

Step 4: Identify what DBT skills you could use to be more effective in a similar situation (Review steps 1, 2, and 3, and look for ways to insert DBT skills at each step and substep.)

What DBT skills could you have used or could you use next time when similar events take place?

_____

_____

What consequences (or potential consequences) to the target behavior might help you to control or avoid that behavior in the future?

_____

_____

How can you remove access (i.e., burn the bridge) to the target behavior?

_____

_____

What else might you do to get your needs met in an effective way that would not hurt you, others, and/or your treatment?

_____

_____

Step 5: Summarize the problem-solving in Steps 1–4

What were the most important events leading up to the target behavior?

_____

_____

What was the target behavior?

_____

_____

What were the consequences of the target behavior?

_____

_____

What DBT skills can you use and at what stage could you use them to get your needs met more effectively when similar events happen?

_____

_____

What is the earliest point at which you could insert skills?

_____

_____

Step 6: Identify resources/assets you have to implement DBT skills instead of using the target behavior

What resources/assets do you have available that will assist your DBT skill use?

_____

_____

Additional input from your therapist, group, or significant other(s):

_____

_____

Dialectics

Introduction to Dialectics

■ *CORE CONCEPT:* Dialectics are syntheses of opposites that lead to a balance in life.

Dialectics refers to a philosophy that recognizes the tensions and conflicts that happen within us, between us, and in the world at large. In dialectics, we seek to synthesize and resolve these opposite tensions to achieve more balance in thought and behavior.

To use a straightforward example, many of us view situations as cut and dried, or black and white. However, life is typically more complicated than the all-or-nothing dichotomies we get caught in. Using dialectics, we see the relative truth on both sides and the resulting synthesis moves us away from the extremes of black and white into shades of gray. We then discover the middle ground and/or what we previously missed in our thinking, in our behavior, and in how we relate to others. This discovery leads us to more effective behavior.

A few basic assumptions make up dialectics:

- We experience opposing tensions, often perceived as contradictory. As noted above, these dialectical tensions can be internal or can happen between people, and they may arise only in certain situations. For example, many people in therapy experience tension between doing what is familiar (staying the same) and doing something new (change).

- Each position in tension or conflict has its own truth or validity, depending on the vantage point. There is no such thing as absolute or complete truth, and even the most contradictory ideas or forces have their own validity and are interrelated. No one position can exist without a relationship to another, with each part making up a larger whole. In the present example, there are valid reasons to stay the same and valid reasons to change, and all of those reasons are intertwined.

- Resolution of dialectical tensions or conflict occurs when one opposing force gradually or suddenly overcomes another, creating movement, change, a new synthesis, and ultimately a new dialectical tension. In this "stay the same versus change" example, each resolution point between the tensions leads to a movement of one type or another. Choosing to try something different, such as using a skill, is an easily seen change. But even choosing to stay the same creates change too, though it is not always as easily seen. For example, resisting change and continuing to do what is familiar may lead to an escalation of a problem. As the problem escalates, the push for change might become more pronounced, creating a new dialectical tension.

- We all continually experience opposing tensions that evolve, and we make the most effective choices when we seek to understand the dialectic nature of these conflicts, carefully consider our options, and remain open to adjusting our course with the winds—controlling what we can while accepting what we cannot.

As you proceed through treatment, you may experience a couple common dialectical tensions.

Self-acceptance versus making personal changes

The inter-relatedness of these concepts is apparent. Self-acceptance is often the prerequisite to making personal changes (and is change itself). There are times and places for both. DBT therapists consider the movement between acceptance and change to be the most fundamental dialectic in DBT.

Doing your best versus needing to do better

At any given time you (and others) are doing the best that you can with what you have. When you allow this assumption, you find compassion and self-acceptance. Yet doing your best is dialectically counterbalanced by the need to do better. That is the reason you are practicing skills: to create a more satisfying life.

Confusing? Like any philosophy, dialectics can be difficult to understand. The following pages continue to detail basic principles of dialectics, list frequent dialectical conflicts, highlight dialectics in other DBT skills, and provide opportunities for understanding and practice. In time you will be thinking and acting dialectically!

Dialectical Principles

■ *CORE CONCEPT*: Following these dialectical principles will lead to dialectical thought and behavior.

Step out of the black and white

Thinking in black and white is characterized by extremes in which we take on either one position or the opposite, or bounce back and forth between them. It is either–or, all or nothing. Try to avoid extremes unless an extreme response fits your priorities, goals, and values and the needs of the situation as viewed from Wise Mind (this will be rare). Examples of extremes include:

- You either intensely love or hate your partner, friend, coworker, etc.

- You think you or someone else is all bad or all good.

- You approach others in an overly strict or overly lenient manner.

- You do not start a task or change unless you think you can do it all at once.

- You separate viewpoints into right and wrong categories.

I am black and white with the following people and/or in the following situations:

_____

Move into shades of gray in thoughts, behaviors, relationships, and situations

Thinking in shades of gray is characterized by understanding other perspectives and adopting middle-ground behaviors. Exploring the "grays" can seem risky when you are used to black and white, but discovering the complexity of people and the world is part of dialectics. Examples of moving into the gray include:

- You show respect and love and/or regard to your partner, friend, coworker, etc. even when he or she performs behaviors you do not like.

- You recognize that you and other people have both positive and negative qualities.

- You approach others in a centered manner, observing and respecting boundaries and being appropriately flexible as needed.

- You start tasks and initiate changes that you are able to do now.

- You avoid separating viewpoints into right and wrong categories and notice the relative truth of different viewpoints. You seek to understand rather than judge.

I can move into shades of gray with the people and situations listed above by:

_____

Be flexible and adaptable

Meet other people and situations where they are at and learn to do what is needed. Recognize and respect that there are many ways of seeing things and many ways to approach the same situation, bringing options to your life. Without losing your center, practice bending from time to time, just as a strong tree bends in heavy winds. To illustrate flexibility and adaptability:

- You decide to "go with the flow" instead of trying to control everything.

- You let other people have their way at times and/or compromise.

- You try a new or novel way to accomplish a task or goal.

- You listen and find the validity in a viewpoint you disagree with (i.e., you find something to agree with about the viewpoint).

- You remain open to what each moment has to offer.

I can be more flexible with people, in situations, and in life by:

_____

_____

Act from your values and do what works!

Although dialectics often call for entering the grays, being flexible, and finding the middle ground, *true balance comes from maintaining a solid core*. Dialectics do not mean being wishy-washy, being a chameleon, or having an "anything goes" attitude. Remember to stay centered within yourself and in relation to other people and the world through connecting with your values and doing what is effective for the moment, in both the short and the long term. This includes practicing dialectical abstinence with harmful and/or addictive behaviors.

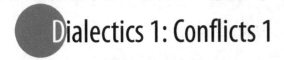

Dialectics 1: Conflicts 1

CORE CONCEPT: Identify shades of gray in common dialectical conflicts.

The following are common examples of dialectical tensions. For each conflict, identify what is valid about each side of the dialectic and then identify middle options. You can write notes here, write on a separate sheet of paper, or plug a conflict into the worksheet Dialectics 2: Conflicts 2. If a conflict does not seem to apply to your life, imagine how it might in a different situation or for a different person.

Self-acceptance versus change:

_____

Wanting a different life while resisting change:

_____

Being the real you versus being vulnerable to others:

_____

Structure versus freedom:

_____

Novelty versus predictability:

_____

Fear of needing people conflicting with fear of being independent:

_____

Desire to succeed while actively destroying your progress:

_____

Setting goals that are too easy or goals that are too hard:

_____

Caring for others and still maintaining boundaries:

_____

Balance focusing on yourself versus focusing on others:

_____

Letting go of control to gain control:

_____

Seeing only pros or only cons of a situation:

_____

Not being a doormat and not being demanding:

_____

Asserting your values while respecting the values of others:

_____

Being too passive or too aggressive:

_____

Both being capable and asking for help:

_____

Being too private versus being an open book:

_____

Doing your best and needing to do better:

_____

Balance of "old" self with "new" self:

_____

"Want-tos" versus "have-tos":

_____

Taking a situation personally when it is not about you:

_____

Wanting perfection and knowing you are human:

_____

An all-or-nothing approach to anything:

_____

Picking your battles:

_____

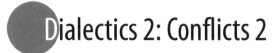

Dialectics 2: Conflicts 2

CORE CONCEPT: Use this worksheet when stuck in a dialectical conflict.

Describe your conflict (be specific):

_____

Describe the other skills you need to be dialectical (e.g., Wise Mind, Nonjudgmental Stance, FAST, GIVE, DEAR MAN):

_____

Describe your current "place" on the dialectic and how it makes sense (find the context and validate it!):

_____

Describe the opposite (or another) position and how it makes sense (find the context and validate it!):

_____

Describe the balance or synthesis of both positions and how this dialectic makes sense:

_____

Describe your specific dialectical action plan (your movement toward change):

_____

Describe how your life will be different when you resolve this conflict:

_____

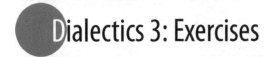

Dialectics 3: Exercises

CORE CONCEPT: Practice these exercises to be more dialectical in your life.

The following exercises can bring about dialectical balance and assist you in seeing options in your life. Remember that in dialectics we can see both sides: Experiencing a difficult problem or crisis does not mean that we are hopelessly stuck, and seeing another side of the problem or crisis does not invalidate how serious or painful it is to you. Remember to validate yourself and look across the dialectic.

Dialectical exercise 1: What is going right?

Often we focus on what is wrong and neglect the other side of the dialectic. Asking what is going right, well, or in your direction, however small, helps to bring another perspective and balance.

EXAMPLES:

- Someone does poorly on a test but also has an opportunity to use a tutor or complete an assignment to gain extra credit, or may be doing well in another subject or area.

- A significant problem occurs at work but you have the knowledge and/or support to address it effectively.

- Your child has a disability but shows resiliency and a positive attitude.

If you feel down, what is going right, well, or in your direction?

Dialectical exercise 2: What are your resources?

We often think of our limitations and overlook the resources that will help us reach our goals.

EXAMPLES:

- You are out of shape but have running shoes, exercise equipment, a gym membership, or a safe place to walk.

- You experience depression but have a therapist, self-help books, and DBT skills to practice.

- A person cannot currently get ahead in his or her current job but has access to classes to advance his or her career or has in-demand job skills and can look for new employment.

With any particular problem, what are your resources?

Dialectical exercise 3: Is there a silver lining?

Few things in the world are all good or all bad. When a painful situation occurs, consider whether there is a silver lining. Sometimes problems and even tragedies reveal opportunities.

EXAMPLES:

- A person is served divorce papers and now has the opportunity to reinvest in hobbies and other interests given up during the marriage or has the opportunity to find a more suitable mate in time.
- You lose your house in foreclosure and find relief in not struggling to make a high mortgage payment every month.
- You change schools but have the chance to have a fresh start and make new friends.

Pick a current problem you are experiencing. What is the silver lining?

Dialectical exercise 4: The dialectics of control

Some people have more of an external locus of control. They think that things happen to them, they frequently blame others, and they miss opportunities to make effective changes that are actually under their control. Other people have more of an internal locus of control and believe that they have influence over their environment and can take charge of their choices and lives.

EXAMPLES:

- One person believes he will fail a test no matter how hard he studies whereas another person believes that her preparation will make a significant difference in the outcome.
- One person thinks she cannot ever be happy and does little to try to improve her life whereas another person invests himself in creating a happy life.
- You blame others for the problems in your life instead of taking responsibility for your choices and behavior.

Think about a problem you have. Where is your locus of control and would you be more effective if you shifted it?

Dialectical exercise 5: All or something!

Often we get in all-or-nothing places in regard to change. All or something means that, if you cannot totally throw yourself into the change process, at least do something that moves you closer to a goal. Some movement is preferable to no movement!

EXAMPLES:

- A person who wants a healthier lifestyle overhauls his diet and starts exercising every day.
- You are overwhelmed by a dirty and disorganized home so you clean one part of one room.

- One person fills out and practices a skills plan to solve a problem while another person starts reading and thinking about skills to practice someday.

Think about a problem you have. How can you throw yourself totally into change or at least do something toward the change?

Dialectical exercise 6: Compassion for others

We can often be harsh in our assessments of others, holding them to high standards and being judgmental. Sometimes compassion is a better route for both others and ourselves. Note that being compassionate does not mean that people automatically get a "pass" for ineffective behavior. We can be both compassionate and accountable, which is dialectic.

EXAMPLES:

- You get cut off in traffic. Rather than getting angry, you think that the offending driver may be having a bad or stressful day.

- Your child is having a tantrum and you remember that being a toddler is no walk in the park.

- A person's boss is critical of her employees. That person recognizes that the boss is overwhelmed by too much responsibility and wants the business to do well.

Think about a person with whom you are struggling. How can you be compassionate toward this person?

Dialectical exercise 7: Movement through scaling techniques

Sometimes it is difficult to imagine big changes happening in your life. When you struggle with thinking about large changes, you can conceptualize smaller changes using scaling techniques. Start by listing the severity of your problem from 10 (extreme problem) to 0 (no problem). After you have rated your problem, consider what you would be doing differently in terms of behavior if the problem improved by one or more points. Then commit yourself to your new behavior(s) to create the incremental change.

EXAMPLES:

- An overweight person rates his problem as an 8. He concludes that when his problem is at a 6 he will be going to his local health club at least three times a week. He commits to going to the club.

- You are depressed and rate your depression's severity at a 10. You think that at a 9 you will be actively sharing and talking in your program group. You start to talk more in program.

- A parent has a child with behavior problems rated at a 7. The parent says that when the problems are below a 5 she will be having more fun with her child. The parent starts engaging in more playtime with her child.

Think about a problem you have and rate it from 10 to 0. What behavior(s) will you be doing when the problem improves by two points? Remember to do what you identify!

Dialectics Applied to Other Skills

■ *CORE CONCEPT:* Dialectics are central to DBT skills.

We can apply dialectics to many of the skills and concepts learned in DBT. Even when dialectics are not explicitly mentioned, it may be useful to think about how they apply.

In the Mindfulness module, balancing emotion and reason to enter Wise Mind is a dialectic.

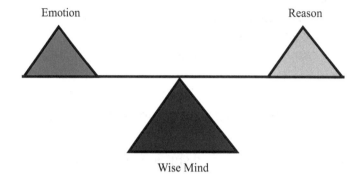

It is common for emotions and reason to conflict with one another, and finding the balance between emotion and reason in a given situation depends on what works. When we go too far in one direction—way into Emotion Mind or way into Reason Mind—the need for the opposite is created. To reach a resolution we need to respect both emotions and reason, and creating balance between the two is what brings us to Wise Mind, that centered place where we can validate our emotions *and* make effective choices.

Another example in the Mindfulness module is the dialectical balance between attending to emotional (or other) pain in life versus redirecting attention to a pleasant distraction. There are times to relate mindfully to your pain and times to turn your mind to other people, to your environment, or to a skill from another module. Again, what we chose to be mindful of is based on effectiveness: Attend to what is needed in the moment without judgment.

In the Distress Tolerance module there is a basic dialectic tension between tolerating a problem and surviving it through the use of distress tolerance skills versus actively working on solving the problem. Distraction is helpful when you cannot solve the problem in the short term, but it becomes counterproductive if it becomes overused and you continue to distract from problems you are actually able to resolve. In other words, there are times to distract yourself from problems and times to get down to solving them.

There are other dialectics in the Distress Tolerance module too, such as using distress tolerance skills that are energizing versus using distress tolerance skills that are soothing, or getting into distress tolerance skills that are self-focused versus getting into skills that focus on other people. Yet another example from distress tolerance is the Pros and Cons skill, which is a dialectical exercise in and of itself. The very nature of Pros and Cons highlights how choices can have both upsides and downsides to consider when resolving conflicts, making choices, and solving problems.

In the Emotion Regulation module, dialectics can be seen in achieving balance through self-care skills that include regulating diet, sleep, and exercise. To use self-care, we frequently have to make difficult choices that involve compromise. Choosing a healthy diet may result in giving up certain foods you love, getting enough sleep may mean going to bed early and missing out on other activities, and engaging in exercise often requires prioritizing it over other demands. Some emotion regulation skills also strike natural dialectical balances, such as Build Positive Experience (fun) counterbalancing Build Mastery (responsibility) and Opposite to Emotion (acting opposite to ineffective behaviors that emotions pull you into) counterbalancing Mood Momentum (continuing to engage in behaviors that generate positive emotions that you want).

Next, dialectics underscore the skills in the Interpersonal Effectiveness module. In particular, the skills GIVE and DEAR MAN require a dialectical balance in order to be effective.

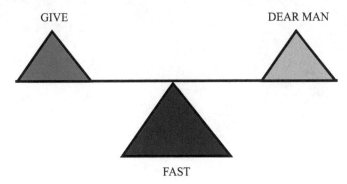

The balance between others' wants and needs (captured by the GIVE skill) and our wants and needs (captured by the DEAR MAN skill) is important for successful relationships. If you get too focused on others or too focused on yourself, conflicts are likely to arise. To resolve those conflicts, you will need to reestablish balance in your relationships. To find an effective balance, we often we rely on our FAST skills (e.g., being fair and sticking to values) to guide how much GIVE versus DEAR MAN we use in relationships.

The examples mentioned above just scratch the surface. As you work through this book, try to notice how dialectics apply to other skills and their use too.

Module 2

Mindfulness

Introduction to Mindfulness

■ *CORE CONCEPT*: Mindfulness is the pathway to an effective and enjoyable life.

Mindfulness means choosing to pay attention to this present moment, on purpose, without judgment. Mindfulness allows us to gain awareness of our emotions, thoughts, bodily sensations, behaviors, relationships, and environment. As we become more mindfully aware in our lives, we can make more informed and effective choices to build more satisfying lives. Neuroscientific research clearly shows that mindfulness makes positive and lasting changes to our brains.

Central to mindfulness is the concept of taking hold of one's mind. This means concentrating our attention on what we choose rather than having emotions, thoughts, or other experiences control us. Training yourself to collect, unify, and direct your attention creates containment in your mind.

Mindfulness skills open doors to acceptance, experience, and connection to yourself and the world. This approach is additive and allows for more complete and richer information and experience to guide us. It is also different from some of our default ways of being: disconnected, judgmental, and alone. These default approaches reduce our experience because we label, categorize, and quickly move on without seeing and connecting to the bigger picture.

As we learn mindfulness, we must remember that it needs to be practiced with other skills and nurtured. The concepts behind mindfulness can be straightforward, but being mindful in our lives requires attention and disciplined practice over time. Like all worthwhile pursuits, our efforts dedicated to mindfulness will reap great benefits if practiced daily.

The Mindfulness module teaches us the core skills to get us to Wise Mind. From Wise Mind, we can live centered and balanced lives using both our hearts and minds. We can also stay One-Mindful in the present, visiting the past and future by choice and connecting with ourselves and the world in a nonjudgmental fashion. Ultimately, we can use mindfulness to slow down and find peace, contentment, and enjoyment in everyday life.

Myths About Mindfulness

■ *CORE CONCEPT*: Misconceptions about mindfulness can interfere with the effective practice of these skills.

Many people, therapists included, have misconceptions about what mindfulness is and what it is not. Sometimes these misconceptions get in the way of engaging in mindfulness practice. Below are some of the most common myths about mindfulness.

Mindfulness is Buddhist (or some other philosophy or religion)

While a large variety of philosophies and religions promote mindfulness practices, mindfulness is best thought of as a human activity that is owned by no group or person. Mindfulness belongs to us all, and, furthermore, mindfulness and its benefits are supported by robust research that clearly shows its psychological, emotional, physical, and performance-based benefits.

Mindfulness is all new-age-y, wavy-gravy, or (insert your judgment here)

For some reason, mindfulness seems to conjure images of people in flowing robes, sitting in serene settings, existing in some unreal world disconnected from your or my reality (admittedly, many photos showing people practicing mindfulness promote those stereotypes). The facts are that mindfulness is for everyone and that people across all races, ethnicities, cultures, religions, occupations, and socio-economic statuses practice mindfulness.

Mindfulness is a fad or trend

Mindfulness has been around since the dawn of consciousness, making the Beatles or Rolling Stones look like fads by comparison. Not much stands that test of time. When the end of the world comes, only cockroaches and Keith Richards, practicing mindfulness, will remain. Enough said.

Mindfulness takes a lot of time

While some advocates of mindfulness stress 45 minutes (or more) of meditation or other mindfulness practice daily, the fact is that you can achieve benefits from taking just a few minutes (or even moments in some cases) to re-center yourself mindfully in the moment. When you consider how much time we all spend distracted by problems, taking a few minutes to breathe or otherwise practice mindfulness is a great trade-off.

People who practice mindfulness are always mindful (and effective)

A mindfulness student once saw his teacher eating while watching TV. Angry at the apparent hypocrisy of doing more than one thing at a time, the student challenged his teacher. "You always teach One-Mindfulness, lecturing 'when you walk, walk, when you pray, pray, and when you eat, eat,' and now I see you both eating and watching TV!" The teacher calmly replied, "When you eat and watch TV, eat and watch TV."

Mindfulness does not create perfection, and practitioners will likely experience the benefits but will certainly not always be in the moment. Further, seeking to be ever-mindful means you are clinging to a goal and as such are not in the moment.

Mindfulness is done only during meditation or other mindfulness practice

This myth is one of the biggest, and it is analogous to saying people only move their bodies when they exercise. Think of meditation and other mindfulness practice as exercise for the brain, building the skills needed to collect and focus your attention and then guide your behavior. Just as physical fitness is about developing a healthy body, meditation and other mindfulness practices are about building healthy mental processes so you can be mindful in the moments of everyday life.

Mindfulness is only about pleasure, peace, and relaxation

While mindfulness can be pleasurable and promote peace and relaxation, mindfulness is also about relating to experiences that can be aversive, uncomfortable, and even painful. Think about how often we try to escape these types of experiences only to make them worse! Perhaps, paradoxically, using mindfulness to accept and relate to what is painful can transform the painful experience; mindfulness is fundamentally acceptance based and nonjudgmental, which alleviates the helping of suffering we often dump on pain.

Mindfulness can turn off problems, or otherwise make them go away

Mindfulness is not about turning anything on or off. Rather, it is about deciding what to focus on and when. What mindfulness can offer is a way to attend to something other than your problems when you choose to take a break, and a way to focus on your problems when you decide to—but with a different approach that can reduce your suffering, as mentioned above.

People with attention deficit, racing thoughts, intrusive thinking, or other problems cannot practice mindfulness

Mindfulness does not turn problems off or make them go away, but it is a set of skills you can practice to eventually minimize the impacts of these problems on your life. For example, if your problem is racing thoughts, you can simply notice when they distract you (gently and nonjudgmentally) and then turn your mind to the chosen focus of your attention. If your problem is attention deficit, then practicing the skill of (re)focusing your attention (i.e., mindfulness) is perfect for you!

Children, people with cognitive disabilities, and (insert another category of people) cannot do mindfulness

Watch young children eat, play with their toys, and explore. They are engrossed, and *there*. This is mindfulness. People of most developmental and cognitive levels have the ability to focus their attention and connect to the present moment, and can have that ability fostered. To this end, having a parent, friend, or loved one practice mindful engagement with them will gently pull along their mindfulness skills, even if they cannot explain mindfulness conceptually. For those without abstract thought, we simply make explanations of mindfulness more concrete. As an example, with young children we can simply say "smell the flowers and blow out the candles" to engage them in the mindful practice of breathing.

You are unable to do mindfulness

See above, and also remember that you already practice mindfulness sometimes, with some things, in some places. Where and with what do you find yourself totally connected and inhabiting the moment? Maybe it is when you play an instrument or sport, or when you are doing a hobby, or into the flow of your work. Maybe it's when you're in your garden, when you're cooking, or when you're connecting spiritually. Use existing times of mindfulness to branch out and develop your skills, remembering that mindfulness is like any other skill set: You get out of it what you put into it. Practice your practice, and the rewards will come with time.

States of Mind

■ *CORE CONCEPT*: Wise Mind is the dialectical balance between emotion and reason.

We experience three primary states of mind: Emotion Mind, Reason Mind, and Wise Mind.

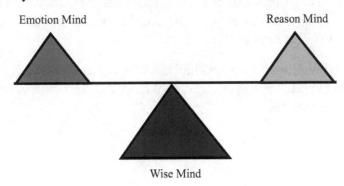

These states of mind exist on a continuum, with Wise Mind being a balance of emotion and reason. Each state of mind is neither "good" nor "bad," although we often think in these terms. However, these judgments are relative and depend on the context of the situation. Instead of judging, seeing what "works" in a given situation is more useful, and you will usually find a balance is best.

Remember that, in dialectics, an extreme contains the seed of the opposite. When we are too far into Emotion Mind, the need for reason arises, and vice versa. We are most effective, most of the time, in Wise Mind.

In a Wise Mind place, we validate our emotional experience *and* integrate our ability to use reason. As described in the introduction to this module, we use our heart and our head, being fully present in the moment. In Wise Mind we can reflect without judgment, live our true intentions in spite of how we feel, and *be* in our experiences without being consumed by them.

Wise Mind is grounded in our values (see FAST in Module 5: Interpersonal Effectiveness) and meets the reality of situations effectively. In Wise Mind, we can overcome our conditioned reactions and be responsive instead. *We all have a wise mind!*

The Path to Wise Mind (WM)

■ *CORE CONCEPT*: The What and How skills lead us to Wise Mind.

Wise Mind is less elusive when we understand the skills used to lead us there: Observe, Describe, and Participate are the What skills. In other words, these three skills are *what* we do to get to Wise Mind. Nonjudgmentally, One-mindfully, and Effectively are the How skills. In other words, these three skills are *how* we apply the What skills to get to Wise Mind.

Although each What and How skill is described individually, remember that they work together to refine our connection with experience and bring us to Wise Mind. To orient yourself to use these skills, practice the directives of this mantra:

Pause, breath, center . . . enter

What skills

Observe

Notice your experience without adding to it or subtracting from it, without amplifying it or pushing it away. Let the experience pass through like clouds drifting in the sky or scenery passing by a car window. Cling to nothing.

Use your senses to gather information. What is seen, heard, smelled, tasted, and touched? What is happening in your mind and body?

Note your emotions, thoughts, and behaviors as well as other people, your situation, and the environment—look inside *and* outside yourself. Notice what is happening physically in your body and the associated sensations. Direct your attention and decide what enters and what stays out; open and close your mental windows with intention.

Describe

Outline the details of your observations with specific descriptions. Use words to bring your observations to life. Language frequently makes greater sense of experience than thought alone. Clarify your experience for yourself and others.

Do not get caught in analyzing your thoughts, feelings, sensations, impulses, and urges. Instead, remember that thoughts are just thoughts, feelings are just feelings, sensations are just sensations, and impulses and urges are just impulses and urges. You are not your mind, and these experiences are not commands.

Participate

Observe and Describe bring awareness to experience. Use this awareness to make choices and to become one with your experience. Go from simply watching your experience to being connected to your experience. Ultimately, *be in* your experience. Inhabit it.

Choose whether you want to stay with and relate further to your experience or redirect your Observe and Describe skills. Recognize whether you are participating in symptoms or problems and choose to participate in skills instead. Redirect your attention and what you participate in based on your wisdom of what works and not simply out of aversion to your experience or a desire to escape from your experience.

Practice these skills until they flow naturally from you.

How skills

Nonjudgmentally

Stick to the facts without coloring them with opinions. Focus on who, what, where, when, and how like an objective reporter. Use respectful language to describe yourself, others, and situations. Be impeccable with your words.

Remember that "good" and "bad" judgments are relative and may not be useful. Sometimes what appears to be desirable can be suffering in disguise, and sometimes problems are hidden opportunities.

Stay away from judgments that amplify or reduce experience or get you stuck in a painful experience by adding suffering. Instead, simply accept what is.

When you observe judgments, gently let go of them. We all judge, so do not amplify your judgments by giving them unneeded power.

One-mindfully

Focus on one thing with your complete attention. Distractions from inside and outside you will happen. Practice stepping out of distractions and avoid being consumed by them. Instead, gently notice and let go of distractions that keep you from your focus.

Treat yourself with kindness and compassion as you practice being One-Mindful and accept distractions instead of judging them. Do not trade the present moment for judgment mind.

If your attention gets divided, stop and focus your attention on what you choose to experience. Be in the here and now with one mind.

Effectively

Do what works best based on the demands of the situation as it is and not what you would prefer it to be. Do not spend your energies fighting reality, which does not unfold according to your preferences and desires.

Do not act out of judgments and a need to be "right." Instead, stay connected to your goals, priorities, and values and use them as guides to act as skillfully as possible.

Use Willingness to get from point "A" to point "B" to accomplish your goals. Remove your own complications and barriers to get out of your own way.

Train yourself to be responsive to experience rather than reactive to experience. Doing what works is a reflection of Wise Mind.

Focus on Nonjudgmental Stance (NJS)

◼ *CORE CONCEPT:* Understand judgments and when to let them go.

Judgments (nonjudgmentally speaking!) are not "good" or "bad" or "right" or "wrong." In fact, judgments can be quite useful at times when we need to label, categorize, and move on or when we simply want to communicate quickly.

It is easier to say that the weather is "bad" than Observing and Describing every detail of the forecast to justify staying home during a storm. Similarly, we might say we have had a "good" day to quickly let others know that problems have been minimal or handled effectively.

Judgments have likely been useful in other ways too. If most men or most women have hurt you in life, judgments about that sex might keep you safe psychologically or even physically in some situations.

However, judgments are less effective when they become overgeneralized or rigid and when we are unable to shift them based on new or different information and experiences. Judgments that no longer work cause strong, ongoing negative emotions and interfere with you meeting your wants and needs. If judgments result in you clashing with a variety of people over time, this might be a sign that Nonjudgmental Stance could be worthwhile.

To see whether judgments might be more or less useful, try to see whether they are "Teflon" judgments or "sticky" judgments. We have no personal investment in or strong emotional reactions to Teflon judgments. These types of judgments can be readily revised when we take in more or different information. In fact, these judgments can be useful when we need to quickly make a decision and move on.

Sticky judgments act like tinted or colored glasses that shade almost everything around us. Because we are committed to these judgments, we refuse to take off those glasses to see ourselves, others, situations, and the world in a different light. Sticky judgments do not help us move on but weigh us down like rocks in a backpack. If you find that your "backpack" is full of heavy judgments, it may be time to take it off, put it down, and gently start to remove those rocks (and use one to smash your tinted glasses, metaphorically speaking of course!).

Focus on One-Mindfulness (OM)

■ *CORE CONCEPT:* Direct yourself back to One-Mindfulness when your attention is divided.

We can clarify One-Mindfulness through examples of divided attention and mindlessness. When we find ourselves in these situations, we go back to the What and How skills to be One-Mindful.

Continual partial attention

Many of us go through our days attending to multiple stimuli simultaneously without giving any one thing our full and complete attention. We eat while watching TV and check our email while in the presence of our families. We think about our problems in the middle of a conversation or during an otherwise positive experience. We talk on the phone while driving and choose to distract ourselves from everyday tasks rather than attending to them. We escape the small moments rather than recognizing that life *is* the small moments.

The result is disconnected attention and incomplete connections. When you notice this continual partial attention, stop, make a choice, and focus on one thing. Continued partial attention is also called the "unquiet mind" or "monkey mind."

Multitasking

We have been misled to believe that multitasking is a strength and is desired. In reality, we can only multitask when behaviors are overlearned or automatic. In these cases, we do not use our conscious minds but instead act like robots.

When we try to multitask with behaviors and in situations that require our conscious attention, we are not actually doing more than one activity at once. Rather, we are shifting our attention back and forth. This approach requires much more mental energy and sets us up to make mistakes.

To illustrate, try this multitasking experiment with two independently easy tasks and notice the outcome: First, count from 1 to 26 as quickly as possible, noting the time. Next, say the ABCs as quickly as possible, again noting the time. Add up the times of these two tasks done one-mindfully. Now, try a true multitasking activity. Time yourself as you alternate performing the tasks of counting and reciting the ABCs (i.e., 1 A 2 B 3 C 4 D and so on). Notice the difference in time, energy, and accuracy.

As another example, you may notice that your computer progressively slows as you have more and more functions open. Your computer is programmed to "multitask," but at some point it spends more time switching and reorienting than actually working. It may even shut down. Your computer's limitations mirror our own limited capacity to spread out our focus. Work on doing one thing at a time as a habit.

Automatic behaviors

Automatic behaviors include anything you can do unconsciously or without thought. While not recommended, most of us can drive, carry on basic conversations, and do most activities of daily living with virtually no attention or connection.

Automatic behaviors can be useful at times. In fact, sometimes automatic behaviors can be highly effective, such as when someone automatically follows an overlearned protocol in an emergency situation or when you swerve or hit your brakes to avoid an automobile accident.

The other side of the dialectic is that automatic behaviors remove us from the here and now of life and deprive us of basic pleasures. A great exercise is being mindful of your automatic behaviors, step by step, with intention. Examples include mindfully preparing and eating meals, driving with your full attention, and taking a shower or bath with awareness of the experience. Any thought or behavior in your day can be attended to one-mindfully.

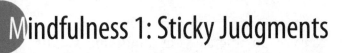

Mindfulness 1: Sticky Judgments

CORE CONCEPT: Use this exercise to let go of sticky judgments.

Describe one sticky judgment about yourself, others, or situations:

_____

_____

_____

Describe how that sticky judgment needlessly upsets you, weighs you down, or holds you back:

_____

_____

_____

Describe how your life will be different without that sticky judgment:

_____

_____

_____

Commit yourself to slowly (or radically!) getting unstuck from that judgment.

_____

_____

_____

Mindfulness Exercises

■ *CORE CONCEPT:* Use these exercises to practice your mindfulness skills.

These mindfulness exercises will strengthen your ability to practice mindfulness and happen to be quite enjoyable too! With all of the exercises, remember to engage each of your senses and to take your time. The text following each exercise just scratches the surface. Go deeper and make the exercise your own!

During your practice, when judgments, other thoughts, or any other distractions occur, do not fuss over them, but gently turn your attention back to the exercise.

1. **Explore a fruit:** Use Observe and Describe to explore an orange. What are the visual features, what does it feel like, and what does it smell like? Now, slowly start to peel the orange and continue to tune in to each sense. Notice any emotions, thoughts, or other experiences that you have during this process, but cling to nothing, instead staying engaged in the activity. Ultimately, you may choose to mindfully eat the orange.

2. **Create with Play-Doh:** Study the Play-Doh container, noticing the writing, colors, and design elements. Slowly peel the lid off the container, and notice the smell. What comes up for you? Notice any associated feelings, memories, or other experiences, and then turn your attention back to the Play-Doh. Feel it in your hands and begin to knead and work it. Notice the texture, the temperature, and whether there are changes in its flexibility as you handle it. Experience the Play-Doh without the need to create anything. (Alternatives: Create what you choose with the Play-Doh, be it an animal, a sculpture, or something else. Let go of judgments as to how the creation is shaping up. Or, imagine you are a child experiencing Play-Doh for the first time. Allow yourself to be immersed in this discovery!)

3. **Connect with a sound:** Put on music; listen to the sounds of waves, nature, or another soothing sound; or pick up on the naturally occurring sounds around you (the hum of an appliance, the sound of traffic, or the bustle of a workplace). Close your eyes and tune in to your chosen sound. Stay with the sound, returning to it when a distraction happens, and perhaps notice how you breathe along with it.

4. **Guided imagery:** Use imagery from a CD, from a website, or recorded from your therapist or another person. Visualize that you are in the place that is being described, hearing the sounds, and feeling the other sensations. Lose yourself in this experience, and, when the exercise is over, bring its benefits back to the present moment.

5. **Create a safe place:** Similar to guided imagery, create a place that is safe and comfortable. It may be a room, a cabin in the woods, or an imaginary land where you are protected by fire-breathing dragons! Use your senses to fully enter the safe place. Notice how it looks, paying attention to even the smallest details. Notice the sounds, or the silence. How does it feel? Stay in this place for a while, and go there whenever you need to soothe and calm yourself.

6. **Sounds of a bell:** Strike a bell or chime, or clang mini-cymbals to create a tone. Listen to the sound until it fades into complete silence. Repeat as many times as you wish. This can be done anytime during the day, before meetings, before meals, or at any other time that you want a break or to return to the moment.

7. **Mindful eating:** Strive to eat mindfully each time you sit down to eat. Notice your food, seeing the shapes, colors, and textures. Smell the aromas. Take it all in before experiencing your first small bite. Our taste buds register tastes more vividly during the first few bites. Eat these bites slowly, experiencing

the tastes, smells, temperature, and textures of each bite. Chew slowly, noticing the release of flavors and the sensations associated with eating. Continue thoughtfully, deliberately, until you notice feeling satisfied, and then stop and reflect. As they say, if you love food, spend some time with it!

8. Mindfulness of smell: Gather a variety of scented candles or essential oils and spend some time exploring the smell of each one. Notice the differences and any reactions you have to each kind of smell. Alternatively, disguise the labels on your candles or oils and see whether you or others can guess each scent.

9. Mindful listening: Pick a song, close your eyes, and listen closely to the music. Follow the lyrics, notice the different instruments, or take in the song as a whole experience. If you have heard the song before, did you notice anything new? Alternatively, pick a song that has a repetitive lyric, phrase, or melody line. Count how many times you hear the reoccurring detail.

10. Mindfulness of touch: Take any object into your hands. Explore the object with your hands and fingers, feeling the shape(s), texture(s), and temperature of the object. This can be done in combination with vision, or done with your eyes closed, focusing exclusively on touch. Alternatively, gather various fabrics such as silk, cotton, wool, and velvet and experience the different feels. Of course, this exercise can be done with any collection of objects (e.g., stress ball, worry stone, sandpaper).

11. Mindfulness of nature/thunderstorms: Put on a nature CD or the sound of a thunderstorm. Listen and notice what emotions, thoughts, and sensations start to come up.

12. Mindful walking: Take a walk outside or around your room. Pay attention to the sensation of your feet in contact with the ground. Let go of thoughts, emotions, and other distractions and just walk, as if being mindful of every step is vitally important. Alternatively, play a game and avoid cracks (or step on them) or count steps between fixed objects such as light poles or mailboxes.

13. Mindful nature walk: Take a walk outside through nature. Notice the sounds and smells. What do you see? Take this time to observe, as if this is the first time you have experienced this scenery and the surrounding elements of nature. When you find yourself getting distracted, come back to the scenery around you.

14. Objects in a bag: Take a bag and add in various types of objects. Make sure the objects are different in texture and shape. Pass the bag around and take turns using your sense of touch to guess what each object is. Observe and Describe the sensations.

15. Making sounds: Go around the group making funny sounds, one person at a time. Pass the sound from one person to another. Notice and release judgments, staying with the game. Alternatively, break into small groups or dyads and create a mantra (word or phrase to repeat) for relaxation, connection, energy, teamwork, or some other concept. Share your mantras and repeat them as a large group for 1 minute each, noticing the connection between the mantra and the resulting emotions and experience.

16. Meditate on an object: Find something in the room to focus on and use that object to ground you while you breathe. It could be a painting, a vase, or any ordinary household object. Fix your gaze on your chosen object, staying with it as you breathe. If you get distracted just pull yourself back to the object of focus.

17. Spaceship: Imagine you have a spaceship that can rocket you to your favorite place, real or imagined. Climb into your ship and count down from 10 to 1 and then blast off to your destination. Stay at your destination awhile and practice breathing, and then ride back home via your rocket ship or another means feeling relaxed and refreshed.

18. Easy and enjoyable sitting mediation: Sit in a comfortable chair, on a park bench, or out on your deck or porch. You are alive! So breathe the air, see your surroundings, listen to the sounds, and feel bodily sensations such as your physical connection to your seat, the air temperature, the breeze, etc. You have no place to be but here. Keep it simple.

19. Mindfulness apps: Search your smartphone, tablet, or computer for free or inexpensive mindfulness apps. Practice each one you find several times, and share them with your friends and family.

20. Breathing colors: Choose two different colors, one to breathe in and one to breathe out. Blue works well for the in-breath, since it matches the cool feeling of the air coming in. Red works well for the out-breath, as it matches the warm feeling of the air leaving your body. However, choose the colors you want, for the reasons you want. Close your eyes and pair each color with its breath.

21. Square breathing: Start by breathing in for four seconds. Hold your breath for four seconds, and then breathe out for another four seconds. Repeat four times.

22. Deep breathing: Breathe in through your nose and out through your mouth. To increase focus and quiet the mind, you can use a mantra such as "in" for when you breathe in and "out" for when you breathe out.

23. Belly breathing: Lie down on your back on the floor or in bed (preferred), or sit upright in a chair. Place a hand on your belly, and as you breathe in watch how your belly expands. Breathing in this way promotes deep breathing, which helps to get oxygen into your system. More oxygen helps us relax our bodies and think more clearly. Set an alarm and breathe deeply for a minimum of 1 minute.

24. Progressive muscle relaxation: Use the classic "squeeze and release" relaxation technique, beginning with your toes and working all the way up to your face. Squeeze each part of your body, holding the tension for a couple of seconds, and then release. Notice both the state of tension for each body part as well as the state of release. Although this exercise works best using your whole body, it can also be condensed to use fewer body parts, such as just squeezing and releasing your hands (making fists and then shaking them out), or by just scrunching up your face before relaxing it. For more directions, search for progressive muscle relaxation scripts online or on YouTube.

25. Body scan: Use Observe and Describe to scan your body from top to bottom, noting areas of tension and discomfort. Gently dismiss judgments that arise, and take a deep breath into each area of the body where this discomfort exists. Do not have an agenda about changing how these areas feel, but do notice differences that happen as you continue to breathe and connect. Also, notice areas of your body that feel relaxed and comfortable. Breathe into these areas too.

26. Rigid body/relaxed body: Stand and tighten your body, assuming a rigid and stiff stance. Hold that pose for 10 seconds or more. Then, relax your body and assume a loose, flexible, and comfortable stance. Identify the different emotions and sensations that came up with each pose.

27. Half-smile (or full smile): Sit in a chair and take a couple of deep breaths. As you continue to breathe, slowly start to turn the sides of your lips upward to make a small smile. Relax your face and take on this more serene look. Notice whether your emotions begin to change, as your face communicates acceptance to your brain. Alternatively, look in a mirror, make a peace sign with your first and middle fingers, and use those fingers to push up the sides of your mouth into a goofy smile. This moment need not be so serious, even if your life sometimes is!

28. Positive memories: Remember a positive event from your life, and use your imagination to transport yourself back to that time and place. Play it in your mind as if it is a movie, and tune in to your senses to fully enter into the memory. Notice what emotions come up as you immerse yourself in the experience. Let this positive memory have an impact on you.

29. Compassion for others: Think of a person who has offended you or others with his or her behavior. Imagine what factors would lead a person to behave in ways that hurt or put off others. Or imagine that person as a child or a baby with innocence. Send this person compassion from your heart, wishing them well in this world. Does sending compassion feel different from holding on to painful feelings about this person?

30. Pictures and judgments: Look at photos in a magazine and describe what comes to mind. What judgments do you notice? Now take a second and describe what you see in a matter-of-fact manner, sticking to the facts. Notice the difference in the experience.

31. Gratitude lists: Make a gratitude list with everything you can think of on it, both big and small. Mediate on the list for several minutes. Note any changes in your emotions. Alternatively, write a thank-you letter to someone, being specific about what the person did to receive your gratitude.

32. 5, 4, 3, 2, 1 senses: To increase your awareness and ground yourself in the present moment, list five things you see, four things you hear, three things you feel, two things you smell, and one thing you taste.

33. Standing like a tree: Stand up and pretend your legs are the roots of a tree, reaching your arms up to be the branches. Start to sway side to side as if you are blowing in the wind. Notice that your legs don't move, keeping you grounded. Imagine yourself being a tree when the winds of life whip up. Be flexible yet grounded, like a strong tree weathers a storm.

34. Finding your center: Sit upright in a comfortable position and take several deep breaths. On the next exhale lean as far to the right as you can without falling over. Inhale and return to center. Then exhale and lean far to the left. Inhale to the center. Slowly start to repeat, leaning less and less every time. When you finally reach the middle, your center, take several deep breaths and notice what it feels like to be in balance.

35. Seeking clarity: Take a jar, fill it with water, and put in fine sand, glitter, or another substance that can be shaken up. Once the lid is tight, shake up the jar. Notice the chaos as the sand or glitter moves about the water, with the water being cloudy or unclear. Then, mindfully watch as everything slowly settles, ultimately bringing clarity to the water. Think about the parallels between Emotion Mind and chaos compared to Wise Mind and clarity.

36. Yoga: Take 5 minutes and assume simple yoga poses (check out a book or video on yoga). Notice your body and remember to breathe as you hold each pose. Just notice emotions, thoughts, and sensations that arise, clinging to none. With practice, this exercise is grounding and relaxing, and promotes regulation of body and mind.

37. Mandalas and coloring books: Mediate on the process of coloring, losing yourself in the activity.

38. Simon says: This game is all about focusing and sustaining attention. Remember to let go of judgments and have fun!

39. Jenga: Focus with one mind as you remove blocks and build the tower higher and higher. Notice your connection to removing and stacking the blocks, immersing yourself in the activity. When the tower tumbles, remember that this is the natural outcome of the game.

40. Categories: Pick a category such as animals or foods and list as many items from that category as possible. In a group setting, go around the circle with each person repeating the items already listed before adding to the category.

41. Picnic game: Start with the phrase "I am going on a picnic and I'm bringing. . ." Go around the circle with each person adding something they are bringing, but only after he or she has said all the items that were mentioned before, in order. For an added challenge, this game can be played listing items from A to Z.

42. Riddles: Buy a book on riddles or search for them online. Contemplate possible solutions. An example: "I am an ancient invention that allows people to see through walls. What am I?"

43. 20 Questions: Play 20 questions with a friend, a child, or your family.

44. Untie knots: Start with string or a shoelace that has been tangled and knotted up. Start to untangle and untie the knots. What emotions come up. Frustration? Impatience? Breathe and practice acceptance as you mindfully complete this activity.

45. Blow bubbles: Blow bubbles and watch as they float through the air, eventually popping. Notice sensations, such as your breathing, the air you blow into the bubble, and any emotions that arise from the activity.

46. Play catch: Play this simple game with the goal of being in the moment.

47. Play catch with categories: Take one ball to throw around a group of people standing in a circle. Pick a category such as countries, music artists, or movie stars. Every time someone catches the ball, they add to the list. If a person cannot add to the list, he or she can create the next category and continue the game.

48. Energy ball: Imagine a ball as a source of negative emotional and mental energy. Hold on to the ball in your hand and take some time to process what it is like to hold on to your negative energy. Do you want to continue to hold on to it? Tell yourself that you have the choice to let the ball go and put it down. Alternatively, decide to bounce the ball off the floor or wall, imagining the negative energy leaving the ball with each bounce, until the ball becomes neutral again.

49. I spy memory game: Find a page in a magazine full of various objects and take 1 minute to mindfully look over the page. After the minute is up, close the magazine and write down all of the things that you remember.

50. Write with your nondominant hand: Create an encouraging or coping statement and write it out 10 times with your nonwriting hand. Notice any frustrations or judgments that come up and practice releasing them. Engage in the process, noting the level of focus needed to have the writing be legible.

51. Attention to small moments: Small moments in our lives include those that we do not typically notice and those we take for granted. A small moment may be having a cup of coffee or a cool glass of water, spending a moment with a child or pet, or performing any everyday activity that goes by without our attention. Enjoyment, peace, and serenity in life happen in the small moments. Each hour, orient yourself to the small moments that you might otherwise miss.

52. Focus on senses: Take time to notice what comes through your five senses: what you see, hear, smell, taste, and/or touch. Your senses are your gateway to the world. (See Self-Soothe in Module 3: Distress Tolerance.)

53. Breathing: We all breathe, and we can all breathe more effectively. Our breath is our anchor and is an excellent way to center ourselves. Take time to breathe mindfully in and out. Stay focused on the sensation of the air coming into your air passages and lungs, holding it, and then letting it out. Use a mantra, such as "in" as you breathe in and "out" as you breathe out, or count each breath from 1 to 10, starting over when you reach 10 or if you lose count.

54. Breathing life cycle: Another way to breathe mindfully is to notice the beginning, middle, and end of each inhalation and exhalation (like how you can hear the beginning, middle, and end of sounds— another mindfulness exercise). Concentrate on the life of each breath going in and out.

55. Quiet/still time: Set time aside each day to be quiet and to experience that quiet. Be One-Mindful with the stillness, finding your center and noticing comfort in the moment.

56. Your favorite song (or album): Listen to your favorite song or album with your full attention. Listen closely to the lyrics and their meaning. Be mindful of each word and phrase. Listen to the sounds of the different instruments. Pay attention to the guitar, bass, drums, vocals, or any other instrument that is central to the music. Notice the production values: Is the song basic or elaborate? Bare bones or highly orchestrated? Be mindful of things you have never noticed in music you have listened to many times.

57. Your favorite show: Watch your favorite TV show, paying attention to the small details. Notice what the actors are wearing, how the sets are designed and decorated, and other elaborate details that go into your show.

58. The room you know so well: Observe and Describe details that you never noticed about your bedroom, living room, office, or any other place in which you have spent a significant amount of time.

59. 10 details: Anyplace, anywhere, pause and Observe and Describe 10 details you would not have otherwise noticed.

60. Turn down the noise (or embrace it): Turn off all extra sources of noise in your home. If you are not mindfully listening to the radio or TV, turn it off. Work on being present without the competition for your attention. If you are unable to turn down certain noises, practice being mindfully aware of them, noticing them without judgment.

61. People (or anything) watching: Be a watcher of people, or of anything that might hold your interest. Remember not to judge what you see, but simply let it into and out of your experience like clouds floating through the sky.

62. One chore/one task: Do one chore or one task, such as washing the dishes or folding laundry, with all of your attention and care. Be One-Mindful with the experience without adding or subtracting.

63. "Holding" a feeling: Hold your present feeling like it is a baby. Calming a distraught baby involves compassion and One-Mindfulness. Babies can tell when we are either frustrated or do not want to be with them in the moment. Our feelings are like babies: They too can tell when we either reject them or are not fully present with them. Holding your feeling and being mindful of it will usually cause it to diminish in intensity. If not, consider distraction skills.

64. Interconnection: Contemplate how you are connected to all of the items around you, to your surroundings, to all of the people in your life, and/or to the universe in general.

65. Relative thinking: Contemplate the upsides and downsides of any judgment without sticking to any conclusions. See how "good" and "bad" depend on the circumstances and are not fixed.

66. 5/60: Plan 5 minutes out of every hour to engage in a mindfulness activity. This may include breathing, doing a scan of your body for tension and then relaxing, or one-mindfully accomplishing any task.

67. Find your center: Before engaging in thoughts and behavior, spend a moment to breathe and find your center. Know that finding your center helps you to access your Wise Mind. Practice the directives of the mantra: Pause, breath, center . . . enter.

68. Write and release: Write what you would like to let go of on paper and shred it, burn it, or place the paper under water and watch the ink wash away and disappear.

69. Lie in the grass: On a day with nice weather, find a patch of lush, green grass in your yard or a park. Lie down, close your eyes, and turn your attention toward the connection and sensations between your body and the grass, feeling yourself supported by the ground. Breathe in the sensations and stay there awhile. Following the exercise, notice what you are feeling. Alternatively, keep your eyes open and gaze at the sky, watching the clouds float into and out of your field of vision. Contemplate the connection between yourself, the earth, and the sky. Take your time in this place, and breathe.

70. Practice compassion for yourself and others: Sit or lie down in a comfortable spot, and turn your attention to your breathing. As you breathe say to yourself over and over, "May I experience peace and happiness." Once you have settled into mediating on this mantra, change the mantra to focus on another person by saying, "May (Person) experience peace and happiness." Continue to breathe as you meditate on this thought from your heart. Extra credit: Make the person you wish peace and happiness to someone you dislike.

71. Report on your experience or surroundings: Write or narrate what is happening right now with your emotions, thoughts, physical sensations, and/or behavior. In doing so, pretend that you are a reporter giving an objective account to your audience. Notice what it is like to Observe and Describe your experience in this somewhat detached manner.

72. Explain a task (and then participate in it): Take any daily task or chore, such as making coffee, sweeping a room, or watering plants, and break it down into its component steps. Imagine that you would have to explain how to do this to a child or even an alien, and go into minute detail. Now, actually engage in the task or chore, noticing each step and participating in it mindfully.

73. Look through a new window: Pick a window in your home, school, or office that you never (or almost never) look through. Sit down and spend 5 or more minutes gazing through the window, observing what is outside. Notice the scenery and whether anything is happening outside the window. Describe the scene and/or action to yourself and connect with it. Extra credit: Contemplate the "windows" in your life you do not or refuse to look through. What would you notice if you chose to look through one or more of these windows?

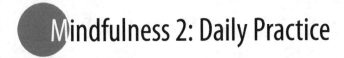

Mindfulness 2: Daily Practice

CORE CONCEPT: Use this worksheet to track daily mindfulness practice.

Pick mindfulness exercises from the examples above (or from another resource) to use in your daily practice and to record on this worksheet. Notice how you feel and/or your urge level before and after each mindfulness exercise.

Exercise: _____

Distress/urge level before: _____ Distress/urge level after: _____

Exercise: _____

Distress/urge level before: _____ Distress/urge level after: _____

Exercise: _____

Distress/urge level before: _____ Distress/urge level after: _____

Exercise: _____

Distress/urge level before: _____ Distress/urge level after: _____

Exercise: _____

Distress/urge level before: _____ Distress/urge level after: _____

Exercise: _____

Distress/urge level before: _____ Distress/urge level after: _____

Exercise: _____

Distress/urge level before: _____ Distress/urge level after: _____

Mindfulness 3: 10 Days to a 10-Minute Meditation Practice

CORE CONCEPT: Use this simple and doable method to develop a meditation practice.

Carving out time to develop a meditation practice seems daunting for most people. Often, we feel either like we do not have the time or that it will not matter unless we commit a serious amount of time to it. Fortunately, 10 minutes can usually be found either by reorganizing our schedules or via the time-saving benefits of practice, which are less time stuck in mental health symptoms and more efficiency approaching the tasks in our lives. Further, research also shows that even brief amounts of meditation make real differences in life.

To get started, schedule a time and place to practice, perhaps setting an alarm on your watch or phone to remind you until it is a habit. The time can be whenever suits you, although some people prefer to start or end their day with it. In fact, one way to solve the time problem for busy people is to simply wake up 15 minutes early to have quiet time for the practice. That 15 minutes of lost sleep is a good trade-off for the benefits of meditation. Whenever the time is, do try to make it a quiet, less hectic time, although that is not essential if that is not possible in your environment. In terms of place, pick somewhere that is comfortable. It may be a chair where you can sit with an upright posture, or it may be lying down on the floor or bed. Remember that this is simple and doable meditation, so do not needlessly complicate the process!

When you sit or lie down during your meditation time, the only task is to close your eyes and focus on your breath, which has been waiting for you the whole time. Naturally, distractions will arise. You will notice emotions, thoughts (maybe a lot of them, including judgments), bodily sensations, and other distractions in your environment. When you notice these distractions, simply refocus on connecting with your breath, over and over again. If you so choose, you can add in a mantra to focus your attention on the breath. Perhaps you say silently to yourself "in" when you breathe in and "out" when you breath out. Be sure to set a timer so you do not have to think about time in a practical way (thoughts about time may still come up as distractions).

That's it! Do this and you are officially meditating. Follow this simple 10-day schedule below to build up to 10 minutes of meditation per day. Note that, if you would like to start smaller, you can simply halve the amounts of time (i.e., building to 5 minutes of meditation). Check in on your general distress or urge level before and after the meditation, and briefly journal about your experience if you choose. After 10 days congratulate yourself. You did it!

Day one: Meditate for 1 minute.

Distress or urge level: Before _____ After _____

Describe your experience:

_____

Day two: Meditate for 2 minutes.

Distress or urge level: Before _____ After _____

Describe your experience:

_____

Day three: Meditate for 3 minutes

Distress or urge level: Before _____ After _____

Describe your experience:

_____

Day four: Meditate for 4 minutes

Distress or urge level: Before _____ After _____

Describe your experience:

_____

Day five: Meditate for 5 minutes

Distress or urge level: Before _____ After _____

Describe your experience:

_____

Day six: Mediate for 6 minutes

Distress or urge level: Before _____ After _____

Describe your experience:

_____

Day seven: Meditate for 7 minutes

Distress or urge level: Before _____ After _____

Describe your experience:

_____

Day eight: Meditate for 8 minutes

Distress or urge level: Before _____ After _____

Describe your experience:

_____

Day nine: Meditate for 9 minutes

Distress or urge level: Before _____ After _____

Describe your experience:

_____

Day ten: Meditate for 10 minutes

Distress or urge level: Before _____ After _____

Describe your experience:

_____

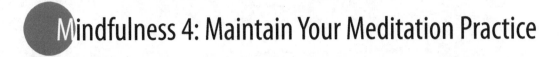# Mindfulness 4: Maintain Your Meditation Practice

CORE CONCEPT: Use this worksheet to maintain your meditation practice.

Track your daily meditation on this worksheet, noting how you feel before and after each meditation. Note that you can give yourself credit for shorter meditation times too.

Monday meditation

Distress/urge level before: _____ Distress/urge level after: _____

Tuesday meditation

Distress/urge level before: _____ Distress/urge level after: _____

Wednesday meditation

Distress/urge level before: _____ Distress/urge level after: _____

Thursday meditation

Distress/urge level before: _____ Distress/urge level after: _____

Friday meditation

Distress/urge level before: _____ Distress/urge level after: _____

Saturday mediation

Distress/urge level before: _____ Distress/urge level after: _____

Sunday meditation

Distress/urge level before: _____ Distress/urge level after: _____

Module 3

Distress Tolerance

Introduction to Distress Tolerance

■ *CORE CONCEPT*: Distress tolerance helps us cope with crisis without making our situation worse.

We sometimes cope with intense emotions in ways that make our situation worse or cause us to neglect our long-term priorities, goals, and values. This coping may work in the short term, but it sabotages our long-term Life Vision. For example, drinking, using drugs, or engaging in self-injury often relieves stress, tension, and emotional pain, but none of these ways of coping are sustainable in our lives. Further, ineffective coping behaviors often cause additional emotional intensity and pain in the long term. Distress tolerance skills provide alternatives to help us cope in the short term without making our situation worse, and they keep us true to our priorities, goals, values, and Life Vision.

One key to distress tolerance skills is making sure that we consistently practice them when we are not in distress. Skills work when we work the skills because practice is how we gain competency with skills. Trying to use skills in a crisis without previously practicing them would be like trying to hit a home run in a big ballgame when you have never picked up a bat. Fortunately, distress tolerance skills are often enjoyable to do in and of themselves, so practicing them does not have to feel like a chore.

Another key to distress tolerance is putting a proactive plan together. We often end up reacting to life situations rather than having a plan for how to respond to them. It is difficult to be effective when we react rather than respond, and the plan we create while in Reason Mind or Wise Mind provides needed balance and direction when in extremes of Emotion Mind.

Luckily, we can simply look to our past to make plans for our future. From our histories, we can identify our vulnerabilities and triggering situations and create a responsive plan that combines the effective coping behaviors we already do with the new skills we are learning. Note that your distress tolerance plan will include skills from the other modules too, as you have to combine skills from all modules to be most effective.

Once you have an effective distress tolerance plan, you can more easily strike the dialectical balance between mindful acceptance and tolerance of emotions (especially painful ones) and effective distraction. With that balance, you can validate your emotions while you also cope in healthy ways.

Distress Tolerance: Guidelines for Use

■ *CORE CONCEPT*: Understand when and how to use distress tolerance to increase effectiveness.

Distress tolerance skills are more effective when the guidelines listed here are followed. Like other skills, the effectiveness of distress tolerance is based on knowing when to use these skills and on recognizing their limitations.

As a rule, distress tolerance is used when we cannot solve a problem. If we *can* solve a problem and it is an okay time to do so, solving it will usually be the best strategy.

However, there are times when we have the solution to our problem but it is not a good time to solve it. In these cases, we can use distress tolerance until we can solve the problem at a better time.

At other times, we need to use distress tolerance to soothe our emotions before we can solve a problem effectively. In other words, sometimes we know the solution and it is an okay time to proceed, except we are not in Wise Mind enough to be effective. In these cases, we might benefit from distress tolerance before problem-solving.

Ask yourself the following three questions to help you to decide between solving a problem and using distress tolerance:

- Am I able to solve the problem? Yes or no. If no, use distress tolerance.

- Is it an okay time to solve the problem? Yes or no. If no, use distress tolerance.

- Am I in Wise Mind enough to solve the problem? Yes or no. If no, use distress tolerance.

If you answer yes to all three questions, work on solving your problem instead of using distress tolerance.

If you answer yes to these three questions but avoid attending to and solving your problems, you will eventually end up overwhelmed. It is important to avoid the use of distress tolerance to distract from life, because excessive use of distraction leads to our problems piling up.

When we cannot attend to or solve our problems, distress tolerance skills replace unhealthy coping behaviors such as self-injury, drinking and drug use, and other behaviors that can damage self-respect or cause other short- and long-term problems.

Nonetheless, we are sometimes reluctant to give up our unhealthy coping behaviors even when we know they are destructive to ourselves or others. If you are unsure about giving up a behavior, you may start by simply increasing your options through learning and practicing distress tolerance skills. Over time, you may have the confidence to let go of your old ways of just surviving.

As you learn and practice these skills, remember that they are meant to be used in the short term. We need to have many distress tolerance skills ready to use in cases when a crisis lasts for a long time, so keep adding more of these skills to your "toolbox." The more we explore and practice the skills in this module, the more we can manage ourselves and our lives—maybe even proactively changing our vulnerabilities and emotions.

Finally, remember to use your mindfulness skills along with your distress tolerance skills. Distress tolerance skills are much less effective if we continue to focus mentally on our crisis. Mindfulness of the skills we use is the foundation for successful use.

As you start to use distress tolerance skills, it is helpful to consider the following dialectics: Attend to the problem versus distract from the problem, and be mindful of the emotion versus be mindful of the distraction. The key to navigating these dialectics is considering the most effective choice in the moment.

Distress Tolerance 1: Crisis and Safety Plan

CORE CONCEPT: Develop a plan to manage crisis and safety issues.

Begin to fill out this plan and continue to add to it as you learn more skills. Treat this plan as a "living" document: It needs to be continuously reviewed, practiced, and updated.

Make several copies and always know where to find your plan. It is hard to know what to do when you are in the heat of the moment. That is why you have a written plan.

Give copies to the people in your support system and discuss your use of the plan proactively. Again, practice, practice, practice—practice makes you prepared to be effective in life.

My reasons for managing crisis effectively and/or staying safe: List all of your priorities, goals, values, and people that matter to you. These are your "whys" that motivate you to use the plan:

_____

_____

_____

My strengths and resources: List what you have going for you. Ask for help if you are unsure:

_____

_____

_____

Warning signs: These are the signals that you may be in crisis or unsafe or about to be in crisis or unsafe. Be as specific as possible. Look to your history for clues:

_____

_____

_____

Feelings: Ask yourself what you are/were feeling before or during this time:

_____

_____

_____

Thoughts: Ask yourself what you are/were thinking before or during this time:

_____

_____

_____

Behaviors: Ask yourself what you are/were doing and/or not doing before or during this time:

_____

_____

_____

Sensations: Ask yourself what you are/were experiencing physically or in your body before or during this time:

_____

_____

_____

Environment: Ask yourself what your environment is/was like and/or what is/was happening in your environment before or during this time:

_____

_____

_____

Key triggers: Ask yourself what sets off a crisis and/or being unsafe for you:

_____

_____

_____

Barriers to skill use: List what will get in the way of using your skills and this plan _and_ list the skills you will use to address each barrier:

_____

_____

_____

Burn the bridges: Write how you will remove the means to act on urges (be specific):

_____

_____

_____

Self-care skills to use: List all of the ways you can care for yourself during this time:

_____

_____

_____

Distress tolerance skills to use: List specific behaviors:

_____

_____

_____

My personal support system: List names and numbers of people/resources you can call, when they are accessible, and the specific interpersonal and other skills you will need to use these supports:

_____

_____

_____

My professional support system: List names and numbers of people/resources you can call, when they are accessible, and the specific interpersonal and other skills you will need to use these supports:

_____

_____

_____

My medications and dosages:

_____

_____

_____

My hospital of choice:

_____

_____

_____

My commitment: I commit to practicing my plan proactively and during times of crisis. I further commit to be safe and call 911 or go to the hospital *before* acting on suicidal urges.

Signed by Client: _____ Date: _____

Original to client; copy to chart

Distract with ACCEPTS

■ *CORE CONCEPT:* Mindfully practice distraction skills when in high distress.

When we experience distress or a crisis or feel unsafe, we have a few choices. We can work on problem-solving, be mindful of our painful emotions, or work on distraction skills.

Use the acronym ACCEPTS to remember the building blocks (**A**ctivities, **C**ontributing, **C**omparisons, **E**motions, **P**ush Away, **T**houghts, **S**ensations) of this skill. These building blocks are described in further detail in the paragraphs that follow.

Activities

Activities help you to decrease depression, anxiety, and other symptoms and can create positive emotions. You need to plan activities as part of your daily routine and follow through with the plans. For ideas, consult the Activities List in Module 9: Building a Satisfying Life.

Activities work best when they engage you physically and/or mentally. Remember mindfulness skills (and the other distress tolerance skills, too) need to be used in connection to activities.

You may have difficulty with activities because you lack interest or energy. When writers have writer's block, they continue to write anyway, because inspiration finds us when we are at work. If we wait to be interested, we might wait a long time. You can control the choice to engage in activities, and in time interest and enjoyment will follow if you do not obsess on them. In other words, mindfully engage in activities without concern for being caught up in interest or enjoyment. Nonetheless, starting with activities that have been interesting and enjoyable in the past is a good strategy.

Use Opposite to Emotion when energy is low and/or DEAR MAN to get others to help you get kick-started. The first law of physics applies: A body at rest tends to stay at rest, and a body in motion tends to stay in motion.

Describe how you can use **Activities**:

_____

Contributing

Contributing gets you out of yourself and your distress and into participating with others and in the world. We all need a break from ourselves sometimes. Contributing also helps you feel connected and less alone, and it creates positive feelings.

Contribute in small but impactful ways: Smile at others, give compliments, hold a door, or do a favor. Thoughtful and unexpected acts of kindness, random or not, fit the bill. Let someone else have a parking spot or move ahead of you in line. Assist others, be part of a team effort, and participate. Simply listening to others can be a great contribution, too. Also consider longer-term ways of contributing, such as volunteering.

Describe how you can use **Contributing**:

_____

Comparisons

Comparisons bring perspective to your current situation. You can compare yourself to other times when you have dealt with more difficult problems or been less effective with skills. You can also compare yourself to others who struggle with even greater problems than you. It is important to remember to validate ourselves as we use comparisons—we can experience tough times *and* have perspective through this skill.

Describe how you can use **Comparisons**:

Emotions

Seek out activities, events, and thoughts that create feelings that are different from the painful ones you are experiencing. Remember that emotions can be influenced by what you choose to do and what you choose to think about.

Listen to music that creates specific emotions: loud and fast music when fatigued, calming music when anxious or upset, and uplifting music when sad. Watch favorite shows or movies, fondly remember fun times (without comparing them to your current situation), or work on a project.

Alternatively, sometimes we can use emotions to validate our feelings. For example, we can listen to melancholy music when sad. However, be careful not to get stuck! The concept is self-validation, not wallowing.

Describe how you can use **Emotions**:

Push Away

Put away distress by mentally locking it in a box and putting it on a shelf in a locked room. Make the imagery as vivid as possible, practicing it over and over. Say "this is a tomorrow problem" and then focus on something else. Or, write something down about the problem and put it away in a drawer or someplace where you will remember to find it when you are ready.

Remember to take out your distress or problem at a safe time in the future to attend to it. Putting and pushing away is a short-term strategy.

Describe how you can use **Push Away**:

Thoughts

Mindfully focus on distracting thoughts. You can only think about one thing at a time, and your distress may diminish when you think about something else. The classic example is counting to 100 when angry; thinking about something else (counting) allows us to cool down and be more rational.

Read a magazine or book, do Sudoku or other puzzles, or think about inspirational sayings and quotes. Bring your thoughts mindfully to other distress tolerance skills or activities.

Describe how you can use **Thoughts**:

_____

Sensations

Sensations include anything that is physically vigorous or actively awakens your senses. The skill is different from the Self-Soothe skills in that it seeks to stimulate rather than relax.

Take a brisk walk or engage in exercise, such as running or weight-lifting. Get into a hot or cold bath or shower or splash cold water on your face. Engage your senses with loud music, bold colors, or strong tastes or smells.

Some people hold ice cubes or a frozen orange when in distress as a substitute for self-injury because the physical pain distracts from the emotional pain. These practices can work in a "harm-reduction" approach, meaning they can be used as safe step-down techniques when you are trying to stop self-injury but are not yet completely ready. Remember that ultimately the goal is to learn that you do not need physical pain to cope with emotional pain.

Describe how you can use **Sensations**:

_____

Distress Tolerance 2: Activities

CORE CONCEPT: Use this worksheet to monitor your activities and their benefits.

Activities provide healthy distractions and create enjoyment. Getting active alleviates the symptoms of mental illness and provides alternatives to ineffective behaviors. Use this worksheet to list activities you plan to do for each day of the week. Notice how you feel and/or your urge level before and after each activity.

Monday: _____

Distress/urge level before: _____ Distress/urge level after: _____

Tuesday: _____

Distress/urge level before: _____ Distress/urge level after: _____

Wednesday: _____

Distress/urge level before: _____ Distress/urge level after: _____

Thursday: _____

Distress/urge level before: _____ Distress/urge level after: _____

Friday: _____

Distress/urge level before: _____ Distress/urge level after: _____

Saturday: _____

Distress/urge level before: _____ Distress/urge level after: _____

Sunday: _____

Distress/urge level before: _____ Distress/urge level after: _____

Self-Soothe (SS)

■ *CORE CONCEPT:* Create relaxation with a mindful connection to the senses.

Self-Soothe involves entering into the world around us through our five main senses individually or in a multisensory way. We can also soothe ourselves mentally and spiritually. Remember that Self-Soothe requires the use of mindfulness skills.

Sight

Notice what is around you and see the details. Look at pictures or take your own photos. Look at art or do your own drawing or another artistic pursuit that involves vision.

See people, pets, and your favorite possessions and be mindful of what is attractive or visually pleasing. Alternatively, see the beauty in "ordinary" objects or your everyday surroundings.

Look at nature and the landscape around you. See trees and leaves sway and blow in the wind. Look at the sky, the sun, the moon, and the stars. Watch a candle or fire.

Describe how you can self-soothe with **sight**:

_____

Sound

Listen to sounds that comfort you, or notice complete silence. Concentrate on pleasant music, white noise, or the sound of a washing machine or dishwasher if those sounds please you. When listening to music, isolate and focus on each instrument or voice with intention.

Close your eyes, be still, and hear what is happening in your environment. Listen for novel sounds or for sonic patterns and rhythms you never noticed before.

Describe how you can self-soothe with **sound**:

_____

Smell

Put on a favorite cologne or perfume and breathe it in. Smell clean and fresh laundry or sheets. Use incense or other scented products you enjoy. Close your eyes and inhale, choosing to linger on the smell.

Deeply inhale the smells of cooking or baking and your food before eating it or without eating it. Like with sound, noticing the absence of smells can be soothing for some people. Take a deep breath of fresh air (Willie Nelson (2006) says it is the greatest natural high).

Describe how you can self-soothe with **smell**:

_____

Taste

Enjoy each small bite of food or sip of a drink mindfully. Eat one piece of candy or have a small treat with your full attention. Pretend it will be the last time you will eat something and savor each morsel.

Do not mindlessly eat to comfort yourself or eat excessively to self-soothe; these approaches are not skillful.

Describe how you can self-soothe with **taste**:

_____

Touch

Touch and pet a dog or cat or other animal. Use DEAR MAN to ask for a hug or massage from someone, or rub and stroke your own neck or body. Put oils or lotions on your skin.

Wear comfortable clothing or get under a warm, soft blanket or clean, cool sheets. Mindfully notice what your body is in connection with and seek out what pleases it.

Describe how you can self-soothe with **touch**:

_____

Multisensory

Integrate your senses into a rich experience. Make a special meal with nice dishes, place settings, candles, and relaxing music. Spend time outside, focusing on each sense, deciding what sense to attend to in the context of the total experience. Go to a movie with intricate sound and visuals while also noticing the smells of popcorn and the comfort of the seat.

While we can experience each sense individually, the idea here is to create a holistic sensory experience where you chose to attend to each element in connection to the whole. Notice how each sense can complement the others in a total experience.

Describe how you can self-soothe by **combining senses**:

_____

Mind sense

Engage in those parts of your mental life that bring you relaxation and happiness. Examples include peaceful thoughts, affirmations, and meditations as well as daydreams and fantasies.

Describe how you can self-soothe through your **mind sense**:

_____

Spiritual sense

Your spiritual sense is an individually defined sense of connection to a higher power, spirit, or nature. This sense, less tangible than the others, can create peace, serenity, and well-being.

We self-soothe with a spiritual sense through mindful reflections, rituals, and contemplation.

Describe how you can self-soothe through your **spiritual sense**:

_____

Distress Tolerance 3: Self-Soothe Application

CORE CONCEPT: Use this exercise to overcome barriers to the practice of Self-Soothe.

For most of us, the concept of Self-Soothe is straightforward, but allowing ourselves to engage in these skills or addressing other barriers may be more difficult. Use this worksheet to identify Self-Soothe skills and other skills to overcome barriers.

Describe how you can use Self-Soothe skills:

_____

_____

Describe barriers to Self-Soothe skills (e.g., judgments about self, judgments about deserving, environmental factors):

_____

_____

Describe other skills you will use to address each barrier:

_____

_____

Describe how your life will be different when you practice Self-Soothe:

_____

_____

IMPROVE the Moment

■ *CORE CONCEPT*: Make the here and now better when in distress.

Like ACCEPTS, these skills provide healthy distractions.

Use the acronym IMPROVE to remember the building blocks (**I**magery, **M**eaning, **P**rayer, **R**elaxation, **O**ne thing or step at a time, **V**acation, **E**ncouragement) of this skill. These building blocks are described in further detail in the paragraphs that follow.

Imagery

Your mind is powerful. Think of times when you have distressed yourself with negative imagery. In contrast, you can harness the power of positive imagery to feel better and more relaxed. Concentrate on a scene in your mind (a beach, the forest, a safe and happy place). Your mind can convince your body that it is there.

Use guided imagery with a CD, app, or YouTube video. Enter a daydream. Consider practicing imagery before bedtime as part of your sleep routine. Practice skill use in your mind's eye (this has been proven to be effective in sports).

As distractions creep in, gently let them go and refocus.

Describe how you can use **Imagery**:

_____

Meaning

Validate that the cloud is there *and* find the silver lining. Is there an opportunity in this problem? What is the lesson or the learning that will come from your difficulties? Victor Frankl, renowned existential psychiatrist and concentration camp survivor, once said, "If you can find a why, you can tolerate almost any how." List your reasons for surviving crisis.

Describe how you can use **Meaning**:

_____

Prayer

Pray for strength and resolve in distressing times. Seek connection with and guidance from your higher power. Avoid "why me?" or bargaining prayers as those prayers tend to demoralize us rather than build us up.

As an alternative, "talk" to anyone important to you: A deceased relative you loved, a person you admire (whether you know him/her or not), or anyone who helps you feel connected outside yourself.

Describe how you can use **Prayer**:

_____

Relaxation

Practice breathing exercises, self-soothe skills, progressive muscle relaxation with each major muscle group, or anything that calms you. Engage in activities you find relaxing every day.

Describe how you can use **Relaxation**:

_____

One thing or step at a time

When overwhelmed, go back to the most important priority again and again. If you have many problems, pick the most important one to focus on or the one you have the most resources to solve. In the context of solving problems, taking one step at a time helps to manage your distress.

Describe how you can use **One Thing or Step at a Time**:

_____

Vacation

Most of us cannot take a real vacation when in distress or maybe even at all. Vacation means taking a break when we are in distress or even before we are in distress. Step outside, breathe fresh air, and take a short walk. Spend 10 minutes listening to music or surfing the internet. Talk with a friend or coworker. "Take a load off." Plan some time for yourself as part of your routine.

Remember to keep these "vacations" brief. We want to take a break from problems but not let them continue to build.

Describe how you can use **Vacation**:

_____

Encouragement

We all talk to ourselves, so we might as well say something positive! Validate your feelings and then encourage yourself like you would a close friend. Life is not impossible; it just feels that way sometimes. Be mindful of your self-talk and make it positive.

Describe how you can use **Encouragement**:

_____

Pros and Cons (P&C)

■ *CORE CONCEPT:* The Pros and Cons skill leads us to Wise Mind decisions.

We can use Pros and Cons any time that we struggle with a decision. This skill allows us to weigh the options in light of expected results in both the short and the long term. Pros and Cons is proactive and leads us to Wise Mind before we commit to any action. Moreover, if we use Pros and Cons to decide whether we want to engage in a harmful behavior, often we will find that the urge has subsided by the time the exercise is complete.

To use this skill, start by identifying your basic choices. Examples include drinking or using drugs versus staying sober, using self-injury versus staying safe, and practicing an old behavior versus practicing a skill.

When you have identified the basic choices, plug them into the worksheet that follows. After you have determined both short- and long-term pros and cons, check to see whether you are in Wise Mind and make a decision. If you find that you are not in Wise Mind, table your decision and try another skill.

Pros and Cons (P&C) Application Example	
My Basic Choices Are: Using self-injury versus using skills	
Short-Term PROS of Self-Injury	**Short-Term CONS of Self-Injury**
Numbed my feelings! Worked Blood grounded me	Missed chance to use plan WORRIED about upcoming group Had to hide it
Long-Term PROS of Self-Injury	**Long-Term CONS of Self-Injury**
None really	Lost trust Lost self-respect More scars Shame sets me up
Versus	
Short-Term PROS of Skill Use	**Short-Term CONS of Skill Use**
No need to lie or cover up Feel good if I make it No hassle with blood and stuff NO BEHAVIOR ANALYSIS!!	Hard and might not work Don't know Maybe more emotional pain
Long-Term PROS of Skill Use	**Long-Term CONS of Skill Use**
RESPECT! Learn to handle life and get somewhere	More expectations? Pressure, I don't know

My Decision: Skills, I guess!!

Distress Tolerance 4: Pros and Cons

Pros and Cons (P&C) Application	
My Basic Choices Are _____ versus _____ .	
Short-Term PROS of _____	**Short-Term CONS of** _____
Long-Term PROS of _____	**Long-Term CONS of** _____
Versus	
Short-Term PROS of _____	**Short-Term CONS of** _____
Long-Term PROS of _____	**Long-Term CONS of** _____
My Decision:	
_____	

Grounding Yourself (GY)

■ *CORE CONCEPT:* Grounding exercises bring you back to the here and now.

Grounding exercises assist us when we drift from the present moment or when we struggle with dissociation, feeling unreal, or PTSD symptoms. Leaving reality is a skill when reality would be too painful for anyone bear. At the same time, leaving reality is less effective when we are distressed but not in imminent psychological and/or physical danger. In these situations, we need to develop more useful coping skills.

Practice these exercises proactively, and they will decrease symptoms of dissociation and derealization. Remember to bring your mindfulness skills along:

- Open your eyes and Observe and Describe your surroundings in detail.

- Who or what is around you? You are here, now. The more detail, no matter how minor, the better.

- Work your senses: Name what you see, hear, smell, and touch right here and now, again using as many details as possible.

- Use the Sensations skill from ACCEPTS. Practice the variations of Sensations.

- Observe your body in contact with your chair. Feel your back, behind, and back of your legs in connection with the chair. Feel your arms in connection with the armrests or your lap. Feel your feet firmly planted on the ground. Now think about how your body is connected to the chair, which is connected to the floor, which is connected to the building, which is connected to the earth.

- Breathe slowly and deeply, counting your breaths.

- Get up and stretch out, feeling your body and moving about.

- Repeat a mantra such as "this is now and not then."

List other ways to ground yourself:

_____

_____

_____

_____

_____

_____

Radical Acceptance (RA)

■ *CORE CONCEPT*: Acceptance decreases suffering.

At times, we have great pain due to trauma, difficult life circumstances, and losses. Suffering is part of everyone's life.

If we are unable to accept situations that cause pain, the result is being stuck and trapped in chronic suffering. Refusal to have a relationship with our suffering creates unending suffering. Paradoxically, we decrease suffering by being willing to accept it and relate to it rather than fight it. We may still have pain to tolerate, but there will be a qualitative difference in our experience of it. Further, acceptance instead of resistance releases our resources to move forward.

When you find yourself in pain, you have four basic choices.

1. Change the situation that is causing you pain

This change may involve ending a hopeless relationship or leaving a dead-end job, or it might involve seeking medical advice or trying to solve some other problem. Changing the situation involves a realistic appraisal of what is and what the options are, grounded in values. Ask yourself: What would you be willing to do to end your suffering?

2. Change how you see the situation or what you think about it

Can you find the upside, silver lining, or meaning in the pain? Would more dialectical thoughts help? Remember that our minds can be powerful in overcoming obstacles, including suffering. Is it a tragedy or "good practice"? Is it a terrible situation or a situation to teach strength, patience, or resilience?

3. Radically accept the situation

Give up fighting reality and release your psychological and emotional resources to move forward. When you accept the situation, you might still have to tolerate pain but you are no longer adding to it. Radical Acceptance means you are willing to experience a situation or state without trying to change it, protest it, or escape it. You will be in a relationship with the pain.

4. Stay stuck in suffering until you are ready to accept reality

Radical acceptance springs from deep within ourselves and requires that we continually orient ourselves toward accepting.

Remember that acceptance is *not* approval, liking it, or giving in. When we recognize, acknowledge, and accept a problem or reality, we actually take control of our lives and emotional health. Acceptance is freedom because it allows us to be effective with what is rather than to stay stuck in denial. Acceptance is the prerequisite to change.

It is helpful to know that Radical Acceptance is a process similar to Kübler-Ross' (2005) stages of acceptance:

1. **Denial:** Not believing our loss, problem, or situation is real.

2. **Anger:** Being angry about why this has or is happening to us.

3. **Bargaining:** Trying to make a deal with someone or a higher power to change reality.

4. **Depression:** Feeling despondent as reality sets in.

5. **Acceptance:** Acknowledging reality without fighting.

These stages do not always happen in sequence. Instead, we often go back and forth in the process, sometimes getting stuck in one stage and/or skipping others. When you experience these stages and emotions, you are in the process of acceptance.

In the words of William James, "Be willing to have it so. Acceptance of what has happened is the first step to overcoming the consequences of any misfortune." Allow it to be so and experience the pain. *You are not and do not need to be the story of your suffering.*

Distress Tolerance 5: Radical Acceptance

CORE CONCEPT: Use this exercise to practice Radical Acceptance in a painful situation.

Describe a situation that causes suffering:

_____

_____

Describe what you can realistically change through problem-solving and/or shifting your thoughts:

_____

_____

Describe what you may need to radically accept:

_____

_____

Describe other skills you may need to practice Radical Acceptance of this situation:

_____

_____

Describe how your life will be different when you have radically accepted this situation:

_____

_____

Everyday Acceptance (EA)

■ *CORE CONCEPT*: Adopting an accepting attitude each day will change your life.

Radical Acceptance is the skill used to deal with painful and difficult-to-accept situations. Starting to practice acceptance in everyday situations will orient you to the practice of Radical Acceptance when life gets extremely difficult. But what is meant by Everyday Acceptance? Consider the following examples:

- You have to wait in a long line.

- Your spouse, partner, or friend is in a lousy mood.

- The delivery person is 30 minutes late.

- Your coworker makes a mistake.

- A guitar string breaks.

- Homework is assigned.

- A friend cancels a date.

- Dinner is not your favorite.

- Your favorite sports team is losing.

- You run out of paper towels.

- The weather does not fit your plans.

- A task needs to be completed.

- Someone cuts you off in traffic.

- MTV shows only 10 seconds of your favorite video.

- You forget to save changes to a computer file.

- You step in gum.

- A dish breaks.

- Your toddler acts like a toddler.

- Gas prices have risen.

- Your partner forgot to pick up milk.

We often cause ourselves to feel frustrated, annoyed, anxious, and stressed out by these common inconveniences. Instead, we can save our resources by meeting these small realities with Everyday Acceptance rather than resistance.

Do not confuse this approach to life with giving in, being walked on, or remaining helpless. Many of these problems have solutions or interventions that are needed (e.g., using assertiveness, running to the store, changing the channel, setting a boundary). However, the use of Everyday Acceptance allows us to have the emotional balance to solve our everyday problems more effectively. Let it be so, and then deal with it effectively.

Willingness (W)

■ *CORE CONCEPT*: Use willingness versus willfulness when stuck.

Many of us learned that "where there is a will there is a way." In other words, our shortcomings come from a lack of willpower.

This belief system is the opposite of what DBT teaches. Sometimes we need to exert our will, but often Willingness is more effective. With willfulness, our options are limited, whereas with Willingness, options to reach goals and solve problems open up through our ability to be creative and flexible. Where there is Willingness there is a way.

This approach works because Willingness aligns us with the realities of a situation rather than pitting ourselves against them. Fighting reality (or anything) rarely creates an effective outcome. Think about power struggles and how ineffective they can be for everybody involved.

Meeting others and situations where they are at instead of where we wish they were frees us to be effective. The parallels to Radical Acceptance and Everyday Acceptance are apparent. Willingness also fits with Effectiveness in the Mindfulness module. Check your priorities, goals, and values to help find your Willingness!

When faced with a problem (and/or when stuck in willfulness), ask yourself what you are willing to do to:

- End your suffering

- Solve a problem—yours, someone else's, or a shared one

- Create a satisfying life.

With time and practice, you will find that Willingness allows you to be more peaceful and effective in life.

Distress Tolerance 6: Skills Practice

CORE CONCEPT: Use this worksheet to monitor your use of distress tolerance skills and their benefits.

Many people develop a few distress tolerance skills and then quit actively exploring and practicing new skills. Just as carpenters, computer programmers, artists, mechanics, students, therapists, and other people work to acquire new tools and techniques, you need to continue to work on new distress tolerance skills to be effective in challenging situations. Use the checklist spaces below to list new distress tolerance skills to practice today or this week, and be sure to check them off after you have practiced them. Notice how you feel before and after each distress tolerance skill.

☐ Distress tolerance skill: _____

    Distress/urge level before: _____ Distress/urge level after: _____

☐ Distress tolerance skill: _____

    Distress/urge level before: _____ Distress/urge level after: _____

☐ Distress tolerance skill: _____

    Distress/urge level before: _____ Distress/urge level after: _____

☐ Distress tolerance skill: _____

    Distress/urge level before: _____ Distress/urge level after: _____

☐ Distress tolerance skill: _____

    Distress/urge level before: _____ Distress/urge level after: _____

☐ Distress tolerance skill: _____

    Distress/urge level before: _____ Distress/urge level after: _____

☐ Distress tolerance skill: _____

    Distress/urge level before: _____ Distress/urge level after: _____

TIP

■ *CORE CONCEPT*: Behaviors that tip your physiology can help you cope with intense emotions.

Intense emotions create intense physiological responses. For example, anger and fear create muscle tension, increased blood pressure, rapid breathing and heart rate, and the release of adrenaline. On the other end of the continuum, depression causes physiological responses such as body aches and pains as well as general loss of energy and fatigue.

Purposefully changing, or "tipping," your physiology can help you to tolerate or even change intense emotions. The acronym TIP describes these strategies. Some of these strategies "shock" the system, some of them use up or conserve energy, and some of them relax the body.

Remember that the TIP skills, like other skills, need to be used mindfully and carefully. The key is tipping your body chemistry and physiological responses in *healthy* ways. Avoid extremes of these strategies that could cause pain or injury.

Used thoughtfully and in balance, TIP skills will be an effective addition to your distress tolerance toolbox.

Temperature

Step out into chilly or cold weather (climate permitting!); place an ice pack on your forehead; fill a sink with extremely cold water (using ice, ice packs, or frozen vegetables) and dunk your face or whole head. By submerging your face in cold water you can stimulate the "dive reflex," a natural set of physical responses that include slowing the heart rate and conserving energy.

Alternatively, you can affect body temperature by taking a hot shower or bath, going in a sauna, or wrapping yourself in warm blankets.

Note how changes in temperature affect emotional responses.

Intense exercise

Walk briskly, run, or sprint; go for a fast bike ride; lift weights or work out with kettlebells; do jumping jacks, push-ups, or other exercises that do not require special equipment; dance.

Vigorously move your body!

Progressive relaxation

Breathe deeply and mindfully for several minutes (or longer); one by one, systematically tense each major muscle group (face, shoulders, arms, hands, torso, buttocks, legs, and feet) for several seconds and then release the tension. Noticing the extremes between tension and release can deepen the sense of relaxation. You can also use guided imagery or search YouTube and the internet for some outstanding demonstrations in progressive relaxation.

Module 4

Emotion Regulation

Introduction to Emotion Regulation

■ **CORE CONCEPT**: Emotion regulation lowers vulnerability and brings balance to your emotions.

Emotions serve many important functions. They provide information about ourselves in relation to other people, situations, and the environment, teaching us and influencing and motivating our behaviors. Emotions also provide the foundation for relationships, being essential for attraction, compassion, and being connected to other people. We would not have the motivation or desire to participate with family, friends, or other people without emotions and what they bring to our relationships. That said, intense and dysregulated emotions sometimes short-circuit their purposes and can be painful and lead to ineffective behavior. Consider these dialectical examples related to emotions:

- A low level of anxiety about a test might motive a person to study and be successful, but a high level of anxiety might paralyze the person and stymie success.

- Anger that is proportional and effectively directed can motivate people to solve issues in relationships or to champion a cause, but intense anger can destroy relationships or sabotage action related to a cause.

- Attraction can motivate you to initiate a healthy and respectful relationship, but sometimes attraction can keep you going back to a harmful relationship.

- Depression can be informative about what needs to change in your life, such as adopting a healthier lifestyle or making a life change, but intense depression can immobilize you and make change difficult.

To achieve balanced and regulated emotions that provide benefits, we use emotion regulation skills. Emotion regulation has several purposes. First, we want to identify our emotions and then, more importantly, we want to understand the process by which they happen. When we see how events and interpretations color our emotions, we can make changes that influence our emotions differently to release ourselves from negative emotional patterns.

Second, we want to learn how to change our relationship to our emotions. Instead of judging or attempting to "get rid" of negative feelings, we want to accept them and try to understand their messages. A curious and understanding approach to our emotions can replace fear and suffering, and, as we begin to relate to emotions differently, we can learn to "hold" them mindfully. Mindfulness of emotions reduces suffering because it does not involve adding to emotional pain, although we often need to dialectically balance this approach with other skills.

In addition to influencing emotions differently and changing our relationship with them, we can also work on decreasing our emotional vulnerabilities through more effective self-care skills and through scheduling positive experiences. Further, we can learn how to continue positive feelings through Mood Momentum and get unstuck from negative feelings through Opposite to Emotion.

To begin, understand that emotional health and well-being involve a dialectical balance between physical and mental health, and then start to practice self-care skills that decrease vulnerability to intense emotions through regulating them.

Well-Being

■ *CORE CONCEPT*: Well-being is a balance between physical and mental health.

Well-being is a state characterized by feeling comfortable, content, healthy, and happy. Well-being does not just happen. Rather, it is created by taking a holistic approach to our health with the understanding that our minds and bodies are interconnected with profound mutual influence. It is difficult to have a general sense of well-being without prioritizing and balancing both physical and mental health.

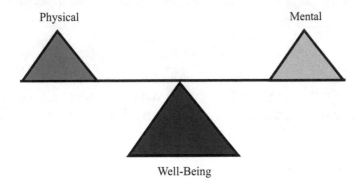

The PLEASED skill in the next section teaches important self-care skills to improve and maintain physical health so we can feel better all around. As we learn PLEASED, we should consider how we can improve our well-being through our goals for both physical and mental health.

Describe your goals for improving **physical** health:

_____

Describe your goals for improving **mental** health:

_____

Describe how you see your goals for physical and mental health being interconnected:

_____

Describe how your life will be different when you improve your well-being:

_____

Pleased (PL)

■ *CORE CONCEPT*: Self-care skills reduce emotional vulnerability and promote well-being.

Self-care is the foundation of feeling well and being ready to weather emotional storms.

Use the acronym PLEASED to help you remember the building blocks (**P**hysical health, **L**ist resources and barriers, **E**at balanced meals, **A**void drugs and alcohol, **S**leep between 7 and 10 hours, **E**xercise 20 to 60 minutes, **D**aily) of this skill. These building blocks are described in further detail in the paragraphs that follow.

Physical Health

Attend to your physical health to feel well. That means staying current on your health through regular medical checkups and engaging in proactive skills and behaviors that keep your body as healthy as possible. It also means treating illness when it arises and complying with medical advice. Take medications as prescribed, consult with your prescriber if medications are not working or side effects are intolerable, and make life changes to minimize use of medications with the advice of your physician. Always consider how your physical health may be impacting your mental health.

List resources and barriers

Resources include skills you might already use (such as O2E, Pros and Cons, and Willingness), people who support you, having a growing knowledge base about health and wellness, and having practical means of increasing self-care (e.g., having a physician, owning exercise equipment, and having access to healthy food). Consider your resources for each part of the PLEASED skill.

Barriers also abound with PLEASED skills. Identify barriers that interfere with any part of effective self-care and develop a plan to use skills to address those barriers.

Eat balanced meals

Eat three balanced meals plus a couple of healthy snacks mindfully throughout the day. Fruits, vegetables, whole grains, and lean protein are must-haves. Eat "whole" (unprocessed or minimally processed) or single-ingredient foods when possible. Drink eight full glasses of water a day. Avoid eating too much or too little and minimize sugars, saturated fats, and food or beverages with little or no nutritional value. Replace "diets" with lifestyle changes and keep current on reputable nutritional information. Start small and build on success. Consult with a physician or nutritionist if needed. Read the next section—Focus on Nutrition and Exercise—for more information.

Avoid drugs and alcohol

The risks associated with drugs and alcohol, along with the emotional, physical, relational, financial, and other effects, can make their use problematic. If you find you need larger amounts to reach a "desired" effect and/or experience an inability to cut down or quit use, you probably need some help and support. Refer to the Addictions module for more information.

Sleep between 7 and 10 hours

Sleep is important to regulate our moods and to maintain physical health. Find an amount of sleep that works for you. Refer to the suggestions in the Sleep Routine section for more information.

Exercise for 20 to 60 minutes multiple times weekly and move throughout the day

Exercise for a minimum of 20 minutes three to five times per week. Balanced exercise will positively impact almost any symptom of mental illness. Find natural ways to move about, such as taking stairs, parking at the far end of a parking lot, gardening, cleaning, and playing with pets or children. Humans are not biologically designed to be sedentary, so movement is vital. Consult a physician if you have any concerns about starting an exercise routine. See the Focus on Nutrition and Exercise section for more information.

Daily

PLEASED skills need to be daily habits for you to reap their tremendous benefits. Record PLEASED skills on a diary card (see the Diary Card section in Getting Started) and/or include them in written routines and schedules.

Focus on Nutrition and Exercise

◼ *CORE CONCEPT:* Use these guidelines to improve your nutrition and exercise habits.

Poor nutrition and a lack of exercise are leading causes of and contributors to illness and diseases such as heart disease and diabetes. While the links between nutrition, exercise, and mental and chemical health issues are less well established (but getting there), it is absolutely naive to think that what we put into our bodies and how we move (or do not move) our bodies has little effect on our well-being. In fact, the smart bet is that what we eat and the amount of movement we get have major and profound effects on how well we feel physically, psychologically, and emotionally. The good news is that, just as poor nutrition and exercise cause and contribute to problems, an emphasis on eating well and getting exercise can be healing and lead to better overall health.

The first step toward changing your lifestyle (some people call it a "healthstyle") is making a commitment to be in it for the long haul, for life. *There are no shortcuts. It takes effort and consistency.* But it is worth it. As the adage says, "If you do not make time for your health, you will have to make time for illness."

If you have a long way to go or are already suffering from obesity and/or other health problems, you should strongly consider seeing your physician and getting a referral to a dietitian or nutritionist as well as getting cleared for an exercise program.

Below are some tips and guidelines to get you started on better nutrition and exercise habits. These lists are not meant to be exhaustive, though following them consistently will get you on the road to wellness.

Nutritional tips and guidelines

Humans were not biologically designed to eat many of the foods that are created, processed, and marketed to us, and we are certainly not designed to eat these foods in the qualities that they often get eaten. These tips and guidelines will get you on a better path:

- Drink at least eight glasses of water a day. Water detoxifies, is essential for our bodies, and is needed for physical energy and for mental attention and concentration. What if you don't like the taste of water? Remember that our tastes change with time and water might become your favorite drink. Alternatively, you can lightly flavor your water with cucumber, lemon, or another healthy addition. Avoid drinking calories in any form. Juices, sodas, and flavored coffees add needless calories with limited or no nutritional value. Black coffee and tea are ok in moderation, but be careful in regard to caffeine.

- Try to stick to whole and minimally processed foods. Can you picture where that food came from? There is no cookie, cracker, or jelly donut tree! Shopping on the exterior of the super market creates a focus on whole, single-ingredient foods. As a general rule, avoid foods in boxes.

- Cut out foods that have little or no nutritional value and/or are actively harmful. Examples include candy, pastries, donuts, and chips. Start to think about sugar that does not occur naturally in foods as *poison*. Research shows that excessive sugar consumption is a leading cause of obesity, diabetes, and liver disease. Other foods with little nutritional value that cause harm include fried foods and foods with a lot of saturated fat, both of which cause heart disease. Stop eating fast food. Stop stocking unhealthy foods in your home.

- Eat at least six servings of fruits and vegetables a day. At most meals at least half of your plate should be fruits and vegetables. In time, you will come to enjoy these foods if you do not already. If you are on a budget then buy seasonal selections or buy frozen fruits and vegetables, which are much cheaper but retain the nutritional value. Eat these foods first to crowd out less healthy options.

- Eat starches and grains in moderation. These should not cover more than a fourth of your plate. Some of the most healthy choices are whole-grain cereals, whole-wheat breads and pastas, brown rice, and quinoa. Sweet potatoes and yams are also healthy choices.

- Limit dairy to no more than three servings a day, favoring low-fat milk, unsweetened yogurt, and lower-fat cheese such as mozzarella or cottage cheese.

- Limit meat to six ounces or less per day, favoring lean cuts of beef and pork or poultry without the skin. A serving of meat is about the size of a deck of playing cards and should take up no more than a fourth of your plate. Incorporate fish into your diet and consider meat alternatives such as lentils and tofu.

- Overall, maximize fruits and vegetables and increase fiber while you limit saturated and trans fats, sugar, and sodium. Follow the adage "eat not too much, and mostly vegetables."

- Have a "crowd out" instead of a "cut out" state of mind: Focus on healthy foods first and crowd out poor food choices. When you focus on eating what is good for you first, there is less temptation to eat much of what is not good for you. It works!

- Do not let yourself get too hungry. Preplan healthy snacks such as nuts, vegetables with hummus, or a piece of fruit.

- Consider taking a multivitamin and/or other supplements, but remember that they *supplement* healthy eating and cannot be a replacement for it.

- Create a meal plan to stay focused. Track your food choices and consumption. Worry less about calories and instead focus on the *quality* of food you eat. You can treat yourself from time to time with less healthy food, but the treats have to be the exceptions and not the rule. Obtaining and maintaining a healthy weight is roughly 80 percent what you eat and 20 percent movement and exercise.

- Use your mindfulness skills to slow down and be present while you eat. Enjoy your food, notice the flavors and textures, and stop eating before you are overfull. Be mindful of the portion sizes you choose to have and the amount of food you eat. Eat because you need the nourishment and not to soothe emotions or manage stress (with the exception of using Self-Soothe with Taste with a *morsel* of food).

- Remember that consistency and time are the keys to having a healthy lifestyle and enjoying the benefits of eating well.

Exercise tips and guidelines

Humans were not biologically designed to be sedentary. These tips will get you moving down a better path.

- Exercise for at least 20 minutes multiple days a week at a moderate intensity. Moderate intensity means that your heart rate is elevated but that you are still able to carry on a conversation. Break up the time if needed; three 10-minute sessions can have the same benefits as 20 minutes straight. Brisk walking, perhaps with occasional stretches of jogging or running, works for a majority of people. Schedule and prioritize your exercise time. Get a walking or workout buddy, and keep each other on track.

- Mix it up and have fun. Try biking, light weights, kettle bells, or yoga, or join a particular exercise class or even a sports league. Sign up for a fun run and set a personal goal. Reward your efforts.

- Use technology (e.g., a Fitbit, an online program, fitness apps, or a pedometer) to track and inspire efforts.

- In addition to scheduled exercise time, it is important to move around throughout the day. Every waking hour take 5 to 10 minutes to get up, do some light stretching, and walk around.

- Find natural ways of increasing movement. Take a walking break, park at the far end of a parking lot, take the stairs, carry your groceries, do housework, garden, or play with your children or a pet.

- Sometimes when you exercise your hunger spikes. Eat a healthy snack. Do not fall into the trap of thinking that exercise gives you a free pass with what you eat or that you can double your portions. *You cannot exercise yourself out of poor eating choices!*

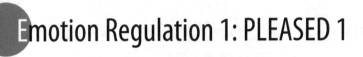

Emotion Regulation 1: PLEASED 1

CORE CONCEPT: Use this worksheet to problem-solve and establish PLEASED skills.

Describe your motivation to improve self-care skills (think of priorities, goals, and values):

_____

_____

Describe your strengths and resources in using PLEASED:

_____

_____

Describe your barriers to using PLEASED:

_____

_____

Describe the skills you will use to address your barriers:

_____

_____

Describe your action plan to start today (share your action plan with others and get started!):

_____

_____

Describe how your life will be different when you use effective PLEASED skills:

_____

_____

# Emotion Regulation 2: PLEASED 2

CORE CONCEPT: Use this worksheet to monitor your use of the PLEASED skills.

Improving your PLEASED skills significantly impacts how you feel and lowers your vulnerability to feeling negative and intense emotions. PLEASED skills also require daily attention and follow-through. Use the checklist spaces below to list your PLEASED behaviors and be sure to check them off when they are completed. Notice how you feel before and after each PLEASED skill.

☐ PLEASED skill: _____

    Distress/urge level before: _____ Distress/urge level after: _____

☐ PLEASED skill: _____

    Distress/urge level before: _____ Distress/urge level after: _____

☐ PLEASED skill: _____

    Distress/urge level before: _____ Distress/urge level after: _____

☐ PLEASED skill: _____

    Distress/urge level before: _____ Distress/urge level after: _____

☐ PLEASED skill: _____

    Distress/urge level before: _____ Distress/urge level after: _____

☐ PLEASED skill: _____

    Distress/urge level before: _____ Distress/urge level after: _____

☐ PLEASED skill: _____

    Distress/urge level before: _____ Distress/urge level after: _____

Sleep Routine

■ *CORE CONCEPT*: A consistent sleep routine is essential to better sleep and health.

Often we try to solve sleep difficulties with medication without trying behavior interventions. While medications have their place, using them as a daily, long-term strategy without trying behavior interventions is probably a poor choice. Further, if you suffer from nightmares, developing a relaxing sleep routine to enable you to go to bed in a peaceful rather than stressed-out state is one of your best strategies. Also note that sleep avoidance will exacerbate nightmares because of what is called "REM rebound." REM rebound is the scientific finding that sleep-deprived people will eventually have a spike in dream sleep that is characterized by more intense and vivid dreams. Again, the remedy is avoiding avoidance and instead focusing on a relaxing and consistent sleep routine.

The following guidelines will greatly improve sleep for most people. However, to be effective, these guidelines must be used nightly for a period of weeks and maintained over the long term. Your efforts will reap benefits and will probably be enjoyable, too.

- Create a sleep routine that begins at least 1 hour before going to bed. Like landing an airplane, healthy sleep involves getting into a pattern and getting the landing gear down well ahead of time. A sleep routine should consist of relaxing activities that cue the mind and body for sleep. Deep breathing, muscle relaxation, and mindfulness work well in a sleep routine.

- Establish consistent sleep and wake times and stick to them, even on weekends. Avoid using the "snooze" button on your alarm clock.

- The bed should be for sleeping and intimacy only. Wakeful activities in bed confuse the mind and body, and the bed no longer becomes a cue for sleep and rest.

- Create a relaxing environment. A clean and uncluttered environment with fresh bed linens and comfortable blankets and pillows will help to create the conditions for sleep. Also, block out sources of light and keep the temperature at a comfortable level, preferably a few degrees cooler than during daytime.

- Avoid alcohol, caffeine, and nicotine for 4 hours (or more) before bedtime.

- Avoid heavy meals and spicy foods before bedtime.

- Turn down your lighting and power off electronics at least 1 hour before bedtime.

- Avoid any stimulation before bedtime, including arguments or conflict, vigorous activity, or anything else that is likely to activate your mind or body.

- Get exercise during the daytime.

- Avoid daytime napping.

- Keep a notebook by your bed for ideas, concerns, or other thoughts you may want to remember tomorrow.

- Practice peaceful imagery or deep breathing as you are falling asleep.

- Minimize catastrophizing when you struggle with sleep. Use your mindfulness skills to refocus your thoughts.

- If you are unable to sleep after 20 minutes, get up and do something boring and/or relaxing until you are sleepy and ready to return to bed.

List other ways to create an effective sleep routine:

_____

_____

_____

Build Mastery (BM)

■ *CORE CONCEPT:* Complete tasks to feel competent and in control.

We all have those daily tasks that lead us to feel competent and in control when they are completed. The flip side is that, when these tasks build up, we feel more overwhelmed and out of control.

For example, basic activities of daily living (see Using ROUTINE (RO) in Module 9: Building a Satisfying Life) often need our attention. The following brief list includes basic Build Mastery activities for many of us:

- Hygiene (e.g., brushing teeth, cleaning self, wearing clean clothes)
- Doing the dishes
- Shopping for food and necessities
- Cleaning whatever needs it
- Doing laundry
- Accomplishing important tasks or chores
- Opening mail and/or paying bills
- Completing homework or work tasks
- Tending to our children and/or pets
- Maintaining a certain level of organization
- Answering emails and voice messages.

Describe daily tasks that help you feel competent and in control when completed:

_____

_____

_____

Build Mastery skills also include taking on realistic challenges and working toward goals. Here are some examples:

- Practicing virtually any skill
- Developing a hobby
- Exercising
- Taking steps to resolve a problem

- Accomplishing tasks outside your comfort zone

- Dealing with an interpersonal issue

- Standing up for yourself

- Volunteering

- Doing your best in a tough situation.

Technically, any attempt to be effective or any accomplishment could be a Build Mastery technique.

Describe other ways you can Build Mastery:

_____

_____

_____

Be mindful of your efforts and give yourself due credit. We frequently dismiss those things in life that we "should" be doing or are expected to do. We invalidate ourselves by saying those efforts are no big deal and are not worthy of recognition. Alternatively, we minimize their importance or get into judgments about what we did not do as a way to erase our efforts.

As a rule of thumb, if you tend to judge yourself when you think you have not made enough of an effort or have not accomplished something, then you deserve credit for the effort or accomplishment when you do try and when you get something done. Using Build Mastery skills helps us feel better, decreases our emotional vulnerability, and increases our self-respect.

Emotion Regulation 3: Build Mastery

CORE CONCEPT: Use this worksheet to monitor the use of your Build Mastery skills.

Certain activities and behaviors lead to us feeling competent and in control (or overwhelmed and out of control when we neglect them). Build Mastery behaviors may vary day to day or week to week. Use the checklist spaces below to list your Build Mastery behaviors for today or this week, and be sure to check them off when they are completed. Notice how you feel before and after each accomplishment.

☐ Build Mastery behavior: _____

    Distress/urge level before: _____ Distress/urge level after: _____

☐ Build Mastery behavior: _____

    Distress/urge level before: _____ Distress/urge level after: _____

☐ Build Mastery behavior: _____

    Distress/urge level before: _____ Distress/urge level after: _____

☐ Build Mastery behavior: _____

    Distress/urge level before: _____ Distress/urge level after: _____

☐ Build Mastery behavior: _____

    Distress/urge level before: _____ Distress/urge level after: _____

☐ Build Mastery behavior: _____

    Distress/urge level before: _____ Distress/urge level after: _____

☐ Build Mastery behavior: _____

    Distress/urge level before: _____ Distress/urge level after: _____

Model of Emotions

■ *CORE CONCEPT:* Knowing how emotions happen helps us influence them.

Emotions seem to happen out of the blue for many people, complete with ineffective and reactive behaviors that flow from those emotions. Fortunately, you can learn to influence and even change many emotions and resulting actions by understanding how emotions happen in the first place. The model of emotions below will assist your efforts. At any given time you can stop and use your mindfulness skills to reflect on this model and how it relates to your emotions, and then make any necessary changes.

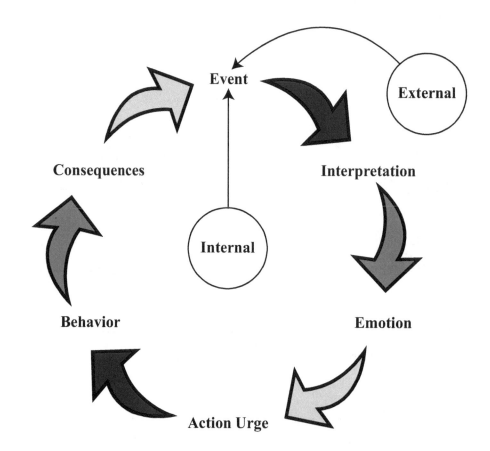

Event

Events begin the cycle of emotion, and they can be internal (within us) or external (in our environment). Use your mindfulness skills to connect an emotion to its source.

Interpretation

How we interpret events has a tremendous influence on what we feel. Step back and Observe and Describe the available facts to check your interpretation (also called self-talk or automatic thoughts) of the event. Ask yourself whether the interpretation works in the situation, and consider other ways of looking at the situation. Is the interpretation from Wise Mind? Is Nonjudgmental Stance needed? Are there dialectical alternative interpretations?

Emotion

Use Observe and Describe to notice your emotional experience. What is happening in your body (e.g., muscle relaxation or tension, heart rate)? What is happening externally with your body (e.g., facial expressions, posture)? What are you communicating both verbally and nonverbally? Use the available information to name your emotion. Remember to Observe and Describe the emotion nonjudgmentally.

Also, try to see whether another feeling is underneath what you Observe and Describe on the surface. For example, hurt or embarrassment might underlie anger or guilt, and shame might underlie depression. Getting to the emotions underneath the surface emotion increases understanding, and increased understanding creates more options.

Action urge and Behavior

What is the emotion urging or pulling you toward? Or, is a behavior already happening? From what state of mind are your action urges and behaviors flowing? Remember to validate your emotion(s) and choose behaviors from a centered, Wise Mind place. Participate with Effectiveness and respond rather than react. Delay your behavior if you anticipate that it will be ineffective.

Note that some action urges can be effective and it is important to act on those, but other actions should not be acted on because they will be ineffective. Can you think of examples of each?

Consequences

Observe and Describe what consequences result from your behavior. Evaluate what worked and what did not work, and learn from your experience.

Emotions and choices in response to them influence what happens with subsequent events, perpetuating the cycle. Use this knowledge to continue positive emotions with Mood Momentum or break out of ineffective emotions with Opposite to Emotion.

Emotion Regulation 4: Feelings Model

CORE CONCEPT: Use this worksheet to discover how emotions (and emotional patterns) happen.

Describe the **event**: What happened; who, what, when, and where?

_____

_____

Describe your **interpretation**: What judgment, evaluation, self-talk, or belief was activated?

_____

_____

Describe your **emotion**: What is happening physically? What body language do you detect? Put a name on the emotion; using a feeling chart if needed. Identify underlying emotions, too, if possible:

_____

_____

Describe your **action urge**: What action, inaction, or communication are you being emotionally pulled toward? Would it fit Wise Mind? This is a moment of CHOICE:

_____

_____

Describe your **behavior**: What action or inaction can be made? Participate using Effectiveness:

_____

_____

Describe the **consequences**: What consequences occurred? Include other emotions, thoughts, actions, and inactions, and their effect on relationships and situations. How did the results set up the next event (e.g., did a pattern continue or did the cycle change?):

_____

_____

Basic Emotions and Their Opposites

■ *CORE CONCEPT*: Emotions have dialectical opposites with intensities on a continuum.

Following is a list of basic emotions and their opposites. Start to think about and discuss emotions to gain a better understanding of them, using the diagram below.

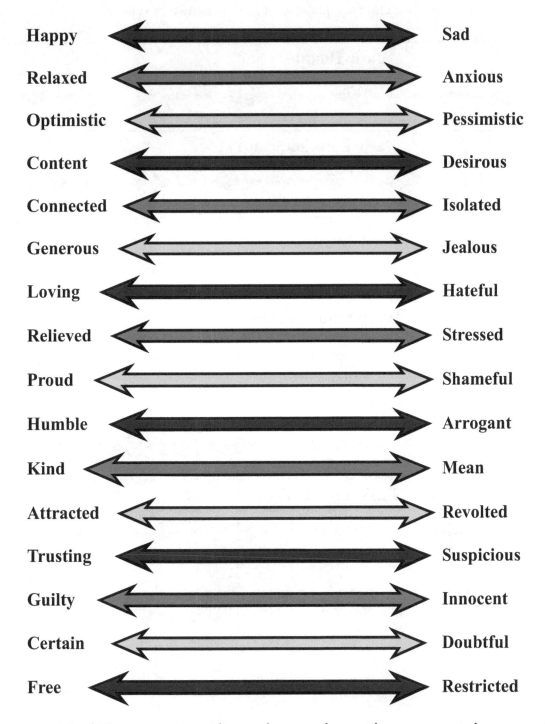

Happy	Sad
Relaxed	Anxious
Optimistic	Pessimistic
Content	Desirous
Connected	Isolated
Generous	Jealous
Loving	Hateful
Relieved	Stressed
Proud	Shameful
Humble	Arrogant
Kind	Mean
Attracted	Revolted
Trusting	Suspicious
Guilty	Innocent
Certain	Doubtful
Free	Restricted

Note that we use Mood Momentum to continue or increase the emotions we want to keep around and Opposite to Emotion to decrease the emotions we want to change.

Emotions on a Continuum

■ *CORE CONCEPT*: Identify lower intensities of an emotion for early intervention.

Emotions come with various intensity levels. Use Observe and Describe to notice lower-intensity emotions for early and proactive skill use. Although it is important to use skills with emotions of all intensities, skills work best when emotions are at their lower intensity levels.

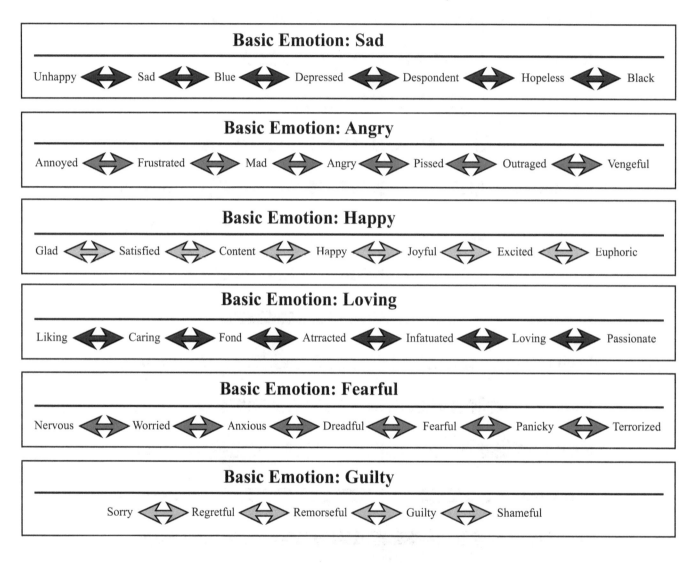

Remember that we can rate any emotion on a continuum from 1 to 10 (low to high) or simply observe it as low, medium, or high. Also remember that we Observe and Describe emotions with Nonjudgmental Stance to avoid adding to or intensifying them.

Changing Your Relationship to Emotions

■ *CORE CONCEPT:* Making an attempt to understand emotions changes our relationship to them.

Emotions are not good, bad, right, or wrong. The first step to changing our relationship to emotions is to become curious about them and use Nonjudgmental Stance. What purpose do they serve?

Emotions exist so we can connect and relate to other people and create meaningful relationships. They allow us to share joy and love with those around us and to be compassionate and empathic with others. Our emotions also communicate quickly to people around us without needing words. Emotions bring us together.

Emotions motivate us not only in relationships but also in other aspects of life. Often, they provide us with intuitive information that motivates our behavior without our thought. This emotional guidance can be highly effective in certain situations. It can even enable us to overcome seemingly impossible obstacles.

When our emotions seem to cloud our lives, such as when we are depressed or anxious or angry, it is important to remember that those emotions are still giving us important information. Rather than judging our emotions, we want to practice acceptance of them and open our minds to listen to their messages. When we reject emotions or try to "get rid" of them, it often has the effect of intensifying them; the message is not getting through, so it needs to get louder.

When others invalidate our emotions, those emotions often become more intense. Self-invalidation has the same effect. Practice nonjudgmental acceptance of your emotions and listen to their messages. Also, remember that emotions are not facts and that a healthy relationship to emotions comes from Wise Mind.

Mindfully "Hold" Emotions to Soothe and Reduce Suffering

■ *CORE CONCEPT*: Mindfulness of our emotions can soothe them.

When we try to get rid of, fight, or judge our emotions, we risk adding suffering to emotional pain. Like any rejection, these approaches create a negative counter-response. Our emotions are a part of us with information to share, and refusal to accept them increases their intensity.

Willingness to be with your emotions soothes them. It is like truly listening to a friend's concern or sitting with another person's distress without having to fix it. *Not* trying to fix your emotions and instead simply being present with them is a solution. Even strong emotions often do not require immediate action.

You can be present and "hold" your emotions through mindfulness. Holding emotions means that you recognize them as a part of your experience while also recognizing that they are not you. When we simply *be* with our emotions, we open ourselves to their ebbs and flows nonjudgmentally and usually find that the intensity subsides.

Observe your emotions without getting stuck, and practice Radical Acceptance when they are painful. If you do find your emotions to be overwhelming in the moment, change strategies and use distress tolerance skills. You can go back to mindfulness of your emotions when their intensity subsides a little.

You will find that emotions have important information for you, and they soothe themselves when we listen to them. Be open to relating to and learning from what your emotions have to say.

Build Positive Experience (BPE)

■ *CORE CONCEPT:* Positive events create positive emotions.

Emotions such as happiness do not just happen but are a byproduct of what we think and what we do: Positive events build positive emotion. As straightforward as this concept seems, it can be difficult to put into action when you are experiencing difficult times. Nonetheless, the bottom line is that *you have to invest in positive behaviors to have positive emotions.*

A lack of interest and energy can be barriers that prevent us from engaging in positive events. It is important to know that you cannot wait to feel interested and energetic. Instead you have to throw yourself into positive events in spite of these difficulties, and interest, energy, and enjoyment will eventually follow in time. This process works best when you invest in positive experiences without a strong desire or need to control the outcome and let positive emotions happen organically.

Other barriers sometimes exist too. For example, if you feel like you do not deserve positive experiences, if you worry about expectations, or if you dread the end of a positive experience, then treat these issues like distractions and use mindfulness to instead focus on the positive experiences.

Take a moment to look at your barriers and make a plan for how you will address them.

Describe your barriers to using Build Positive Experience:

_____

Describe the skills you will use to address each barrier:

_____

We can think of using Build Positive Experience in a few ways. We have positive experiences that are possible right now, positive experiences that we can plan and look forward to in the short term and positive experiences that we work toward step by step in the long term.

Positive events right now

What can be a positive event in the here and now or immediate future? Maybe it is a conversation, hearing or telling a joke, or helping someone. It might be taking a break, taking a quick walk, or taking a few minutes to practice mindfulness. You may find that the positive event is simply soaking in some sunshine, seeing rain wash everything clean, or feeling a warm breeze.

There is an enormous number of positive events that are possible now, sometimes occurring naturally around you without any effort on your part. You just need to turn your mind toward them and be open to participating in the experience with your full attention.

Positive events planned in the short term

These positive events can include a regular family meal, an outing alone or with a friend, a Friday movie night, or anything you can plan and schedule over the short term.

Start by listing the interests, hobbies, and activities you like to do (or used to do) and add activities to try from the Activities List in Module 9: Building a Satisfying Life. If you have a short list, you may have to develop some additional interests through trying out a lot of new activities with an open mind. Plan time for these positive events in your schedule and follow through with them.

Short-term positive events need to be regular occurrences and planned daily to be effective. Having regular positive events to look forward to moves you toward a satisfying life.

If interest and energy are low, it may take weeks to experience the benefits. Do not give up on the process or enter into judgments about not getting the desired outcomes right away. Participating in the journey will eventually get you to the destination.

Positive events to work toward in the long term

Make a list of your long-term priorities and goals. It may be going to school, learning a craft, making a career change, taking up an instrument, being in great physical shape, or having a vision for making a difference in the world.

Pick something from your list and break it down into manageable steps. Plan and schedule time to work on that first step, and follow through on it. As you accomplish each step, give yourself credit and plan the next step. A thousand-mile journey starts with a single step.

Your work toward long-term positives is a major part of building a satisfying life. Remember that some steps can be hard or frustrating. Do not give up, and stay focused on what you want in the long term.

Positive event planning, scheduling, and your routine

You may not know what to do to Build Positive Experience or how to plan these experiences. As stated earlier, first, you should identify possible positive experiences and schedule them, or they are less likely to happen (see the Activities List and Using ROUTINE (RO), both in Module 9: Building a Satisfying Life). Then you have to follow through with your plan using Opposite to Emotion when needed.

Mindfulness and positive events

Using Build Positive Experience requires your mindfulness skills to be effective. Stay focused on the event and not when it will end, how your expectations might change, or anything else that could take away from the experience.

Describe how your life will be different when you effectively use Build Positive Experience:

_____

Emotion Regulation 5: Build Positive Experience

CORE CONCEPT: Use this worksheet to monitor the use of Build Positive Experience.

Identify at least one positive experience for each day this week, including the details of where and when you will participate in those experiences. Also record your distress and/ or urge levels before and after the mindful participation in each positive experience. Notice how positive experiences tend to be beneficial to improving emotions and managing urges. Check off the completion of your daily use of Build Positive Experience (BPE).

☐ **Monday** BPE: _____ Where and when: _____

    Distress/urge level before: _____Distress/urge level after: _____

☐ **Tuesday** BPE: _____ Where and when: _____

    Distress/urge level before: _____Distress/urge level after: _____

☐ **Wednesday** BPE: _____ Where and when: _____

    Distress/urge level before: _____Distress/urge level after: _____

☐ **Thursday** BPE: _____ Where and when: _____

    Distress/urge level before: _____Distress/urge level after: _____

☐ **Friday** BPE: _____Where and when: _____

    Distress/urge level before: _____Distress/urge level after: _____

☐ **Saturday** BPE:_____Where and when: _____

    Distress/urge level before: _____Distress/urge level after: _____

☐ **Sunday** BPE: _____Where and when: _____

    Distress/urge level before: _____Distress/urge level after: _____

Attend to Relationships (A2R)

■ *CORE CONCEPT:* Use Attend to Relationships to keep relationships healthy and to create positive emotions.

Life events, problems, and symptoms can disrupt our relationships. We may have neglected friends and family or have simply lost track of those connections. At other times, we may have actively damaged relationships or burned others out with our struggles. We may be lonely, and isolation tends to create and maintain unwanted emotions.

Attending to relationships is a way to Build Positive Experience that tends to create positive emotions over time. When you use this skill, remember to also use the skills in the Interpersonal Effectiveness module, Nonjudgmental Stance, and Opposite to Emotion.

Remember that we get out of relationships what we put into them. Actively invest in friends, family, co-workers, neighbors, etc., and the dividends will follow.

Emotion Regulation 6: Attend to Relationships

Start with two lists of people: those who are currently in your life and those from the past who you would want in your life again. Only list people with whom you currently have or previously had an overall positive connection. *Do not list unhealthy people or people with whom you have had hopeless relationships.*

These people are in my life now:

_____

Describe how you can better attend to each person and how you can repair relationships if needed:

_____

These are people from my past with whom I would like to be reconnected:

_____

Describe how you can reconnect with at least one person on this list, how you can attend to that person, and how you can repair the relationship if needed:

_____

If you find that your lists are short, you are not alone. Many of us need new people in our lives for a variety of reasons; start thinking about making new relationships.

_____

Describe your resources and places where you might reach out for new relationships:

_____

Describe the other skills (in addition to Attend to Relationships) you will use to start making new relationships:

_____

Describe how your life will be different when you effectively use Attend to Relationships:

_____

Mood Momentum (MM)

■ *CORE CONCEPT:* Notice positive moods and choose skills and behaviors to keep them going.

We influence emotions with the behaviors we choose. When we Observe and Describe an emotion that we want to continue to experience, we can use Mood Momentum. This skill directs us to stay involved in events and thoughts that keep our positive emotions around so we can benefit from the momentum of already feeling well.

Emotions tend to unconsciously draw us to behaviors that are congruent or fit with them. Mood Momentum is a mindful effort to choose these mood-congruent behaviors when they will be helpful. Ways to continue positive moods include the following:

- Engage in using Build Positive Experience.

- Balance using Build Positive Experience with using Build Mastery.

- Use mindfulness to reflect on a positive emotion.

- Engage in using PLEASED.

- Balance active positive events with relaxing positive events.

- Engage in healthy relationships.

- Work on a responsibility and stay mindful of your efforts and accomplishments (and distract from judgments).

- Practice mindfulness exercises.

- Work on a hobby or project or try something on the Activities List in Module 9: Building a Satisfying Life.

- Think of other ways you can use Mood Momentum.

An important aspect of Mood Momentum is to pick from a variety of positive experiences, activities, and behaviors to keep it interesting. Even the most fun or relaxing event will eventually reach the point where it no longer creates a positive effect. We benefit most from Mood Momentum when we take a balanced approach, switch up our strategies, and keep it fresh.

Opposite to Emotion (O2E)

■ *CORE CONCEPT:* Use Opposite to Emotion (also known as Opposite Action) to get unstuck from ineffective behaviors that arise from certain emotional states.

We get stuck in negative or ineffective emotional states partly as a result of mood-congruent behavior. Mood-congruent behavior occurs when, without awareness, we fall into behavior patterns that keep certain emotions around. For example, when we feel depressed, we may perform the following actions or inactions:

- Get isolated (e.g., be disconnected from relationships, not answer the phone, miss social engagements and appointments)

- Be inactive (e.g., stay in bed or on the couch, not participate in hobbies or potentially positive experiences, let the chores at home and other responsibilities pile up)

- Engage in stuck thinking (e.g., focus only on the negative, ruminate, want to die)

- Neglect self-care and hygiene

- Eat and sleep too much or too little

- Decide to stop therapy and medications

- Engage in other behaviors that perpetuate negative emotional states.

Unfortunately, these automatic reactions to depression keep us depressed and may even make it worse. This is where Opposite to Emotion is helpful. This dialectical skill directs us to act in ways that are the opposite of the behaviors toward which our difficult emotions pull us. For the depressive examples just given, we would use Opposite to Emotion to:

- Reach out to others with whom we have relationships for help and positive experience

- Get moving by doing activities, hobbies, and important tasks; use ROUTINE, the Activities List in Module 9: Building a Satisfying Life, Build Positive Experience, or Build Mastery, or engage in distress tolerance skills

- Practice dialectics, take a Nonjudgmental Stance, or use Encouragement

- Use PLEASED

- Go to therapy appointments and discuss medication issues with your prescriber before making changes

- Use other skills to address additional behaviors that perpetuate negative emotional states.

See the following explanations and examples for ways to use Opposite to Emotion to address common difficult emotions.

Opposite to Emotion with anxiety or fear

We tend to avoid when we feel anxiety and fear. We also tend to ruminate on anxious thoughts. Avoidance gets reinforced because it protects us from distress. However, the more we avoid, the more our anxieties build over time and the more we end up feeling overwhelmed. In addition, avoidance results in our world getting smaller and smaller.

Using Opposite to Emotion means approaching our fears one step at a time and learning to tolerate the distress that comes with it. To do this effectively, we use mindfulness to desensitize ourselves and distress tolerance when we feel too overwhelmed. The more we approach rather than avoid, the more our nervous system learns to be "bored" and the less anxious we feel.

With some fears we might not go one step at a time, instead choosing to jump fully in. Going all in to approach a fear is like jumping into a cold swimming pool: At first it is shocking, but then your system acclimates. Whether you take on a fear one step at a time or go all in depends on the situation, so choose your strategy according to what will be most effective for you.

Last, we can also learn to accept our anxious thoughts rather than fight them or catastrophize about them. This approach takes the power out of the thoughts.

Opposite to Emotion with anger

We often want to lash out with words or behavior when we feel anger, and we may replay the situation we are angry about over and over in our minds. Using Opposite to Emotion includes avoiding the person you are angry with until you calm down while also being kind and compassionate to others, choosing to spend quality time with our pets, friends, and/or family, and being careful to be gentle and not to displace our anger onto others.

Additionally, we might imagine compassion for the person we feel anger toward (which is difficult to do sometimes). Remember that most people (including ourselves) do not want to make mistakes and do not want others to be angry at them, no matter how unskillfully they act. Compassion can be dialectically balanced with accountability.

We can also distract ourselves from angry thoughts and from replaying situations that cause anger by using the Thoughts skill. Count to 100 or recite the alphabet, or focus on thoughts that are the opposite of angry thoughts.

However, Opposite to Emotion with anger does not mean denying or stuffing anger, because this sets the stage for rage. After you have calmed your anger by using Opposite to Emotion, see whether the emotion fits Wise Mind and use interpersonal effectiveness skills to address the situation with others if needed.

Opposite to Emotion with guilt and shame

We feel guilt when we have done something to hurt ourselves or others or when we make mistakes. Often we try to avoid or hide from others when we feel guilt, or we try to blame or otherwise avoid accepting responsibility for our actions.

Using Opposite to Emotion means addressing what we did or the mistake that we made with whoever was affected. We apologize and try to make the situation better if possible. If we cannot make the situation better, we try to do something better somewhere else; this is a symbolic way to right a wrong. Be committed to not repeating the same mistakes and develop a plan to act differently in the future.

Remember that a genuine apology is for the benefit of the other person and not a means of avoiding consequences. Other people may still be upset for a time after your apology. Be patient with the process. Accept consequences with grace unless they do not fit the situation as evaluated in Wise Mind. *Do not participate in guilt or consequences that are out of proportion with the situation.*

After you have completed the steps listed here, let go of the situation and the thoughts that caused the guilt. Use Radical Acceptance.

Sometimes guilt does *not* fit Wise Mind. For example, we have a right to say no and to have boundaries, and we do not need to feel guilty for exerting this right. At other times, we experience guilt in the absence of wrongdoing for a variety of reasons. Examples include feeling guilty for practicing Self-Soothe skills, for having a good time, or for taking time for ourselves. This type of guilt leads us to avoid behaviors such as saying no, setting boundaries, and participating in beneficial activities.

When we have guilt that does not fit Wise Mind, the Opposite to Emotion is to approach rather than avoid. Keep practicing saying no, setting boundaries, and participating in activities until you no longer feel guilty. Remember to use REASON and Encouragement to address your thoughts and judgments that prompt guilt. We need to coach ourselves in these situations!

We feel shame when guilt is not addressed, when we have done something serious, or when something serious has happened to us. Shame involves experiencing judgments about being damaged, unlovable, or unforgivable as a person.

We can also feel shame for how we look or who we are as people even when it does not fit Wise Mind. This type of shame frequently originates from others' judgments and from being mistreated. Shame causes us to hide, and hiding keeps the shame around.

Using Opposite to Emotion with shame involves coming out of hiding and talking about what causes us shame with *someone safe, nonjudgmental, and accepting.* As we work through shame, we can often open ourselves up to more and more supportive people and begin to heal. The process of working through shame also requires a Nonjudgmental Stance and distress tolerance skills.

Opposite to Emotion with other emotions

We can use Opposite to Emotion with other emotions too. For example, you might feel attraction or love toward someone who is not worthy of it or who mistreats you, and those emotions keep you engaging in the ineffective relationship. In this case Opposite to Emotion would involve avoiding this person, blocking his or her advances to engage in the relationship, and reminding yourself why the person is not healthy for you. You might also approach other relationships.

As another example, we have times when we feel jealous and go on the offensive toward the person we are jealous of or try to overcontrol the people involved in the event causing the jealousy. In this situation the Opposite to Emotion would be avoiding going on the offensive and letting go of the tendency to control others.

A last example is feeling unmotivated or like you do not "feel like" doing a behavior that you know will be helpful. You consequently avoid doing what you know to be effective, whether that is doing the dishes, going for a walk, engaging in a conversation, or doing whatever is needed. We all have these moments, usually every day. Of course you can use mindfulness to explore the reasons you don't feel like doing the thing you are avoiding, but the Opposite to Emotion is to follow the Nike slogan and 'just do it'. An oversimplification? Maybe, but there is a reason that this almost 30-year-old slogan resonates with so many people.

In your use of Opposite to Emotion, consider one final note. Whether or not your emotion or the intensity of it is justified depends on the situation, the facts, and other potential factors. Opposite to Emotion is not meant to invalidate the real emotions we experience. Instead, Opposite to Emotion is intended to get us unstuck from prolonged and overly intense emotional states by recognizing behaviors that do not work and instead choosing those opposite behaviors that are more effective. In other words: Do less of what does not work and more of what does in order to change your emotions.

Emotion Regulation 7: Opposite to Emotion

CORE CONCEPT: Use this worksheet to practice Opposite to Emotion.

Describe your current emotion:

_____

_____

Describe what actions (or inactions) this emotion is pulling you to do (what is mood congruent?):

_____

_____

Describe the predicted outcomes from these actions (or inactions):

_____

_____

Describe how you can use Opposite to Emotion:

_____

_____

Describe the predicted outcomes from your use of Opposite to Emotion:

_____

_____

Describe how your life will be different when you effectively use Opposite to Emotion:

_____

_____

Do your A-B-Cs: Accumulate Positives, Build Mastery, and Cope Ahead

■ *CORE CONCEPT:* The A-B-Cs keep you balanced in the present and immediate future.

The A-B-Cs capture important elements for emotion regulation and health. We do better emotionally when we focus on positives, take care of important tasks and responsibilities, and develop coping plans for troubles we can anticipate. Of course you will also notice the parallels between A-B-Cs and Build Positive Experience, Build Mastery, and developing skills plans.

Use the acronym A-B-C to remember the building blocks (**A**ccumulate positives, **B**uild Mastery, and **C**ope ahead) of this skill. The building blocks of this skill are described in the following paragraphs.

Accumulate Positives

Positives are consistently around us if we open ourselves to them. However, we often hold on to a negative and let it overshadow our other experiences. For example:

- We remember one person who treats us rudely and fail to recognize several people who treat us with kindness and respect.

- We stay fixated on a problem and do not notice what has gone well or according to plan.

- We overfocus on negatives and fail to notice positives happening naturally in our environment.

The first part of accumulating positives is to recognize the positives that go unnoticed. Add those up!

Next, involve yourself in activities and build positive experiences that you can do right now. Check the Activities List in Module 9: Building a Satisfying Life, choose an activity and do it, or use the Build Positive Experience skill. Engage in what is happening around you, including attending to people and relationships with the Attend to Relationships skill. Be mindful and participate in the moment.

Longer term, think about your priorities, goals, and values. What is important to you and what do you want to work toward? Work on the Building a Satisfying Life module.

Build Mastery

Do what makes you feel competent and in control. Take care of your home environment or throw yourself into completing a task that has gone undone. When you have completed a chore or task or when you have taken a step toward a larger goal, take a few moments to appreciate the accomplishment and give yourself credit. See the Build Mastery skill for more details.

Cope Ahead

Most of us have hot-button situations in which we are vulnerable to ineffective behaviors. Think of one of these situations. Next, imagine yourself in this situation, but, instead of imagining your ineffective reactions, picture yourself responding and coping with your skills. Continue to replay the coping response to the situation over and over in your mind. This is called "imaginal rehearsal." After you have visualized how to cope ahead, write down the details of your hot-button situation and the skills you imagined using to deal with it effectively.

Take the information and skills you imagined and formulate a written plan for coping that you can refer to later.

Your Emotions and Your Body: Discovering the Connection

■ *CORE CONCEPT:* Your emotions and body communicate and influence one another.

Our minds, including emotional experiences, and our bodies are connected and can influence one another for better or worse. The good news is that, when you are aware of the connection, you can mindfully influence your emotions for the better. Consider the following examples:

- Depressed people frequently slouch and avoid eye contact. Sitting up straight with a confident posture and making eye contact are incompatible with depressed emotions. Changing how you hold your body and making eye contact can make a difference in the level of depression you feel.

- When life is difficult you can adopt a serene expression on your face, often referred to as a half-smile. The half-smile communicates acceptance to your mind, making changes in the emotional impact of your difficulties. Alternatively you can look in the mirror, make a "V" with your first and second fingers, and push up the corners of your mouth. Maybe this is a silly example, but give it a try. Doing something silly can be a great break from feeling an intense emotion!

- Anxious or angry people can decrease the intensity of these emotions through practicing muscle relaxation, deep breathing, and being mindful of how they are holding or communicating with their bodies.

Of course positive emotions are also reflected in our bodies. Any time you are aware of your emotions, or your body, check in on how they are influencing one another and make adjustments accordingly.

Module 5

Interpersonal Effectiveness

Introduction to Interpersonal Effectiveness

■ *CORE CONCEPT*: Interpersonal skills lead to healthy relationships.

Interpersonal effectiveness enables us to make and maintain relationships, resolve conflict when it occurs, and get our and others' wants and needs met effectively in a balanced manner.

This module has three main sets of skills: FAST, GIVE, and DEAR MAN. FAST skills build self-respect. You have a relationship with yourself, and the way that you talk to yourself and the behaviors you choose affect how you feel about yourself. FAST skills orient us to make choices and act in relationships in ways that increase our self-respect. Self-respect is based on actions grounded in our priorities, goals, and values. Respecting yourself provides the foundation for skill use in your relationships with others.

GIVE skills are other-focused. We want to treat others with care, interest, validation, and respect. This approach allows us to form and nurture meaningful relationships that will enrich our lives. GIVE also enables us to be dialectic in conflicts so we can resolve them effectively.

DEAR MAN is assertiveness that is self-focused. We use DEAR MAN to get our wants and needs met more reliably, to say no, to set boundaries with others, and to negotiate when needed.

We use all three sets of skills to be effective in our relationships. Remember to role-play and practice these skills consistently.

Interpersonal Effectiveness Dialectics

■ *CORE CONCEPT:* Relationships require balance and working the middle ground.

Dialectics are central to healthy relationships. Being too other-focused or too self-focused leads to unmet wants and needs and conflict. Instead, we attempt to find balance in relationships, and that balance differs based on the nature of the relationship along with the context of the situation.

Think of GIVE and DEAR MAN existing on a dialectic:

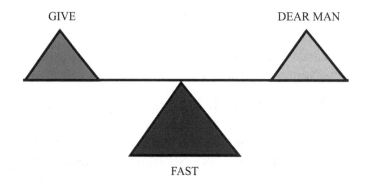

At times we need to focus on others and at other times we need to focus on ourselves. In practice, we are most effective when we blend both sets of skills. The blend between thinking about others versus ourselves is grounded in FAST. We use our values to guide us in relationships to enhance our self-respect and others' respect for us.

To find interpersonal balance, ask yourself three questions when working the dialectic in relationships:

1. What does the other person need in this interaction (GIVE)?

2. What do I need in this interaction (DEAR MAN)?

3. What is needed in this interaction to maintain or build my self-respect (FAST)?

The answers to these questions will be a reliable guide. Remember that all healthy relationships are based on reciprocity. Be willing to balance give and take and to be there for others if you want them to be there for you.

FAST (F)

■ *CORE CONCEPT:* Self-respect and healthy relationships start with you.

FAST skills are focused on our priorities, goals, and values so we can make choices that build our self-respect. Self-respect is the foundation to liking ourselves, and it creates a solid base for us to build and maintain relationships with others.

Use the acronym FAST to remember the building blocks (<u>F</u>air, <u>A</u>pologies not needed, <u>S</u>tick to values, <u>T</u>ruth and accountability) of this skill. These building blocks are described in further detail in the paragraphs that follow.

<u>F</u>air

Be just and take a Nonjudgmental Stance with yourself and others. Avoid extremes and ground yourself in Wise Mind in interactions with others. Think of fair weather as being neither too hot nor too cold and without storms. Keep a moderate climate with others without whipping up bad weather. Use respectful words and actions with yourself and others. Others do *not* need to earn your respect. We treat others with respect because it builds our own self-worth. Respond rather than react in relationships.

<u>A</u>pologies not needed

Do not engage in unneeded apologetic behavior. Do not apologize for having an opinion or for your own viewpoints. You are allowed to disagree. Do not apologize for being you. Avoid apologies for things over which you have no control. Chronic, unnecessary apologies erode self-respect and devalue apologies that are genuinely needed. Note that "no apologies" does not apply to situations that require an apology (e.g., hurting someone).

<u>S</u>tick to values

Use your priorities, goals, and values as guides and ground yourself in them. Choose behaviors and have interactions with others that build your self-respect. Identify what is important to you and stick to it. Know what values are non-negotiable and, when values conflict, work to resolve the conflict through Wise Mind. Live your life grounded in values.

<u>T</u>ruth and accountability

Be honest and accountable with yourself and others. Sometimes we avoid the truth because we are afraid of the consequences, but trying to deceive others destroys self-respect and often causes greater problems. Even if you have a great memory and can keep from getting tangled in a web of lies, *you* will still know the truth. Being accountable is more effective in most cases.

In addition, act in a manner that respects your true abilities and avoid feigned helplessness, exaggerations, and an excuse orientation to life. Take responsibility for yourself.

Interpersonal Effectiveness 1:
Values Application 1

CORE CONCEPT: Identify values and how to express them through behavior.

This is a partial list of values. You might have a value that is not on the list or notice some overlap between values. Review the list and circle your top 10 values. Use your selected values in the exercise that follows.

Acceptance	Cleanliness	Discipline
Achievement	Closeness	Discretion
Activity	Comfort	Diversity
Adaptability	Commitment	Drive
Adventurousness	Compassion	Duty
Affectionateness	Confidence	Education
Altruism	Connection	Effectiveness
Ambition	Consistency	Empathy
Assertiveness	Contentment	Encouragement
Attentiveness	Contribution	Endurance
Availability	Cooperation	Energy
Awareness	Courage	Enjoyment
Balance	Courteousness	Enthusiasm
Belongingness	Creativity	Excellence
Bravery	Credibility	Exploration
Calm	Decisiveness	Expressiveness
Capability	Dependability	Fairness
Caring	Determination	Faith
Challenge	Devotion	Family
Charity	Dignity	Fidelity

Financial independence	Leadership	Respect
Firmness	Learning	Restraint
Fitness	Love	Sacrifice
Freedom	Loyalty	Security
Friendship	Mindfulness	Self-control
Fun	Modesty	Self-reliance
Generosity	Motivation	Sensitivity
Giving	Neatness	Service
Grace	Openness	Sharing
Gratitude	Optimism	Simplicity
Happiness	Order	Sincerity
Harmony	Passion	Spirituality
Health	Peace	Spontaneity
Honesty	Persistence	Stability
Honor	Playfulness	Strength
Hopefulness	Pleasantness	Structure
Humility	Pleasure	Success
Humor	Popularity	Support
Hygiene	Practicality	Teamwork
Imagination	Pragmatism	Thankfulness
Independence	Privacy	Thoughtfulness
Integrity	Professionalism	Trust
Intelligence	Prosperity	Truth
Intensity	Relaxation	Usefulness
Intimacy	Reliability	Warmth
Joy	Religion	Willingness
Kindness	Resilience	Wisdom
Knowledge	Resoluteness	

Once your values are identified, you can describe specific behaviors that you can practice to live your values with intention. The following are examples of how you can complete this exercise:

I value: Truth

Describe three specific ways you can live this value:

 1. Fill out my diary card more accurately

 2. Tell important others when I make a mistake

 3. Stop hiding liquor bottles in the garage

I value: Friendship

Describe three specific ways you can live this value:

 1. Return phone calls from my friends

 2. Respect Tammy's boundaries

 3. Practice GIVE skills in group

I value: Peace

Describe three specific ways you can live this value:

 1. Not yell at my wife and kids when I am angry

 2. Practice MINDFULNESS exercises in the morning and at bedtime

 3. Use RADICAL ACCEPTANCE to stop beating myself up for mistakes

I value: Giving

Describe three specific ways you can live this value:

 1. Give my group feedback on what they are doing well

 2. Donate possessions that I have not used for a year

 3. Be present in my relationships

Now it's your turn.

I value: _____

Describe three specific ways you can live this value:

_____

I value: _____

Describe three specific ways you can live this value:

_____

I value: _____

Describe three specific ways you can live this value:

_____

I value: _____

Describe three specific ways you can live this value:

_____

I value: _____

Describe three specific ways you can live this value:

_____

I value: _____

Describe three specific ways you can live this value:

_____

I value: _____

Describe three specific ways you can live this value:

_____

Interpersonal Effectiveness 2:
Values Application 2

CORE CONCEPT: Identify values and decide which ones you want to express more through your behavior.

This exercise illustrates how values get expressed in your life through behaviors you choose. Each value on the list has two corresponding statements, one that endorses that you already "live" the value and one that endorses a desire to express the value to a greater degree.

For each value your options are to:

- not check either of the statements under the value, meaning that the value is not important in your life

- check only the first statement under the value, meaning that you already express the value in your life

- check only the second statement under the value, meaning that you do not express the value in your life but would like to, or,

- check both statements under the value, meaning that you already express the value in your life *and* would like to express the value even more.

For each statement you check, consider (and perhaps write down) what behaviors you engage in that demonstrate to yourself and others that the value is important in your life. Try to increase behaviors in your life that reflect your core values. Values plus behaviors that reflect them equate to self-respect.

Acceptance

☐ I practice acceptance in my life.

☐ I would like to practice more acceptance in my life.

Achievement

☐ I work toward achieving my goals.

☐ I would like to achieve more of my goals.

Activity

☐ I involve myself in activities.

☐ I would like to be more involved in activities.

Adventurousness

☐ I am adventurous and take safe chances.

☐ I would like to be more adventurous and take more safe chances.

Affectionateness

☐ I show affection toward other people.

☐ I would like to be more affectionate with other people.

Assertiveness

☐ I can be appropriately assertive with other people.

☐ I would like to be more appropriately assertive with other people.

Belonging

☐ I feel like I belong in my family, at work, and/or with people important to me.

☐ I would like to feel more like I belong in my family, at work, and/or with people important to me.

Calm

☐ I am calm with other people and in stressful situations.

☐ I would like to be more calm with other people and in stressful situations.

Capability

☐ I have the skills and abilities to accomplish tasks.

☐ I would like to develop my skills and abilities to accomplish tasks.

Caring

☐ I show caring toward myself and others.

☐ I would like to be more caring with myself and/or other people.

Commitment

☐ I show commitment to my goals and to other people.

☐ I would like to be more committed to my goals and/or other people.

Confidence

☐ I am confident in my abilities and show confidence to other people.

☐ I would like to develop confidence in my abilities and to show it to other people.

Consistency

☐ I follow through with expectations and tasks consistently.

☐ I would like to follow through with expectations and tasks more consistently.

Contribution

☐ I contribute to those around me and my community.

☐ I would like to contribute more to other people and my community.

Cooperation

☐ I am cooperative and work with other people.

☐ I would like to be more cooperative and work with other people.

Creativity

☐ I have creative pursuits and/or can solve problems in creative ways.

☐ I would like to have more creative pursuits and/or show more creative problem-solving.

Decisiveness

☐ I am able to make decisions with relative ease.

☐ I would like to make decisions more easily.

Dependability

☐ I am dependable and people can count on me.

☐ I would like to be more dependable to other people.

Determination

☐ I am determined in reaching my goals.

☐ I would like to show more determination toward reaching my goals

Diversity

☐ I appreciate diversity in culture and/or ideas.

☐ I would like to be more appreciative of diversity in culture and/or ideas.

Education

☐ I engage in learning new ideas and skills.

☐ I would like to engage more in learning new ideas and skills.

Empathy

☐ I understand and share in the feelings of other people.

☐ I would like to better understand and share in the feelings of other people.

Fairness

☐ I act without bias and in an evenhanded way with other people.

☐ I would like to act with less bias and in a more evenhanded way with other people.

Family

☐ I place a high priority on family.

☐ I would like to prioritize my family more.

Financial independence

☐ I adequately support myself (and my dependents) financially.

☐ I would like to better support myself (and my dependents) financially.

Fitness

☐ I maintain good physical health.

☐ I would like to achieve better physical health.

Friendship

☐ I am a true friend to other people.

☐ I would like to be a better friend to other people.

Fun

☐ I regularly have a good time in life.

☐ I would like to have more good times in life.

Generosity

☐ I am unselfish and give toward other people.

☐ I would like to be more unselfish and give more to other people.

Grace

☐ I approach people and situations with grace.

☐ I would like to be more graceful in how I approach people and situations.

Gratitude

☐ I am thankful for other people and what I have.

☐ I would like to be more thankful for other people and what I have.

Happiness

☐ I experience a sense of well-being and contentment in life.

☐ I would like to experience a greater sense of well-being and contentment in life.

Health

☐ I take care of my health.

☐ I would like to take better care of my health.

Honesty

- [ ] I am an honest person.
- [ ] I would like to be more honest.

Humility

- [ ] I am humble about my accomplishments.
- [ ] I would like to show more humility about my accomplishments.

Independence

- [ ] I am able to do things on my own and take care of myself.
- [ ] I would like to be more able to do things on my own and take care of myself.

Kindness

- [ ] I treat others in a nice and concerned way.
- [ ] I would like to treat others more nicely and with more concern.

Knowledge

- [ ] I have information and facts in regard to a number of different areas.
- [ ] I would like to have more information and facts in regard to a greater number of areas.

Leadership

- [ ] I am able to guide other people through my positive example.
- [ ] I would like to better guide other people through my positive example.

Love

- [ ] I share mutual attraction and affection with other people.
- [ ] I would like to have more mutual attraction and affection with other people.

Loyalty

- [ ] I show faith and devotion to people around me.
- [ ] I would like to show more faith and devotion to people around me.

Mindfulness

☐ I practice being in the moment, on purpose, nonjudgmentally.

☐ I would like to practice being in the moment, on purpose, nonjudgmentally, more often.

Peace

☐ I have calm, tranquility, and quiet in my life.

☐ I would like to have more calm, tranquility, and quiet in my life.

Persistence

☐ I work toward goals without giving up until I accomplish them.

☐ I would like to work toward goals until I accomplish them without giving up.

Relaxation

☐ I take time to unwind and relax.

☐ I would like to take more time to unwind and relax.

Reliability

☐ I am dependable and follow through consistently with other people.

☐ I would like to be more dependable and follow through with more consistency with other people.

Resilience

☐ I am able to cope with the ups and downs of life.

☐ I would like to be better able to cope with the ups and downs of life.

Respect

☐ I show respect to myself and other people.

☐ I would like to show more respect to myself and other people.

Self-control

☐ I am in control of my words and behavior.

☐ I would like to have more control of my words and behavior.

Service

☐ I place importance on doing things for other people and/or important causes.

☐ I would like to place more importance on doing things for other people and/or important causes.

Simplicity

☐ I keep my life uncomplicated.

☐ I would like to make my life less complicated.

Spirituality

☐ I involve myself in a spiritual practice.

☐ I would like to be involved or more involved in a spiritual practice.

Stability

☐ I keep myself mentally, emotionally, and behaviorally healthy.

☐ I would like to be more mentally, emotionally, and behaviorally healthy.

Trust

☐ I am seen as reliable, good, and honest by other people.

☐ I would like to be seen as more reliable, good, and honest by other people.

Willingness

☐ I am flexible and do what is needed with other people and in situations.

☐ I would like to be more flexible and to better do what is needed with other people and in situations.

Wisdom

☐ I am seen as knowledgeable and experienced, with sound judgment, by other people.

☐ I would like to be seen as more knowledgeable and experienced, with sound judgment, by other people.

Interpersonal Effectiveness 3: Values Conflict Application

CORE CONCEPT: Use this worksheet to resolve value conflicts.

Most of us know the phrase "that person has their priorities mixed up." It implies that a person's values are in conflict and that an ineffective course of action has been taken. In other words, the person is making choices without considering important priorities, goals, and values.

We frequently have these conflicts. When they happen, we try to decide what will best meet the demands of the situation while still maintaining our self-respect. Use the following exercise to help you resolve value conflicts.

Describe the situation nonjudgmentally:

_____

Describe the priorities, goals, and values that are in conflict:

_____

Rank these priorities, goals, and values from most to least important:

_____

Describe options that either follow your top-ranked value(s) or that show adequate respect across values:

_____

Evaluate the options (see Pros and Cons and SOLVED). Describe a course of action from Wise Mind that maintains or builds self-respect:

_____

Note: Occasionally we must make choices that sacrifice important values. Make these decisions from Wise Mind and only when the outcome is essential.

GIVE (G)

■ *CORE CONCEPT:* Focus on others to build and maintain relationships.

GIVE skills focus on others. We build and maintain relationships by balancing our own wants, needs, and desires with those of the people around us. Everyone benefits from healthier relationships grounded in genuine interest and validation. GIVE is also key to resolving conflicts.

Use the acronym GIVE to remember the building blocks (**G**enuine, **I**nterested, **V**alidate, **E**asy manner) of this skill. These building blocks are described in further detail in the paragraphs that follow.

Genuine

Be honest, sincere, and real with others. Speak and act from your heart with caring and use mindfulness to be with others in the moment. Let others know that you value them and treat them with respect.

Interested

Interest comes from efforts to connect with a person. Let others have the focus. Listen intently to others and pause to make space before responding. Ask questions and listen to the answers.

Be mindful of your nonverbal communication. Our nonverbals communicate a great deal of information to others, both intentionally and unintentionally. Send the nonverbal messages that you want to send to others. Nonverbally, interest is communicated by looking at the person, making appropriate eye contact, and keeping your mannerisms and posture open and relaxed.

Validate

Validation is the nonjudgmental acknowledgment of others' feelings, thoughts, beliefs, and experience. To validate you "walk a mile in someone else's shoes" and see life from his or her perspective. We validate when we find others' truth and how their experiences make sense given their life circumstances and the situation. Remember to validate *yourself*, too.

Easy manner

Remember the idiom "you catch more flies with honey than with vinegar." Having an easy manner means treating others with kindness and a relaxed attitude. It also means not being heavy handed with our judgments, opinions, and viewpoints. Allow space for others.

Remember that we can always raise our interpersonal intensity if necessary but that it is often more effective to start out in a relatively relaxed and laid-back manner.

Last, learn and use polite manners. Being easy-going and polite is kind to others, and actually opens a lot of doors for you too!

Listening (L)

■ *CORE CONCEPT*: Listen in order to demonstrate that you care.

Listening is a skill that requires mindfulness and practice. To listen well, we must let go of distractions, especially our own thoughts, and focus our attention on what is being said in the moment. We also need to practice Nonjudgmental Stance to listen accurately. When we Observe ourselves being defensive or planning what to say in response, we have probably lost some of the accuracy of our listening. Go back to listening using One-Mindfulness and attend to what others are saying.

Many of us have an unconscious resistance to listening. When others say, "listen to me," there is often an implied "agree with me" or "follow my directions." These unconscious assumptions can get in the way. Remember that listening does not have to mean agreement or compliance.

Reflective listening is an effective way to practice listening and to validate. With reflective listening, we mirror (or reflect) back what the other person said, either exactly or by paraphrasing the central themes. Our reflective responses can be brief. The goal is to stay attentive in the conversation and make sure we hear others, sometimes listening to what is "behind" the words.

Reflective listening is a skill that can feel awkward at first. Practice reflective listening in role-plays and in conversations. When using this skill, resist the urge to respond with your own material and instead keep the focus on others through reflection. With time and practice, you will notice that effective listening creates positive changes in relationships and maybe a decrease in conflicts.

VALIDATION (V)

■ *CORE CONCEPT*: Use validation to connect to others.

Validation is a complicated skill. Use this expanded teaching to learn a more advanced approach to the validation component of GIVE.

Use the acronym VALIDATE to remember the building blocks (**V**alue others, **A**sk questions, **L**isten and reflect, **I**dentify with others, **D**iscuss emotions, **A**ttend to nonverbals, **T**urn the mind, **E**ncourage participation) of this skill. These building blocks are described in further detail in the paragraphs that follow.

Value others

Seeking the inherent value in others is essential to validation. Adopt an attitude of acceptance toward others. Demonstrate your caring and concern, and let others know they are important to you.

Ask questions

We ask questions to help clarify others' experience. Ask specific questions about what others are feeling. Ask about thoughts and beliefs. Be genuinely curious about what is behind behaviors. Use questions to draw out others' experience.

Listen and reflect

Listen to others' answers to your questions and reflect back the major themes. Invite others to confirm your understanding (or lack of understanding). Continue to question, listen, and reflect for clarity.

Identify with others

Work to see the world through the eyes of others. How do relationships and the world make sense to *them*? Seek to understand others, identifying when you can and accepting differences when you cannot.

Discuss emotions

Talk about others' feelings and how they affect them from *their* perspective (not how their feelings affect you). Acknowledging the impact of others' experience on them demonstrates understanding.

Attend to nonverbals

Notice others' nonverbal communication to give you information about their experience. Do they look open or closed? Are they making eye contact? Read facial expressions and body language to identify feelings, and then check out your observations with others for accuracy.

<u>T</u>urn the mind

Validation does not mean that we agree with others. Validation means that we nonjudgmentally accept what they feel, think, and experience and how behaviors make sense given their context. Turn the mind toward validation, especially when it is difficult to relate. Turning the mind is especially important in conflicts.

<u>E</u>ncourage participation

Validation can be a difficult process at times, so we need to encourage ourselves and others to be engaged with each other. Do not give up, even when understanding is hard, when you feel disconnected, or when you are in conflict with others.

What Validation Is Not

■ *CORE CONCEPT*: These interactions can be confused with validation.

Validation is complex and takes practice. Another way to improve this skill is to understand interactions that are not experienced as validation. The following ways of relating with others often get confused with validation. Some of these ways of relating can work, but we want to minimize their use or use them in balance with accurate validation.

Personalizing others' experience

Keep the focus on the other person. One or maybe two self-statements that communicate your similar experience can be validating, but, when we start to tell our own story, the focus leaves the other person.

Getting too absorbed

Validation is about connection with others' experience *but not getting absorbed into it*. We can validate without taking on others' distress. *Be with* others in distress without *being* their distress. Also avoid taking on someone as a "project." We can show concern and connection without being responsible for the feelings of others.

"Fixing," offering solutions, or giving advice

These strategies are effective in some situations, but they are on the opposite end of the dialectic from validation. Most of us do not need our situations to be fixed, or we already know how to do it ourselves. Instead, we are looking for acknowledgment and understanding.

Cheerleading and encouragement

These approaches can be effective in balance with validation, but they can feel dismissive or condescending if a person has not been validated first.

It is also useful to avoid looking on the bright side, stating that the situation could have been worse, or one-upping others to try to put their issues into perspective (or accomplish something else). These approaches do not usually work well. Even if what the other person is saying does not seem like a big deal to you, remember that it may be a big deal to him or her.

Agreeing or giving in

You can validate others' experience even if you disagree, are in conflict, or want a change to happen. Validation can be a starting point for change.

DEAR MAN (DM)

■ *CORE CONCEPT:* DEAR MAN is used to get wants and needs met.

The DEAR MAN skill focuses on us. We use DEAR MAN to get our wants and needs met, to say no, and to set boundaries. This skill is the DBT version of assertiveness. Before describing the components of DEAR MAN, it is important to establish some assumptions and guidelines to increase the effectiveness of this skill:

- **Others cannot read your mind:** This includes your closest friends and family. Assume that others are oblivious to you and that they cannot tell how you are feeling or know what you want or need. It often feels personal when others have no clue what we want or need, and we may get frustrated and blame others. However, we need to proactively and clearly *ask* for our wants and needs, say *no* when appropriate, and *maintain* our own boundaries.

- **Effective communication of your wants and needs requires words:** Do not sigh, sulk, cop an attitude, get destructive, withdraw, or otherwise communicate without thoughtful words *and* expect it to work effectively. It is true that our behaviors communicate volumes, just not clearly.

- **DEAR MAN does not always work, even when done effectively:** DEAR MAN increases the probability that you will get your wants and needs met, but it does not guarantee it.

- **You must be mindful of your DEAR MAN goals before you begin:** Decide what is important and what is negotiable before you use DEAR MAN.

- **Remember to balance DEAR MAN with GIVE grounded in FAST:** Attending to others (GIVE) makes them more willing to assist, accept it when you say no, and respect your boundaries. Keep track of priorities, goals, and values in relationships (FAST).

Use the acronym DEAR MAN to remember the building blocks (**D**escribe, **E**xpress, **A**ssert, **R**eward, **M**indful, **A**ppear Confident, **N**egotiate) of this skill. These building blocks are described in further detail in the paragraphs that follow.

Describe

Use Observe and Describe to outline the situation in nonjudgmental, descriptive language. Identify the facts that will support your request, your reason for saying no, or your need for a boundary. Stick to facts when you describe the situation.

Express

Share your opinions and feelings if they are relevant and will help others to understand the situation. Sometimes you may choose not to include this step.

<u>A</u>ssert

Ask clearly for what you want or need, say no, or set your boundary. Establish your DEAR MAN goals up front so you know what you want out of the situation and work to be straightforward and matter of fact. The Assert step is essential. Otherwise, no one will know what you want or need.

<u>R</u>eward

Let others know what is in it for them. How will meeting your wants and needs, accepting your refusal, or respecting your boundaries benefit the relationship? Try to focus on rewards rather than threats. Create opportunities for others to feel positive about their help or respect for you. However, sometimes we need to discuss consequences instead of rewards. Again, be matter of fact, but avoid ultimatums that will box everyone in, and especially ultimatums you cannot or will not follow through with.

<u>M</u>indful

Stay focused on your DEAR MAN goal(s). Others will often try to change the subject or throw in comments to derail you. When this happens, one strategy to consider is a "broken record" approach, which means repeating your request or limits over and over again. (Notice how children do this effectively with their parents.) Also be aware of when the broken record technique is not working or is inappropriate to the situation, and switch strategies accordingly.

<u>A</u>ppear Confident

Act as if you feel confident even if you do not. Pretend you have the confidence you have seen someone else model. Use an assertive tone of voice, make eye contact, and use confident body language. Be mindful of your facial expression (keeping it relatively neutral) as well as your posture and overall personal appearance. Use nonverbal communication to your advantage. Write down and practice your DEAR MAN skills before using them so you feel more confident in the actual situation.

<u>N</u>egotiate

Negotiation means that we strike compromises and are willing to give to get. Decide what compromises make sense if you cannot meet your desired DEAR MAN goal(s). If you get stuck, turn the issue over to the other person for options to solve it; for example, say, "What do you think will work?" Turning the tables shifts the dialectical balance and can get the process moving again.

Negotiation is a dialectical strategy to get wants and needs met by meeting someplace in the middle. In some cases, you may decide in Wise Mind that negotiation is not an option.

Note that, while the building blocks of DEAR MAN work together, some of the components can also be used independently in certain situations. For example, you can Assert without using any other DEAR MAN building blocks. Use as much or as little of DEAR MAN as is required by the situation.

DEAR MAN Alternative: ASSERT

■ *CORE CONCEPT:* ASSERT provides an alternate model for assertiveness.

In addition to DEAR MAN, assertiveness can be taught through a variety of models. The following model may be more straightforward for some clients to learn or may provide a supplement to the DEAR MAN skill.

Use the acronym ASSERT (**A**sk or **S**et boundaries, **S**ay what is needed, **E**ye contact, **R**espectful, **T**iming) to remember the building blocks of this skill. These building blocks are described in further detail in the paragraphs that follow.

Ask

You cannot be assertive without speaking up. You need to ask clearly for what you want and/or need. Do not hint or beat around the bush. Be direct and confident in your request. Or. . .

Set boundaries

Say "no" and set other interpersonal boundaries when necessary. Do not expect others to know or recognize your boundaries. Again, be direct and confident.

Say what is needed

No more or less. Some situations may be benefited by you sharing your feelings, opinions, or detailed explanations. Other situations do not require elaboration. Tailor the amount you share to the context at hand, based on what will be most effective.

Eye contact

Look others in the eye when you speak without staring or having too intense a gaze. Eye contact communicates interest, confidence, and respect in Western cultures. However, be sensitive to other cultures and religions that view eye contact differently. Adjust the amount of eye contact you use accordingly.

Respectful

Choose respectful words, have a respectful tone, and be polite. Disrespectful words and tone will sabotage your efforts to be assertive and reach your goal(s).

Timing

Be thoughtful about timing. Some assertive statements need to happen in the moment, and others will be more effective when you choose timing that benefits your assertiveness goal(s). Generally, address issues that require assertiveness when you and others are in a Wise Mind place.

DEAR MAN: Factors to Consider

■ *CORE CONCEPT:* These factors can increase your effectiveness with using DEAR MAN.

The effectiveness of DEAR MAN relies on many different factors. The factors below will assist you in fine-tuning your DEAR MAN skills.

Be in Wise Mind

Wise Mind is essential for the effective use of DEAR MAN. If you are not in Wise Mind, consider soothing your emotions before using DEAR MAN in most cases. (Sometimes using DEAR MAN when in Emotion Mind is needed—for example, if safety is an immediate issue.)

Use GIVE first

Start an interaction with GIVE to increase your effectiveness. Others are more receptive when you consider their feelings, point of view, and situation. GIVE can open doors to use DEAR MAN.

Think about timing

It's been said that "timing is everything." They also say, "there's no time like the present." Dialectically, both of these sayings have truth. Consider whether the timing seems to favor the use of DEAR MAN, but do not use timing as an excuse to put off using DEAR MAN when you need to, especially if the situation is time sensitive.

Direct DEAR MAN appropriately

Make sure you speak to someone who can actually respond to your use of DEAR MAN. Sometimes it is difficult to predict whether someone will respond well to your use of DEAR MAN. Start where you can and be respectful at all times, then move on to a different person if your use of DEAR MAN is not working. Remember that, even if one person may not be able to grant your DEAR MAN request, he or she might have influence with the next person you address.

Do not give up

DEAR MAN is a difficult skill that varies in its effectiveness. Practice it in everyday situations and you will improve your overall assertiveness.

Your DEAR MAN Bill of Rights

■ *CORE CONCEPT:* We have DEAR MAN rights that we can exercise with responsibility.

Review the bill of rights below. Refer to it to encourage yourself to use DEAR MAN. Also, remember that rights require responsibility, so use DEAR MAN mindfully and effectively. Choose your DEAR MAN moments wisely.

- I have the right to be treated with respect.

- I have the right to my own opinions.

- I have the right to express my feelings.

- I have the right to stand up for my values.

- I have the right to disagree with others.

- I have the right to understand a request before agreeing.

- I have the right to ask for information.

- I have the right to take time to think about a request.

- I have the right to say no without guilt.

- I have the right to ask for my wants and needs.

- I have the right to set healthy boundaries with others.

- I have the right to be in Wise Mind before I get into a discussion.

- I have the right to disengage from a conflict.

- I have other rights related to my needs and wants.

List other DEAR MAN rights:

_____

Conflict Resolution

■ *CORE CONCEPT:* Conflict resolution takes a balance of interpersonal effectiveness skills.

We all have conflicts with others, but often we struggle to resolve them effectively or we may even avoid them altogether. Use the following steps to guide you through conflicts.

1. Address issues proactively with DEAR MAN to keep the potential for and intensity of conflicts lower.

2. When in conflict, step back and see whether you and others are in Wise Mind. If you want to win or be "right" more than you want to seek understanding and resolution, you are probably not in Wise Mind. When in Emotion Mind, conflicts are rarely effective. If you or the other person are not in Wise Mind, disengage and discuss the issue later. Use distress tolerance skills before getting back into the issue(s).

3. Consider the relevant issues. Use Wise Mind to consider whether this is a conflict worth having right now with this person. Consider your priorities, goals, and values and the nature of the conflict. Pick your conflicts wisely.

4. Use FAST throughout any interpersonal situation and especially with conflict. Lowering yourself to another's "level" will decrease your self-respect and will rarely result in an effective outcome.

5. Start with listening and GIVE. Think about companies with great customer service. They avoid arguing and listen instead, and then let you know they understand your problem. This approach frequently defuses conflicts.

6. Use Nonjudgmental Stance and you might find that you agree with at least some of what the other person has to say. Breathe and give some space before you respond. Many conflicts escalate because of a mutual lack of listening coupled with rapid-fire responses.

7. Use DEAR MAN effectively. Be clear about your wants and needs, saying no, or setting boundaries. Do so in a matter-of-fact way without name-calling, labeling, judging, or getting into extremes.

8. Use Radical Acceptance when conflicts are not resolved or when others are upset and angry. Not all conflicts have an immediate resolution. Sometimes we need to step away and let it be. When resolution seems unlikely or when the conflict is escalating, gently disengage yourself and agree to revisit it later.

Remember that negotiation and making Wise Mind concessions are useful. Stay away from all-or-nothing approaches and work the dialectic.

Interpersonal Intensity

■ *CORE CONCEPT*: Begin your use of DEAR MAN skills at an effective intensity level.

Effective use of DEAR MAN sometimes depends on our level of intensity. Assertiveness is a dialectical concept, with passivity on one end and aggressiveness on the other:

Levels of Intensity

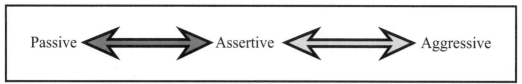

There are times to be more passive or more aggressive, but the most effective level of assertiveness is usually someplace in the middle. When we are too passive, it is easy for others to dismiss us. However, when we are too aggressive, others get defensive and resist our demands. Use Observe and Describe to make a Wise Mind assessment in regard to the intensity needed in each unique situation.

It works well to start at the low-middle end of the dialectic in most situations. From the low-middle end, you can dial up the intensity if needed; it is typically less effective to start out too intense and then try to dial it down.

Consider your baseline interpersonal style when applying interpersonal intensity. If you are normally passive, an effective DEAR MAN level will probably feel uncomfortably aggressive. If you are normally aggressive, an effective DEAR MAN level will probably feel uncomfortably passive. Closely Observe others' reactions and responsiveness and adjust your interpersonal intensity accordingly.

Interpersonal Effectiveness 4: DEAR MAN Application

CORE CONCEPT: Use this worksheet to develop your DEAR MAN skills.

Describe what you want or need, what you need to say no to, or the boundary you need to set:

_____

Describe (stick to facts):

_____

Express (your opinions and feelings if needed):

_____

Assert (be direct and specific):

_____

Reward (what is in it for the other person?):

_____

Describe how you can appear confident:

_____

Describe negotiations you are willing to make:

_____

Making Friends

■ *CORE CONCEPT:* Making friends takes positivity, time, and consistency.

Most of us want to have at least a couple of good friends, and a lot of people struggle with how to create lasting and meaningful friendships. Here are some suggestions for creating friendships to get you started.

Meet people who share similar values and interests to yours

People tend to make friends with other people who are similar, although sometimes quite different people become fabulous friends, so do not limit yourself either. If you have a particular hobby or interest (e.g., music, woodworking, scrapbooking, ham radio, politics), maybe there is a club, group, message board, or another meeting place for people into the same thing. If you have children, seek out other parents with children of a similar age group, or, if you have dogs, visit a dog park or area where people commonly walk their dogs (or take an obedience class; your dog might need it and you will get to learn more about behaviorism).

Get active in your community or involved in particular causes (e.g., social justice, the National Alliance on Mental Illness, issues in your own community). We have to get involved to meet other people.

Meet people around you

People commonly become friends based on proximity. Getting to know the people who live close to you, who you work with, or whose paths you frequently cross is an effective way to develop friendships. These people do not have to be a lot like you as the familiarity that comes with getting to know people over time often bridges differences. However, as mentioned above, you have to get involved with those around you to make friendships.

Be curious, show interest in others, ask questions, and really listen

Most people enjoy it when others take an interest in them. Learning about others is a great way to get to know them and they may reciprocate interest. When taking an interest in others, be mindful of their nonverbal communication and whether they are taking part in the interaction. Also be mindful of boundaries and do not overreach in asking questions. Stay clear of potentially controversial topics such as politics and religion at least at first, unless the context of the conversation or situation naturally leads to these topics.

Practice give and take in relationships

Healthy relationships are based on give and take. Those who take without giving burn out friends. Those who give without getting in return feel hurt and resentful. Strive to have balance in relationships. Be the kind of friend to others that you want them to be to you.

Be a rewarding person to be around

Consistent with behaviorism, your presence around others needs to be sufficiently rewarding or others will disconnect and avoid you. Work on being pleasant and enjoyable to be around, and others will respond. That does not mean that every interaction needs to be positive, or that you cannot rely on others for support from time to time, but if others do not feel at least intermittent rewards, it will be hard to maintain friendships. That is behaviorism.

Do not share too much or too little

People who immediately share their story or intimate, private details of life often scare off others. On the other end of the dialectic, people who are too private can take too much effort to get to know for other people, or others may interpret a private disposition as disinterest (accurately or not). Aim for the middle ground with what you share in relationships.

Realize that people have different social wants and needs

People are a lot like plants. Some need a lot of light and others thrive in shade. Some need only a bit of water, and others need a lot. Some plants have deep roots, and others do not. Plants are diverse, as are people. Think about yourself and people you know. Some are "people persons" and others have fewer people needs. Some people like to get to know others intimately, and others like to keep relationships more superficial. Match yourself to others in ways that work, finding people with similar people needs and accepting differences when they exist.

Take your time

While some people become friends quickly, most friendships develop over time. Be patient. Focus on being a consistent friend to others, and in time friendships with others will materialize.

Build respect over "liking"

If you behave in a respectful manner that leads others to respect you, others will also like you most of the time. However, if you place "liking" above respect, others might like you but there is no guarantee that they will respect you. Strive to earn others' respect in order to build friendships.

TRUST (T) and Relationships

■ *CORE CONCEPT:* Learn how to develop trust in relationships.

People who have been hurt or betrayed and/or who have experienced inconsistent relationships commonly struggle with trust. It is difficult to have rewarding friendships and other relationships if trust does not develop. The information below will help you decide whether people are trustworthy and will assist you in becoming more trustworthy yourself.

Use the acronym TRUST to remember the building blocks (**T**ruthful, **R**espectful, **U**nderstanding, **S**table, and **T**ime) of this skill. These building blocks are described in further detail in the paragraphs that follow.

Truthful

Trustworthy people tell the truth, even when it is inconvenient, difficult, or will result in consequences. Do not give your trust to other people whom you know to be dishonest, and do not erode others' trust in you by being dishonest.

Respectful

Being respectful means that others (and oneself) are treated fairly and with dignity. People who shout, intimidate, bully, are aggressive, or are otherwise disrespectful are not trustworthy.

Understanding

People who care enough to understand others and take their perspectives, wants, and needs into account tend to be more trustworthy. It is difficult to trust those who cannot look outside themselves to care for others too.

Stable

Trustworthy people are stable and consistent, and others can rely on their predictability. By contrast, erratic, unstable, and inconsistent people can be too hard to predict and have poor follow-through, both of which erode trust.

Time

Time is one of the best ways to gauge trustworthiness. Trust should not be automatic; it should be developed over time. For people who have destroyed trust, working the other components of the TRUST acronym over time will help in repairing it.

Boundaries

■ *CORE CONCEPT:* Boundaries keep relationships healthy and safe.

Boundaries exist to define how we are separate from others. A goal in relationships is to be in healthy contact with others without getting too enmeshed or being too disconnected.

It is important to be connected with others while also maintaining our own emotional, psychological, and physical space. Boundaries are dialectical in nature, as we strive to balance our interpersonal needs and comfort zones with those of others. Healthy boundaries allow us to have meaningful relationships without taking on others' distress and problems and without being isolated and alone. Boundaries define who we are as individuals in relation to others and the world.

Like types of fences (e.g., invisible versus picket versus razor wire), boundaries vary based factors such as personality, family, culture, locale, situation, and setting, among other factors, as well as how defined we need to be in relation to others. Our experience, what we Observe and Describe, and our priorities, goals, and values inform us about what types of fences to put up.

Boundaries are complex, and it is difficult to recognize and practice healthy boundaries if we have not seen them modeled by others. We will therefore begin with basic definitions of boundaries as a step toward developing healthy ones.

Definitions and Types of Boundaries

■ *CORE CONCEPT:* Define boundaries in order to practice them.

Physical

Physical boundaries include your body and the space that surrounds it (i.e., your personal space). Physical boundaries can be defined in terms of who is allowed to touch us and in what areas. These boundaries include all levels of physical intimacy and all sexual practices. Additionally, physical boundaries include what goes into us, such as food and drink, and anything else that affects our physical being.

Psychological

Psychological boundaries include information about yourself, your thoughts and beliefs, and your values. These boundaries might include topics of conversation and anything that occupies your "mental" space. Who knows about your inner life and how it is shared (if at all) constitute psychological boundary issues.

Emotional

Emotional boundaries include your feelings and their ability to be leveraged or manipulated (e.g., emotional "hostage-taking" or guilt-tripping). Emotional boundaries also include not taking on others' distress or expecting them to take on yours. Like psychological boundaries, who knows about your feelings and how they are shared (if at all) constitute emotional boundary issues.

Spiritual

Spiritual boundaries include your ability to choose your own religion, higher power, or spiritual life or lack thereof. Who knows about your spiritual life and how it is shared (if at all) constitute spiritual boundary issues.

Biographical

Biographical boundaries have to do with your history and life story. What to tell others about your life depends on many factors. Of course, psychological, emotional, and other boundaries intersect with biographical boundaries.

General

Anything that defines and differentiates you as separate from others (and others from you) is a boundary, and anything needed to keep you healthy and safe interpersonally and in the world constitutes a boundary issue. General boundaries might be where you live, where you work, who your friends and family members are, and other general information about you.

BOUNDARY (BO)

■ *CORE CONCEPT:* This skill guides healthy boundaries.

Healthy boundaries are the foundation of safe and respectful relationships with others, but many people do not know where to start in terms of developing boundaries. The BOUNDARY skill establishes a system to develop effective boundaries.

Use the acronym BOUNDARY to remember the building blocks (**Be** aware of self, **O**bserve others and the situation, **U**nderstand your and others' limits, **N**egotiate sometimes, **D**ifferences exist, **A**lways **R**emember your values, **Y**our safety comes first) of this skill. These building blocks are described in further detail in the paragraphs that follow.

Be aware of self

Use Observe and Describe to notice what you are sharing and what you are doing. Does your behavior fit the situation and your relationships with others? Does your behavior feel comfortable? Notice whether your boundaries are at either extreme, being too closed or too open for the situation and the relationships.

Observe others and the situation

What is happening in the situation and with others? Notice the level of interest, the information shared, and the behavior of others. Do the sharing and the behavior of others seem healthy and respectful? Note that observing others does not mean *copying* others. Keep your self-respect in mind and act accordingly. Observe and Describe what you are sharing and doing in the context of others, and understand that your boundaries exist in relation to those of others.

Understand your and others' limits

We all have important boundaries or limits. Be aware of your boundaries and maintain them from Wise Mind based on the needs of the situation and the relationships between you and others. Also be aware of others' boundaries and respect them.

Negotiate sometimes

In important relationships, we sometimes negotiate our boundaries. Negotiations happen from Wise Mind and rarely involve extreme changes. Avoid negotiating boundaries in unimportant relationships, in new relationships, or to be liked. Put your self-respect above being liked by others.

You may also negotiate your boundaries if there is a benefit in adjusting them. If your boundaries can be too undefined, work on developing tighter limits. If your boundaries can be too rigid, work on developing more flexible limits. Again, make adjustments from Wise Mind.

<u>D</u>ifferences exist

Negotiating boundaries is effective at times, but we need to balance negotiations with a healthy respect for individual differences, too. Differences in boundaries happen due to personality, personal history, culture, religion, situations, settings, and other reasons. Sometimes it is not about negotiating boundaries but maintaining your boundaries while being respectful of others' boundaries. Use Radical Acceptance or Everyday Acceptance with individual differences and learn not to take those differences personally (this is a boundary, too).

<u>A</u>lways <u>R</u>emember your values

The decision to negotiate and adjust your boundaries or to maintain them needs to be grounded in your priorities, goals, and values. Use your values as a compass to guide your boundaries and do not compromise boundaries at the expense of self-respect.

<u>Y</u>our safety comes first

People sometimes compromise boundaries to be liked or to fit in with others. Avoid situations that can harm you emotionally, psychologically, physically, spiritually, or in other ways.

Interpersonal Effectiveness 5: BOUNDARY Application

CORE CONCEPT: Use this worksheet to define boundaries.

Describe your **physical** boundaries:

_____

Describe your **psychological** boundaries:

_____

Describe your **emotional** boundaries:

_____

Describe your **spiritual** boundaries:

_____

Describe **general** boundary issues important to you:

_____

Describe what boundaries may be negotiable in some situations:

_____

Describe what boundaries are non-negotiable to you:

_____

Describe how establishing and maintaining boundaries can build and maintain your self-respect:

_____

Describe how your life will be different when you establish and maintain effective boundaries:

_____

Module 6

Cognitive Modification

Introduction to Cognitive Modification

■ **CORE CONCEPT:** Learning to be flexible with thoughts and beliefs helps us be more effective.

Many of us have been told that it is "all in our heads" or that there is something wrong or inaccurate with our thoughts and beliefs. These viewpoints invalidate our experience. The effect is that we learn not to trust ourselves, and we become defensive and guarded about our thoughts and beliefs. We then feel vulnerable when asked to evaluate them. That sense of vulnerability and defensive stance serve to protect us from further invalidation.

Dialectically, our thoughts and beliefs come from somewhere, and they make sense given the context of that place. Most of the time, our thoughts and beliefs have or have had adaptive functions, and there is a least some kernel of truth to them.

It is not about our thoughts and beliefs being right or wrong, accurate or inaccurate, but about whether they "work" or are functional in a given situation. For example, someone who grew up with critical parents may think that all other people will be critical, too. That thought or belief has worked in the past because it protected the person in a world that could be mean and punishing. However, when thoughts and beliefs become too generalized or extreme, they lose their function at times. In this example, the thought or belief will be less effective when applied to other people in situations other than the original home environment.

As an alternative to globally applying the belief, it may be useful for that person to see whether the general thought or belief about critical people works in specific situations. A dialectical shift in the thought or belief could be more effective in many ways for that person. Dialectical shifts lead to more flexible thoughts and beliefs about ourselves, others, situations, and the world and are at the center of how cognitive modification is done in DBT.

The key to dialectical thinking is being in Wise Mind, where emotions can be validated and reason can be accessed. This module focuses on a cognitive method for shifting thoughts and beliefs and also looks at common "stuck" thoughts and their dialectical remedies.

REASON (RE)

■ *CORE CONCEPT:* Check out your thinking while still validating your emotions.

The goal with our thinking is to have it be flexible in order to be functional. The skill below can be used to check thinking and beliefs while still validating emotions. In time, we can learn to trust our thoughts and beliefs knowing that we can do self-checks and shifts when needed.

Use the acronym REASON to remember the building blocks (**R**ational, **E**motions matter, **A**lternative views, **S**elf-trust, **O**ld beliefs, **N**ew thoughts and beliefs) of this skill. These building blocks are described in further detail in the paragraphs that follow.

Rational

Is the thought or belief coming from reason or Wise Mind? Does it work in the present situation? Remember that we all get stuck in thoughts and beliefs that do not work in certain situations, so be nonjudgmental with yourself. Remember that our thoughts and beliefs make sense given the context from which they originated, even if they do not work in the present situation. Thus, you can both validate why you have the thought or belief and shift it if needed. Check thoughts and beliefs with a trusted friend, family member, therapist, or other person. Be open to shifting a thought or belief to better fit the facts.

Emotions matter (validate)

Remember that emotions are important, as is the information they provide. Sometimes emotions give us the most accurate information while at other times they distort facts and situations. Validate your emotions and learn to notice the difference between when they help and when they hinder effective thinking.

Alternative views (dialectic)

Develop alternative views to consider alongside the original thoughts or beliefs. Take time to evaluate how each alternative view may work in the present situation. Will a different "place" on the dialectic be more effective in the present situation? There are many ways to think about the same situation. Be open to other perspectives and interpretations.

Self-trust (develop)

People who have been chronically invalidated do not trust their own thoughts and beliefs. Begin to notice times when your thoughts and beliefs work well in situations, and give yourself credit. When you learn to trust your thoughts and beliefs during these effective times, you will develop the foundation needed to recognize when shifting thoughts is needed in other situations.

Old beliefs (balanced with)

Respect old thoughts and belief systems. Remember that they have served purposes in past situations. The goal is not to negate old thoughts and beliefs. In time, thoughts and beliefs that are no longer useful will diminish on their own.

New thoughts and beliefs

New thoughts and beliefs will bring new options to how you think about yourself, others, situations, and the world. The ability to think dialectically will become part of your behavioral repertoire, and new thoughts and beliefs will contribute to a more satisfying life.

Cognitive Modification 1: Dialectical Shifts

CORE CONCEPT: Practice dialectical shifts with common thinking styles.

Certain common styles of thinking sometimes benefit from dialectical shifts. For each one, make the concept relevant by identifying when you notice being stuck in a style and how you can shift the thought to be more effective.

Black-and-white thoughts (either/or; dichotomous; or all-or-nothing thinking): Words that signal this type of style are "always," "never," "every," and "all the time," among others. Black-and-white thoughts feed emotional extremes and rarely work well. This approach to thinking leads to rigidity and inflexibility in situations and relationships.

Dialectical shift: If your thoughts seem extreme, think of opposite thoughts or beliefs, and then start to identify middle-ground ways of thinking. You may not believe the opposite thoughts or beliefs, but the intention is to practice flexibility in your thinking.

Describe when you do this and how you can shift:

_____

Regret orientation (woulda, coulda, shoulda thinking; or hindsight bias): It is easy to look back with the information you have now and regret what you did or did not do. As they say, "hindsight is 20/20." Regret orientation keeps us stuck in the past rather than focusing on what we can do effectively right now.

Dialectical shift: Rather than dwelling on past mistakes, focus on what you can do to be effective in the present moment (see Radical Acceptance and Everyday Acceptance).

Describe when you do this and how you can shift:

_____

Mind-reading: Many of us believe we know others' thoughts, and that belief causes us to feel or act in a certain manner. Most of us are not very good mind-readers in reality, so our feelings and actions are not based on very accurate information.

Dialectical shift: When you catch yourself mind-reading, check out your assumptions with other people, especially the person whose mind you are trying to read. Remember to use your DEAR MAN skills.

Describe when you do this and how you can shift:

_____

Minimization: Minimization happens when we take something large or significant and reduce it to something that is very small. We do this to reduce the emotional impact of a situation, but the result is that we end up invalidating our emotions. We also do this when we do not want to face difficult realities.

Dialectical shift: Observe and Describe the situation accurately without adding or subtracting. Remember to validate your feelings.

Describe when you do this and how you can shift:

_____

Magnification: Magnification is the opposite of minimization. It happens when we take something that is small or insignificant and exaggerate it to something that is very large. It is like looking at a kitten through a magnifying glass and seeing a tiger. The result of magnification is amplifying our feelings.

Dialectical shift: Like with minimization, Observe and Describe the situation accurately without adding or subtracting.

Describe when you do this and how you can shift:

_____

Catastrophizing: Catastrophizing is an extreme form of magnification. It involves taking a situation and continuing to build it and build it and build it in our minds into a calamity with dire consequences.

Dialectical shift: Focus on the _one_ situation or problem at hand without exaggerating it. Remember that most situations do not end up with extreme and dire consequences. Take one thing at a time. Alternatively, purposefully catastrophize to the point of absurdity to help yourself see that your fears are not realistic.

Describe when you do this and how you can shift:

_____

Fortune-telling (crystal-ball-gazing): Fortune-telling is the attempt to predict the future, usually in negative ways. It assumes that we already know what is going to happen, and it often causes emotions of anxiety and dread. In reality, most of us are not very accurate at predicting the future.

Dialectical shift: Rather than let a negative prediction of the future paralyze you, focus on what you can do effectively right now to cope with your situation or problem. Stay in the present moment.

Describe when you do this and how you can shift:

_____

Overgeneralization: Overgeneralization involves taking a small bit of information and applying it broadly across all kinds of people and situations.

Dialectical shift: Do not assume that your knowledge fits all people and all situations. Acknowledge when your information does fit, and actively look for times when it does not. Be open to not knowing all of the facts.

Describe when you do this and how you can shift:

_____

Selective information-gathering (selective abstraction; mental filter; or confirmation bias): Sometimes we only gather information that fits with our current thought or belief. This approach tends to validate our thought or belief, but it can lead to ineffective choices due to a poverty of information and viewpoints.

Dialectical shift: Actively gather information and viewpoints that are different from your own. Remember that you do not need to agree with these different perspectives but that they may lead you to greater flexibility and more effective choices.

Describe when you do this and how you can shift:

_____

Labeling (judging): Labeling is an approach that takes a person or situation and reduces it to only a name. Labels fail to look at people and situations in a holistic manner and miss important subtleties or nuances.

Dialectical shift: Gently let go of the need to label a person or situation. Instead, Observe and Describe nonjudgmentally. Understand that the world is more complex than labels and judging.

Describe when you do this and how you can shift:

_____

Personalization: Personalization makes it all about you. Even when situations feel personal, they often are not. We feel the weight of the world when we take so many situations and others' issues and problems personally.

Dialectical shift: Use Teflon Mind. Remember that most of the time it is not about you. Take responsibility for what is yours (if it fits Wise Mind) and gently let go of the rest.

Describe when you do this and how you can shift:

_____

Emotion Mind "reasoning": Emotion Mind reasoning means having your thoughts and beliefs come from an Emotion Mind place without factoring in Reason Mind or Wise Mind.

Dialectical shift: Use What and How skills to access Wise Mind. Alternatively, use distress tolerance skills to soothe your emotions before shifting thoughts and beliefs.

Describe when you do this and how you can shift:

_____

Should statements: These statements get us stuck because they focus on judgments rather than the realities of a particular situation or interaction. Reality unfolds in ways that do not fit our preferences (i.e., what "should" happen).

Dialectical shift: Focus on "what is," not what "should be." Stop "shoulding" on yourself and others.

Describe when you do this and how you can shift:

_____

Discounting positives: Often we focus on the negatives or the downside of situations and are blind to positives. Sometimes we minimize or negate positives about ourselves, others, situations, or the world. Discounting positives is undialectical.

Dialectical shift: Seek out positives, upsides, and silver linings for balance. Own the positives about yourself and give yourself credit. Find the positives in people and situations that seem negative.

Describe when you do this and how you can shift:

_____

Blaming: Blaming makes everyone but us responsible for our problems and difficulties. When we blame, we give up our power and control and are utterly dependent on others to fix a situation (or our lives).

Dialectical shift: Someone or something else may be responsible for a problem, but your power and control come from focusing on how you can influence situations and your life, if only through choosing how you respond.

Describe when you do this and how you can shift:

_____

Defusing: A Mindful Way to Separate Yourself From Thoughts and Beliefs

■ *CORE CONCEPT:* Defusing can lessen the impact of negative thoughts and beliefs.

A technique called defusing, which is a part of acceptance and commitment therapy (Hayes et al., 1999), can help us Observe and Describe thoughts and beliefs more mindfully with less of a negative impact. With defusing, you remove the personalization from your thinking by making small changes in the language of your thoughts and beliefs, effectively separating yourself from them.

To use defusing, you work on describing thoughts and beliefs in ways that are not about you. To illustrate, "nobody likes me" becomes "I am having a thought that nobody likes me"; "I can't do this" becomes "I am thinking that I can't do this again"; "this is stupid" becomes "I am using a judgment word in this moment"; and "I'm so ugly" becomes "I'm thinking that I'm ugly again."

Thoughts are just thoughts and only have the power we give them, and defusing decreases the power thoughts hold. As you practice defusing, you accept rather than judge or fight thoughts and beliefs. By doing so, you remove much of their emotional power and stay unstuck.

Readers who find this approach to thoughts helpful can find additional explanations and applications in books on acceptance and commitment therapy.

Cognitive Modification 2:
REASON and Shifting Thoughts

CORE CONCEPT: Use this worksheet to practice shifting thoughts.

Observe and Describe the thought or belief:

_____

_____

Is the thought or belief rational from Reason Mind or Wise Mind? Is it functional or working right now? Is it an example of a stuck thought? Describe:

_____

_____

Validate your current emotion (it matters too):

_____

_____

Describe at least two alternative viewpoints on the dialectic:

_____

_____

Balance these alternative viewpoints with your original thought or belief. Describe any differences in your thoughts, beliefs, emotions, or behavior:

_____

_____

Module 7

Problem-Solving

Introduction to Problem-Solving

■ *CORE CONCEPT:* A systematic approach promotes effective problem-solving.

Problems of various types and levels of difficulty frequent our lives. If we do not actively work to solve our problems, they grow in number and size, and we end up chronically overwhelmed or even paralyzed by them.

Unfortunately, many of us do not have a method for solving problems. We try to solve them by trial and error or in a haphazard manner. These approaches sometimes work but tend to be ineffective overall.

Another difficulty many of us have is Emotion Mind "problem-solving." We place disproportionate importance on our feelings and the information that comes from them. In turn, we neglect information and facts that would give us a more balanced approach to problem-solving based on more complete information. Therefore, it is beneficial to balance our emotions with our reason to reach a Wise Mind place to work through problems and difficulties. In Wise Mind, we can validate our feelings *and* connect with our priorities, goals, and values to engage in an effective approach to problem-solving.

Problem-solving starts with being aware of problems as they come up and developing a willingness to address them effectively.

Basic Principles of Problem-Solving

■ *CORE CONCEPT*: Use these principles when you approach solving a problem.

Take one problem at a time

Most people have more than one active problem at any given time. It is overwhelming to have many problems, but the reality is that you can only solve one at a time. Start somewhere. You might start with your easiest problem to solve or your most important problem to solve, or you might need to address problems sequentially (i.e., you might need to solve a certain problem first in order to solve a related problem).

Understand and define the problem

Once you pick a problem, specifically define the problem with nonjudgmental, descriptive language. If you do not understand the problem and cannot define it, then it may be difficult to figure out a solution. Be as precise as possible in your definition of the problem.

Research the facts

To better understand and define your problem, you need to do your homework. What information do you need or are you missing? Information is power and is the difference between being uncertain or paralyzed in the face of a problem and seeing a clear pathway to a solution.

What is the cause of the problem?

Identifying and addressing the cause of the problem is sometimes necessary to solving it. Stay nonjudgmental and be sure that identifying the cause of the problem does not lead you to blaming. Getting stuck in "blaming mind" is seldom productive and can often make the problem worse. However, if you are able to be skillful to decrease or eliminate the cause(s) of your problem, do so.

What works (or has worked)?

Have you solved this problem (or one like it) before? If so, what did you do that worked? Do more of the solution behavior(s). In a similar vein, what is different about your behavior, others' behavior, or the environment when the problem is not happening? Do more of what is working when the problem is not happening. From Wise Mind, do what you think is needed to solve the problem with a focus on Willingness and Effectiveness.

What does not work (or has not worked)?

Have you done anything that has contributed to the problem or has not worked in bringing about a solution? What are you doing, or not doing, when the problem is happening? Do less of or eliminate behaviors that have contributed to the problem or have not worked toward finding a solution.

Can you take it one step at a time?

Some problems, especially large or complicated ones, need to be solved sequentially or in steps. Break your problem down into steps that will enable you to reach a solution, and take the first one.

Use Willingness, cooperation, commitment, and follow-through!

Often what is needed to solve a problem does not fit with our preferences. Be willing to put aside your preconceived notions of how you think things should happen in order to do exactly what is needed. Be willing to cooperate and be part of solutions and not part of problems. Work with and not against others in seeking a solution; offer and seek help as needed. Once your action steps toward a commitment are identified, commit yourself to following through.

Using SOLVED (SO)

■ *CORE CONCEPT:* Use this systematic approach to solve problems.

Use the acronym SOLVED to remember the building blocks (**S**tep back and be objective, **O**bserve available options, **L**imit barriers, **V**alues driven, **E**ffectiveness first, **D**ialectical thought and action) of this skill. These building blocks are described in further detail in the paragraphs that follow.

Step back and be objective

Observe and Describe from Reason Mind or Wise Mind. What is the problem in nonjudgmental terms? Stick to the facts: who, what, where, when, how, and why. Write it down.

Observe available options

Brainstorm and list as many options as you can, and then determine what options are available. Remember to accept the realities of both the problem and the possible solutions. Also list the resources you can use at this step. Use DEAR MAN to ask for ideas, help, and guidance if needed.

Limit barriers (emotional and environmental)

Remove barriers that stand between you and a potential solution. Do not get in your own way. Use Radical or Everyday Acceptance, Willingness, and Nonjudgmental Stance. Do not amplify or minimize your problems. Gauge the level of your problem and address it in a manner-of-fact way. Identify whether barriers exist in your environment and address them as needed. Again, use DEAR MAN to ask for ideas, help, and guidance if needed.

Values driven (what are your priorities and goals?)

Use your priorities, goals, and values as your compass. Values will not lead you astray in the long term. They will be the foundation of solutions that work. From your available options, pick the solution that best solves the problem while building or at least maintaining your self-respect.

Effectiveness first

What will work? The most effective solutions will not always be your preferred solutions. Accept that life has problems and solve this one so you can get on to the next one.

Dialectical thought and action

Solutions often involve compromise. Be dialectical with thoughts and actions and remember that effective, values-driven solutions often come from the middle ground.

After following this process, make a decision and take action. Evaluate the outcomes and use the SOLVED process to readjust your approach and the solution to your problem if needed.

Problem-Solving 1: SOLVED

CORE CONCEPT: Use this worksheet to solve problems.

Step back and describe your problem from Wise Mind:

_____

_____

Brainstorm and then describe the options and resources available to you:

_____

_____

Describe your barriers and the skills that you will use to address them:

_____

_____

Describe your priorities, goals, and values and how they can guide your solution:

_____

_____

Use the above information to describe what will work:

_____

_____

Describe your solution and action plan:

_____

_____

Describe how your life will be different when you solve this problem:

_____

_____

Addictions

Introduction to Addictions

■ **CORE CONCEPT:** Understanding addiction is the first step to overcoming it.

Addiction happens when a person compulsively engages in a behavior despite its harmful consequences. Signs of addiction include a preoccupation with the behavior along with a lack of control over it, despite significant negative consequences. Addictive behaviors are typically characterized by immediate gratification or reward followed by delayed costs and harm. Common addictions include:

- Alcohol and/or drug use

- Excessive eating or addiction to certain foods (e.g., sugar, fast food)

- Spending money/shopping

- Gambling

- Harmful relationships

- Exercise

- Internet use

- Sex and/or pornography

People with addictive behaviors often experience tolerance and dependence. Tolerance means that more and more of the addictive substance or behavior is needed to feel the "fix," and dependence means that reducing and/or stopping an addictive behavior causes withdrawal symptoms. Some withdrawal symptoms are physical—such as fatigue, vomiting, and loss of energy—while others are psychological and emotional. All withdrawal is uncomfortable or painful, making the person vulnerable to falling back into the behavior.

Stopping an addictive behavior is difficult, and it often requires the help of a professional and/or a strong and positive support system. Giving up the immediate rewards, facing up to withdrawal and other consequences, and reaching out to others is hard. In the early stages of change you may not even know or want to accept that you have a problem. See the Addiction Checklist worksheet to evaluate your situation. If you question whether your behavior is an addiction, it is also helpful to:

- Complete a Pros and Cons assessment (see Distress Tolerance module) to determine the pros and cons of engaging in the behavior.

- Educate yourself about the risks and costs (physical, psychological, emotional, relational, financial, etc.) of the substance or behavior.

- Try an abstinence holiday from the addictive behavior.

- Be open to an assessment and assistance from professionals.

Recovery from an addiction is possible, even for the most "hopeless" addicts. By making a choice to recover, developing a plan, seeking and accepting support from others, and taking recovery one day (or moment) at a time, you can do it. Start by being honest with yourself and others, practicing your skills to build a new life, and recognizing that for most people (probably including you!) recovery is an everyday commitment for life.

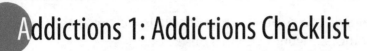

Addictions 1: Addictions Checklist

CORE CONCEPT: Use this checklist to determine whether you struggle with addictive behavior.

People with an addiction show many different signs and symptoms. Review this list and take an inventory of each behavior and/or concern as it relates to your life. Check each item that applies to your addictive behavior. Remember that an honest self-assessment is essential to committing to change an addictive behavior.

☐ **Difficulty stopping the behavior:** Your attempts to stop the behavior have been unsuccessful.

☐ **Withdrawal symptoms:** You experience physical, psychological, and emotional symptoms when coming off the behavior. These symptoms might include cravings, disturbances with appetite and sleep, moodiness, anger, and attention and concentration problems, among others. At an extreme you may experience trembling, sweats, seizures, hallucinations, or even a medical emergency with certain addictive behaviors.

☐ **Health problems:** You continue to engage in the behavior even when it puts you at risk of or causes health problems.

☐ **Legal trouble:** You have been arrested or have had other legal consequences as a result of your behavior.

☐ **Large doses and excessive engagement in the behavior:** You take a large dose of a substance to "get started" or you engage in a behavior in an extreme manner.

☐ **Keeping a supply and/or hidden "stashes":** You maintain a supply and/or hide away substances, pornography, food, or other items in various parts of your home, office, or car.

☐ **Needing the addictive behavior to cope:** You feel unable to deal with the ups and downs of life without substances or your addictive behavior.

☐ **Preoccupation:** You find yourself constantly thinking about and planning to engage in the addictive behavior.

☐ **Hobbies and activities decrease:** You decrease or stop engaging in hobbies and activities you used to enjoy. The addictive behavior has crowded out healthy and fun activities you used to prioritize.

☐ **Missing out:** You choose not to participate in activities in which you cannot also engage in your addictive behavior.

☐ **Risk-taking:** You put yourself in dangerous situations as a result of the addictive behavior.

☐ **Secrecy and isolation:** You hide your behavior and participate in it alone.

☐ **Minimizing and denial:** You downplay the effects of your addictive behavior on yourself and/or others or even outright deny the possibility that your behavior is a problem.

☐ **Financial difficulties:** Paying for your addictive behavior causes strain on your or someone else's finances.

☐ **Relationship problems:** You have conflicts with other people about your addictive behavior.

Abstinence Holiday (AH)

■ *CORE CONCEPT*: An Abstinence Holiday provides a glimpse of life without your addictive behavior.

An abstinence holiday means that you set aside a period of time in which you do not use a substance of abuse or engage in an addictive behavior. To practice this skill you select an amount of time to remain free from your selected behavior in order to Observe and Describe the outcomes. This skill is a form of harm reduction, and it works especially well for people who are unsure about the effect of addictive behaviors in their lives and/or for people who are not ready to give up their addiction "forever." An abstinence holiday can serve as a personal experiment to gauge your level of addiction and the benefits of abstinence.

Abstinence holidays work best when you have established a skills plan for how to deal with urges, how to occupy open time in your schedule, and how to address barriers or problems you anticipate may upset your holiday plans. Just like a literal holiday, you have to put thought into your plans.

Abstinence holidays can be short (e.g., an hour or evening), intermediate (e.g., a week), or a longer period of time (e.g., a month or more). To feel the benefits of moving away from your addictive behavior, it is best to choose a reasonable amount of time to see what happens, knowing that within this time period you can still take on the challenge one moment at a time. The goal is to recognize that your life can be *better* without your addiction than with it.

The following are examples of an abstinence holiday:

- Going 30 days without drinking alcohol

- Turning off all your electronic devices after 5pm for a week

- Avoiding added sugar for 2 weeks

- Going without cutting for the weekend

- Not seeing a harmful friend for a month

- Attending a concert without consuming drugs or alcohol

- Not smoking marijuana for 6 months.

Ready to try life without your addictive behavior for a while? Use the following Abstinence Holiday worksheet to get started.

Addictions 2: Abstinence Holiday

CORE CONCEPT: Use this worksheet to monitor your abstinence holiday.

An abstinence holiday is an opportunity to try life without one (or more) of your addictive behaviors. This worksheet is set up for 1 week, but your holiday can be for any length of time. A good rule of thumb is to plan to go long enough for the average difficulty of abstaining from the behavior (rated from 10, extreme difficulty, to 0, no difficulty) to drop while the average observed benefits increase (rated from 10, great benefits, to 0, no benefits). You want to see that life can be better without the behavior!

If at any time you revert to the behavior, try dialectical abstinence and get back to your plan as soon as possible.

☐ **Monday**

    Average level of difficulty: _____ Observed benefits: _____

☐ **Tuesday**

    Average level of difficulty: _____ Observed benefits: _____

☐ **Wednesday**

    Average level of difficulty: _____ Observed benefits: _____

☐ **Thursday**

    Average level of difficulty: _____ Observed benefits: _____

☐ **Friday**

    Average level of difficulty: _____ Observed benefits: _____

☐ **Saturday**

    Average level of difficulty: _____ Observed benefits: _____

☐ **Sunday**

    Average level of difficulty: _____ Observed benefits: _____

Dialectical Abstinence

■ *CORE CONCEPT:* Some behaviors are so harmful there is no middle ground with them.

In DBT, dialectical abstinence means that you take the undialectical stance that your addictive behavior is so destructive to your life that you commit to only one side of the dialectic: working on abstinence from the behavior. This 100 percent commitment means that your sole focus is on learning and using skills to establish and maintain abstinence.

It is reality that many people who work on abstinence from an addictive behavior have setbacks. If you make a mistake or have a slip, the goal is to remember dialectical abstinence and your 100 percent commitment to avoid a full-blown relapse. You do this by quickly repairing your mistake and completely throwing yourself back into your goal(s). What you want to avoid is giving up and working against yourself by making one mistake a bigger one, or, worse yet, a series of bigger ones. If you were climbing a mountain and lost your footing, you would quickly restabilize, check your anchors, make necessary adjustments, and get back to climbing; you would not just throw yourself off the mountain!

Another helpful analogy is that successful people in any pursuit (e.g., parenting, business, sports) make mistakes, but the key difference between them and less successful people is that they actively learn from mistakes, sometimes mining their greatest opportunities from them. If a parent yelled at his child, the goal would be to learn and practice more skillful parenting, not to yell more or escalate into extremely ineffective parenting. If a businessperson lost an account, she would learn and correct the mistake in the future, not keep making the same error with her other accounts too. And, if a pitcher gave up a home run, he would regroup and continue to try his best to get strikeouts, not just give up and start throwing slow, easily hittable pitches!

Complete commitment to doing better flows from the skills of self-acceptance and being nonjudgmental. Beating yourself up and getting into judgments is counterproductive to your goals and will not help you to do better. Remember the basic assumption that you are doing your best and need to do better, and resolve to learn from mistakes. Use behavior and solution analysis with your therapist(s) and the philosophies promoted in this book to learn from relapses. This approach will improve your progress toward abstinence and a better life.

Note that the concept of dialectical abstinence can be used with many different problems, such as making a 100% commitment not to act on harmful thoughts such as suicide, self-injury, or substance use, and/or not to fall into behaviors that feed into symptoms of mental illness.

Dialectical Abstinence Versus Harm Reduction

■ *CORE CONCEPT:* Harm reduction can be a dialectical choice when someone is not ready for dialectical abstinence.

Some people are unsure whether they want to use dialectical abstinence to completely give up an addictive behavior, but they still want to decrease the harm that the behavior causes them and/or others. Actively choosing to decrease harm without fully giving up an addictive behavior is called "harm reduction." Examples of harm reduction include:

- Use of condoms to lower the risk of disease or an unwanted pregnancy

- Avoiding the use of "hard" drugs while continuing the use of less harmful substances

- Holding on to an ice cube instead of cutting

- Using a clean needle every time intravenous drugs are used

- Participating in opioid replacement therapy

- Using a designated driver, taxi, car service, or public transportation when drinking or using drugs in public

- Switching to electronic cigarettes

- Gambling only a predesignated amount of money.

Ultimately, harm reduction is a compromise that attempts to mitigate damage while not fully protecting yourself from or delaying the deleterious effects of an addictive behavior.

Is harm reduction rather than abstinence right for you? To decide, you need to take an honest inventory and seek advice and guidance from others.

Frequent Dialectical Tensions With Addictions

■ *CORE CONCEPT:* People with addictions commonly experience certain dialectical conflicts.Ocum tam vestess olicavenat, corum perfenaribut publiceres sunimo movidit, dum addum ine int, publi perrace contem P. Habus.

There are certain dialectical conflicts that are common to addictions. See whether any of these conflicts relate to you and brainstorm what approaches or skills could be useful to resolve them effectively. Also think about and discuss other dialectical tensions that frequent your life and how to navigate them effectively.

- Wanting to give up the behavior yet resisting change

- Having ambivalence about giving up an addictive behavior

- Enjoying an addictive behavior while it also causes you suffering

- Being pulled into versus stepping out of unskillful behaviors (related to substance use and/or mental illness)

- Wanting to use yet knowing it will be harmful

- Seeing only one side to a situation

- Being independent yet still needing help

- Taking things personally when it isn't about you

- Having a mismatch between your values and behaviors

- Deciding a relapse means total failure

- Wanting to be like others who don't struggle with addictive behaviors

- Feeling good in the moment but knowing your behavior will lead to feeling lousy later

- Deciding between a lie and the truth

- Wanting respect but not practicing respect

- Telling too much versus too little to others

- Balancing your wants and needs with those of others

- Separating feelings and facts

- Staying nonjudgmental in difficult situations

- Leaving open options to act unskillfully

- Taking an "all-or-nothing" approach to anything

- Indulgence versus restriction

- Balancing emotion with reason

- Having your goals conflict with your current behaviors.

Clear Mind

■ *CORE CONCEPT:* Clear Mind comes from sustained recovery balanced with recognizing the risks of relapse.

For people who struggle with addictive behaviors, three states of mind that supplement Emotion Mind, Reason Mind, and Wise Mind can help guide recovery. These states of mind are Addiction Mind, Clean Mind, and Clear Mind.

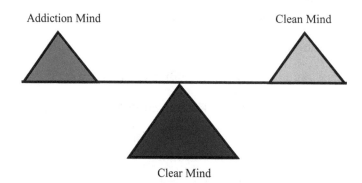

When people are still using or are in the early stages of change, they are frequently stuck in what can be called Addiction Mind. This state of mind is focused on urges and cravings to engage in addictive behavior. Addiction Mind keeps the doors to use open, and people in this state of mind are preoccupied with planning and acting on the behavior. Addiction Mind is distorted and keeps people from seeing the consequences of the behavior, making them ready to deceive both themselves and others in the pursuit of it. According to traditional treatment approaches, being in Addiction Mind is similar to being caught in denial or ambivalence about giving up addictions.

Once people have obtained abstinence through treatment or other means, they can then be stuck in what is called Clean Mind. One example of this state of mind is a "treatment high" in which the person quickly moves forward but neglects underlying issues, making a relapse more likely. Clean Mind is characterized by being naive to warning signs, triggers, and environmental cues to the addictive behavior; not being sufficiently proactive; and not making sufficient plans to avoid relapse. In Clean Mind, people may also fall into the trap of believing that they have enough behavioral control to hang out with friends and in environments where addictions are active, or even go back to "moderate" engagement in their addictive behavior.

As with Wise Mind, ultimately we want to move into Clear Mind. From traditional treatment approaches, Clear Mind is similar to being in the responsive state of sustained recovery. In Clear Mind, strong emotions and urges are nonjudgmentally acknowledged and respected, and people are proactive and make adequate plans about how to handle them. Clear Mind has no illusions about how falling into old behaviors and relapsing can occur subtly and outside awareness without sufficient practice of mindfulness, self-care, and use of resources.

It is key to remember that the path to Clear Mind comes from decreasing engagement in the addictive behavior, achieving abstinence, managing physical and psychological discomfort, dealing effectively with urges, and keeping doors to relapse closed while working on skills to build a satisfying life.

In Clear Mind, the continued practice of effective behaviors happens moment by moment, one day at a time, even after many years of abstinence.

Two Steps to Wise Mind/Clear Mind

■ *CORE CONCEPT:* Follow these two steps to access Wise Mind/Clear Mind.

The following two steps give us the ability to get into Wise Mind and Clear Mind. Note the overlap between this teaching and the Wise Mind and core mindfulness lessons in the Mindfulness module. Use all of these teachings together to increase your mastery of mindfulness and states of mind.

Step One: Observe and describe, nonjudgmentally and one-mindfully

Observing and describing is a process of waking up, being aware of experience, and allowing it to flow. We begin by collecting and unifying our attention and then focusing our concentration. Think about having various mental windows: windows to emotions, windows to urges, windows to physical sensations, windows to behaviors, windows to others and our surroundings, and windows to our senses. Of course, there are other windows too, such as windows to the past (e.g., memories) and windows to the future (e.g., planning). As we become aware and notice experience, whatever it may be, we decide which windows to open and which to close, based on what is explained in Step Two below. As we look through our chosen mental window, we watch without clinging to or pushing away due to either attraction or aversion. In other words, the experience is the experience, no more, no less.

The process of Observing and Describing is intended to be nonjudgmental. While judgments can be useful on occasion (e.g., when we simply need to categorize information and move on, in a dispassionate manner), most of the time they cloud experience, either amplifying or diminishing "what is." The truth about judgments is that they are all relative and what is "good" or "bad" depends on the context of the moment in relation to other moments. For example, problems are opportunities and opportunities have problems. Judgments usually reduce perspective, like looking at the world through a drinking straw. Think about times in which you attached labels to what was being experienced. Chances are something important was missed, and the negative labels probably added suffering to experience and stopped the flow of observation, leading to being stuck. When we are stuck, it is difficult to participate effectively in experience.

Our goal is to describe what we observe in nonjudgmental language, again not adding to or subtracting from the experience. This neutral way of describing uses factual language that is objective, without coloring the experience. In other words, this process of Observing and Describing involves taking in information and reporting it in a matter-of-fact manner.

Observe and Describe is meant to be a One-Mindful process, again, in relation to what is described in Step Two. Metaphorically, be a gatekeeper about what you observe. Gatekeepers decide what to let in and what to let out, and they maintain a watchful focus. Similarly, we direct the focus of our attention and concentration with One-Mindfulness, gently noticing and letting go of distractions, gently closing those windows that blow open.

Step Two: Participate effectively

Observing and Describing creates awareness. When we are not awake to the moments of our lives, we live reactively. Reactive living leads to exacerbation of symptoms and addictive behavior through escape and avoidance and/or mood-congruent behaviors. Once we are aware we have behavioral choice, we can choose to participate in symptoms and/or an addictive behavior, or we can choose to participate in skills and behaviors that are representative of Wise Mind and Clear Mind.

We decide how to participate based on what would be effective, or what "works." Effective participation means removing barriers, from yourself and/or your environment, in order to meet your goals and live your life based on your true intentions and values. All things being equal, how do you best play your cards, meeting the demands of the present situation? How do you move from point A to point B being responsive instead of reactive? *What are you willing to do to have a better life?*

Making skillful choices that work is one part of effective participation. The other part is experiential, connecting and being with experience. Being with experience means getting off the sidelines and into the game, going from reading the lines to playing the part, and moving from sleepwalking through life to living it, moment by moment, starting with this one.

The more you practice the skills and behaviors that are important to creating the life you want, the more you will find those skills and behaviors springing intuitively from Wise Mind and Clear Mind, because they will become a part of you.

Nonjudgmental Stance (NJS), Self-Acceptance, and Change

■ *CORE CONCEPT:* Be both nonjudgmental and accountable with yourself to achieve change.

No one has ever overcome the symptoms of mental illness and/or addictive behaviors through judging oneself or others. In fact, harsh judgments serve to amplify problems and guarantee that people stay stuck in ineffective cycles and patterns. Judgments get in the way of change.

While judgments occasionally have functions, most of the time they skew the way we perceive reality, shutting us down from continued evaluation of the facts and keeping us in a state of elevated emotions and stress. In judgment mind, we default into our reactive and ineffective ways of dealing with life without a real connection of our greater goals and values.

Staying nonjudgmental does not mean evading accountability for choices. It is important to take responsibility for mistakes and for falling into old patterns. Staying nonjudgmental means that, as soon as you have a SLIP (**S**kills **L**earning **I**mproves **P**rogress) into an addictive behavior and/or into symptoms of mental illness, you quickly try to learn from it and make the necessary changes in a matter-of-fact manner, avoiding self-criticism, which can become a vulnerability to engaging in ineffective behavior. A nonjudgmental approach allows you to dialectically create a positive out of a negative.

A Nonjudgmental Stance is a prerequisite to learning self-acceptance. Self-acceptance means acknowledging, without judgment, who you are in this very moment, with all of your faults and shortcomings. When you accept yourself, you free yourself of struggling with your real self. Self-acceptance is not resignation but a process that releases your psychological resources toward the possibility of change.

Acceptance is both the catalyst of change and change itself, allowing you to realize a better life.

One Moment at a Time

■ *CORE CONCEPT:* Taking one moment at a time gets you through the long haul.

An old adage in treatment programs is that someone may not know how to be abstinent from a behavior for a year (or longer), but that person does know how to stay abstinent for a day (or shorter). Whether working on abstinence or simply trying to tolerate something painful, time and progress are more manageable when they are considered in small chunks, one moment at a time.

Take whatever you are trying to commit to and put it into a manageable timeframe. When that timeframe expires, commit to the next manageable timeframe. Over time, you will link these smaller successes into sustained success. For example:

- On a difficult day, commit to not drinking or using drugs for 1 hour (or less) at a time.

- Table the option to attempt suicide or act on self-injurious urges between professional appointments.

- Commit to practicing skills in 10-minute increments.

- Decide to wait on confronting someone (if you cannot be skillful) until the next day.

- Make a commitment to go to treatment one week at a time.

As you look to manage symptoms, urges, and behaviors within smaller timeframes, keep practicing other skills and throwing yourself into the behaviors that will create the life you want. And remember: One moment at a time works best when you are not watching the clock!

Bridge-Burning (BB)

■ *CORE CONCEPT:* You cannot act on a harmful behavior if you proactively remove the means.

Bridge-Burning refers to proactively removing the means of acting on your urges to engage in addictive behaviors. The concept of Bridge-Burning recognizes that relapse into harmful behaviors happens more easily when there is the immediate opportunity to act on impulses. Eliminating the opportunities and/or inserting barriers between urge and action will result in more opportunities to practice skills.

Bridge-Burning with substance use

- Remove all alcohol and drugs from your home.

- Remove all alcohol- and drug-related objects and paraphernalia from your home (e.g., cocktail glasses, corkscrew, pipes, papers, lighters, and/or anything associated with use).

- Erase the numbers of using friends, associates, and dealers from your phone.

- Block the phone numbers of using friends, associates, and dealers from your phone or get a new number.

- Stay away from bars, liquor stores, and locations associated with use, changing your routines and routes to actively avoid them.

- Do not carry cash.

- Tell anyone and everyone that you have given up substances.

- Actively tell others when you experience urges to use.

List other ways of Bridge-Burning to substance use:

_____

Bridge-Burning with self-injury and/or suicidal urges

- Remove razors, lighters, and other self-injury tools.

- Mix up and change rituals associated with self-injury.

- Remove the specific method of acting on suicide.

- Tell others when you are unsafe and need help.

- Spend time with others and in locations in which you would not harm yourself.

- Go to the hospital *before* acting on suicidal urges.

List other ways of Bridge-Burning with self-injury and/or suicidal urges:

_____

Bridge-Burning with spending

- Cut up credit cards (if you need to keep one, freeze it in water so it will take longer to access it or have someone trustworthy hold it for you).

- Have someone trustworthy keep your excess money when urges are high.

- Establish a "waiting period" that you must adhere to before making a decision to buy any nonessential item.

- Stay away from stores, the mall, online shopping, and/or TV shopping.

List other ways of Bridge-Burning with spending:

_____

Bridge-Burning with unhealthy and/or hopeless relationships

- Erase the other person's number from your phone.

- Block the other person's number or get a new number.

- Route emails from the other person to your junk mail folder or block them altogether.

- Tell anyone and everyone that you have moved on from the relationship.

- Fill your free time with activities and healthy people.

List other ways of Bridge-Burning with hopeless relationships:

_____

Bridge-Burning with overeating

- Keep binge and "comfort" foods out of your home.

- Dish out your portions and put the rest away before eating.

- Avoid "all-you-can-eat" restaurants and buffets.

- Eat multiple times a day, mindfully, including healthy snacks.

List other ways of Bridge-Burning with overeating:

_____

Bridge-Burning with gambling

- Avoid places where gambling occurs.

- Limit your access to cash and credit that can be used for gambling.

- Have someone trustworthy hold on to your money when urges are high.

- Block internet access to gambling websites.

List other ways of Bridge-Burning with gambling:

_____

Bridge-burning works best in conjunction with other skills. When we remove the ability to act on harmful behaviors, we need to replace them with something new and skillful. *Be careful not to trade one unhealthy behavior for another.*

Building New Bridges

■ *CORE CONCEPT:* Build bridges to new ways to meet your wants and needs.

Burning bridges removes the means of acting on your addictive behavior. As a rule, anytime you subtract a behavior from your life, you should look to add new behaviors to replace what was lost. This is where bridge-building comes in.

If your addiction made you feel good (in the short term)

- Increase opportunities to laugh (e.g., listen to comedy, watch a favorite sitcom, read a joke book and tell others your favorites).

- Practice Build Positive Experience.

- Boost your endorphins through movement, physical touch, or getting outdoors.

- Practice affirmations.

List other ways of feeling good:

_____

If your addiction relaxed you

- Practice Self-Soothe skills.

- Practice deep breathing every hour.

- Schedule down time in which you can turn off your electronics and not be responsible for anything.

- Learn to let go of the "small stuff."

List other ways of practicing relaxation:

_____

If your addiction involved a ritual

- Start a meditation practice.

- Develop a prayer routine.

- Create morning and bedtime rituals.

- Take morning or afternoon tea time.

List other ways of getting into rituals:

_____

If your addiction had social aspects

- Go to a 12-step meeting.

- Get involved in a cause or advocacy group.

- Develop friendships with people who do not involve themselves in your addictive behavior.

- Make time for small talk with people as you go through your day.

List other ways of being social:

_____

If your addiction involved fun

- Identify new hobbies.

- Get a do-it-yourself guide on something you're interested in doing or creating.

- Join a sports league (softball, bowling, kickball, flag football, etc.).

- Play music and sing and/or dance.

List other ways of having fun:

_____

If your addiction involved the excitement of risks or danger

- Take up an exciting hobby such as trail running, snow-boarding, or rock climbing.

- Join (or form) a band.

- Invest a small amount in penny stocks (but do your homework and avoid scams).

- Work up a comedy routine and show up on amateur night.

List other ways of creating excitement through safe risks:

_____

_____

If your addiction is a way to rebel and break rules

Practice alternative rebellion by:

- Questioning commonly held beliefs
- Speaking your mind or writing a letter to the editor of a newspaper or other publication
- Supporting a fringe cause or political candidate you believe in
- Learning to stand out from the crowd in positive ways.

List other ways to rebel that do not hurt you or other people:

_____

_____

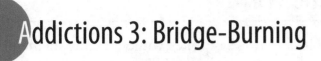

Addictions 3: Bridge-Burning

CORE CONCEPT: Use this exercise to remove the means to act on your harmful behavior.

Describe how you can use the Bridge-Burning skill with a harmful behavior (e.g., self-injury, drinking or drug use, spending, promiscuous sex, overeating). Be specific about how the means to act will be removed:

_____

_____

_____

Describe the new behaviors and skills you will use to replace the old behavior:

_____

_____

_____

Describe how you and others will benefit from effective Bridge-Burning (e.g., how you and others will feel, how it will affect your self-respect, what other practical benefits will occur):

_____

_____

_____

Describe how your life will be different when you burn bridges to your harmful behavior(s):

_____

_____

_____

Urge-Surfing (US): Ride the Wave

■ *CORE CONCEPT:* Go with the ebbs and flows of urges without acting on them.

Urge-surfing is the nonjudgmental acceptance of urges, allowing you to simply notice and ride their ebbs and flows without reaction.

The essence of Urge-Surfing is to understand that urges are a part of our experience and are not commands for action. Often, instead of just watching our urges, we unwittingly intensify them. Judging and catastrophizing are two ways in which we make it harder to tolerate urges. We also have a natural tendency to want to escape urges by fighting them or acting on them. All of these approaches to urges ultimately intensify them.

Trying to fight urges is not unlike struggling to escape quicksand: Frantic efforts lead to sinking. Like fighting urges, escaping discomfort by acting on urges will also cause you to go under in time. This happens because relieving tension with unhealthy behaviors is reinforcing and feeds the cycle of addiction.

The secret is to not panic and react but to float. Riding the ebbs and flows requires us to be willing to have a nonjudgmental relationship with our urges, even when they cause intense discomfort. It may seem counterintuitive, but an acceptance-based relationship with urges, emotions, or any other uncomfortable experience will decrease the intensity of many of these experiences over time. Remember that acceptance is not resignation; instead it is a state of mind in which we acknowledge "what is," freeing up our resources to be responsive and effective.

Practice Urge-Surfing when your urges are at lower levels. Like real surfing, you learn to ride small waves before you can graduate to large swells, and you also learn when the waves are too intense to ride. Keep in mind that Urge-Surfing works well in combination with other skills, such as distraction. Be responsive and switch up skill strategies based on what works.

Emotions, Thoughts, and Situations That Trigger Addictive Behavior

■ *CORE CONCEPT:* Understand what triggers your addictive behavior and plan solutions.

Read and discuss the following triggers for addictive behaviors and check the ones that apply to you. Implement the suggested solutions, and add the information you learn about yourself and what might be effective to your skill plans.

☐ **You feel painful emotions:** Anxiety, depression, anger, hopelessness, guilt, and shame are just some of the emotions that can lead you to engage in an addictive behavior.

Solution: Accept the emotion without judging it, talk to someone supportive, or throw yourself into an activity or distraction. Remember that unhealthy coping of all types feeds painful emotions.

☐ **You find yourself in "high-risk" situations:** You are surrounded by people, places, and things that you strongly associate with an addictive behavior and/or you are in a situation where people are engaging in addictive behaviors and maybe even pressuring you to engage too.

Solution: Would you stay in a burning building? Figure out how you are going to walk out in a calm and orderly manner, using your skills and/or plan(s).

☐ **You have a bad day:** You use a difficult day as an excuse to escape or take a break through addictive behavior.

Solution: We all need to manage stress on bad days, so develop skills to replace your addictive behavior.

☐ **You have a great day:** You use a great day as an excuse to prolong positive feelings through addictive behavior.

Solution: Brainstorm other ways to keep good times going without your addictive behavior.

☐ **You reminisce about the "good old days":** You are nostalgic about your addictive behavior and do not remember any of the corresponding "bad old days" that came with it.

Solution: Gain some balance by recalling the "bad old days" and how your addictive behavior has negatively affected you.

☐ **You minimize the effects of your addictive behavior:** You push away how your addictive behavior affects you and others negatively (e.g., thinking that your addiction is not nearly as bad as that of others).

Solution: Think about the long-term effects of your addictive behavior on your life (e.g., your health or finances). Remember that you probably have no special defenses against the long-term effects of your addiction.

☐ **You experience strong physical sensations and cravings:** Some bodily sensations can strongly motivate addictive behavior.

Solution: Practice Urge-Surfing, Opposite to Emotion, relaxation, or distraction. Seek out healthy pleasures and use Build Positive Experience.

☐ **You experience withdrawal symptoms:** When you have withdrawal symptoms and feel unwell, it can be tempting to use your addictive behavior to feel better again. Beware of this vicious cycle!

Solution: Use Radical Acceptance with withdrawal symptoms and consult a physician if needed. Immediately practice PLEASED and/or self-care skills, and try to get into healthy distractions. The discomfort will pass in time.

☐ **You think that a little bit of your addictive behavior won't hurt you:** In truth you know it definitely will not be just a little.

Solution: Count the times that you held to a little bit of your addictive behavior compared to the times it spiraled into more, or gather this data going forward.

☐ **You "reason" that this is the last time you will do you addictive behavior or that you will change starting tomorrow:** However, your history has proven this to be an unlikely "commitment."

Solution: Read and talk about stages of change and consider where you are and what you need.

☐ **You think that it's unfair that other people can engage in your addictive behavior, so you should be able to too:** However, others may not engage in the behavior with the same frequency, intensity, or duration or suffer the same ill effects as you do.

Solution: Use Radical Acceptance to understand that life is sometimes unfair, and mindfully refocus on skills to Build Mastery or use Build Positive Experience without your addictive behavior.

☐ **You think your attempts to quit the addictive behavior are a "lost cause," or you even think of yourself as a lost cause:** This thinking promotes addictive behavior to "validate" your sense of being worthless.

Solution: Practice Nonjudgmental Stance, use interpersonal effectiveness to ask for support, or throw yourself into a distraction.

☐ **You believe you deserve a celebration:** You think you have earned your addictive behavior through hard work.

Solution: You do deserve a celebration! Think of healthy and positive ways to recognize yourself and your accomplishment.

☐ **You believe you deserve an escape because life has gotten hard.**

Solution: You do deserve an escape! Look at your skills plan or brainstorm with others about healthy pleasures and escapes.

☐ **You think that you have to escape this emotion, urge, or situation because it seems unbearable.**

Solution: Practice acceptance, use distress tolerance skills, or reach out to others for validation and problem-solving. Read this (or another) skills manual until the urge passes.

☐ **You mix up your wants and needs:** Wanting to engage in an addictive behavior is not the same as needing to.

Solution: Who "needs" addictive behaviors other than those who are addicted to them? Get into mindful distractions, relaxation techniques, or other ways to have fun, and use Build Positive Experience.

☐ **You experience myopic thinking and see only a small part of the picture or only today.**

Solution: Get into dialectical thinking, seeing both the forest and the trees.

☐ **You use a small slip to justify a full-blown relapse:** You think, "in for a penny, in for a pound."

Solution: Actively remember your commitments, use dialectical abstinence, take on a Nonjudgmental Stance, and "play the tape through," considering the likely consequences of a full-blown relapse. Do not burn down a house you worked hard to build.

☐ **You think that no one cares for you anyway:** Since you are not worthy of care and concern, you may as well do your addictive behavior.

Solution: Test that theory by talking to your therapist, another program member, a supportive family member or friend, or someone at a crisis intervention center or meeting. Be open to allowing someone to show concern, and do not punish their efforts by arguing or rejecting what is offered.

List your other triggers to your addictive behaviors and effective solutions:

_____

_____

_____

Observing and Describing the Effects of Addictive Behavior

■ *CORE CONCEPT:* Increase mindfulness of the negative effects of your addictive behavior to motivate change.

Addictive behaviors have both varying and similar effects on people's lives. The goal of this exercise is to build awareness about the negative effects that the behavior you engage in has on areas of your life. If you are not sure whether your addictive behavior causes problems for you (or think that it does not), then Observe and Describe the impacts your behavior has on other people who have expressed concern about you. Also "fast-forward" and Observe and Describe concerns you (or others) have about longer-term consequences of your addictive behavior.

Use information from your therapist(s), program members, books, the internet, discussions, and other sources to complete this exercise. If you are not sure whether the information you find is accurate, be sure to inquire further and/or ask someone who knows (e.g., a therapist, physician, or another expert).

Note that this exercise can be done with any addictive and/or problem behaviors, such as alcohol and drug use, chronic suicidal behaviors, self-injury, gambling, overeating, or any other behaviors that cause undesirable consequences.

Addictions 4: Describing the Consequences of Addictive Behaviors

CORE CONCEPT: Use this worksheet to assess how your addictive behavior impacts important areas of your life.

Describe how your addictive behavior affects the following areas of your life.

Mental health:

_____

Physical health:

_____

Spiritual health:

_____

Family:

_____

Friends:

_____

Education and/or self-learning:

_____

Work, volunteering, and/or productivity:

_____

Leisure:

_____

Other areas:

_____

Cycle of Emotions and Ineffective/Addictive Behaviors

■ *CORE CONCEPT:* Understand cycles of addictive behavior to break them.

Emotions and ineffective and addictive behaviors follow a cyclical pattern. Notice how vulnerabilities, triggers, emotions, and action urges pull us into ineffective and addictive behaviors in an attempt to cope. These behaviors usually fall into two categories: mood-congruent behaviors, which maintain emotional or mood states, and escape and avoidance behaviors, which we use to get away from emotional or mood states.

Ineffective and addictive behaviors often meet short-term needs, but their consequences can intensify the emotions that we struggle with in the first place. Further, these behaviors can cause other secondary painful emotions such as regret, guilt, and shame. These consequences then feed into the next vulnerabilities at the top of the cycle. Over time, you become psychologically and/or physically dependent on your addictive behavior to cope.

Study this cycle and use it to identify the specifics of your emotions and your ineffective and addictive behavior cycle. As you understand your cycle, start to think of ways to skillfully intervene at each point of the cycle; each potential problem is an opportunity for practice. Also consider that both ineffective and addictive behaviors and symptoms of mental illness need to be addressed at the same time for your efforts to be effective.

As you learn more about your cycle and its components, consider how you will use that information in your skills plan(s).

Mental Illness and the Ineffective/Addictive Behavior Cycle

■ *CORE CONCEPT:* Symptoms of mental illness and addictive behavior follow recurring cycles that can be interrupted.

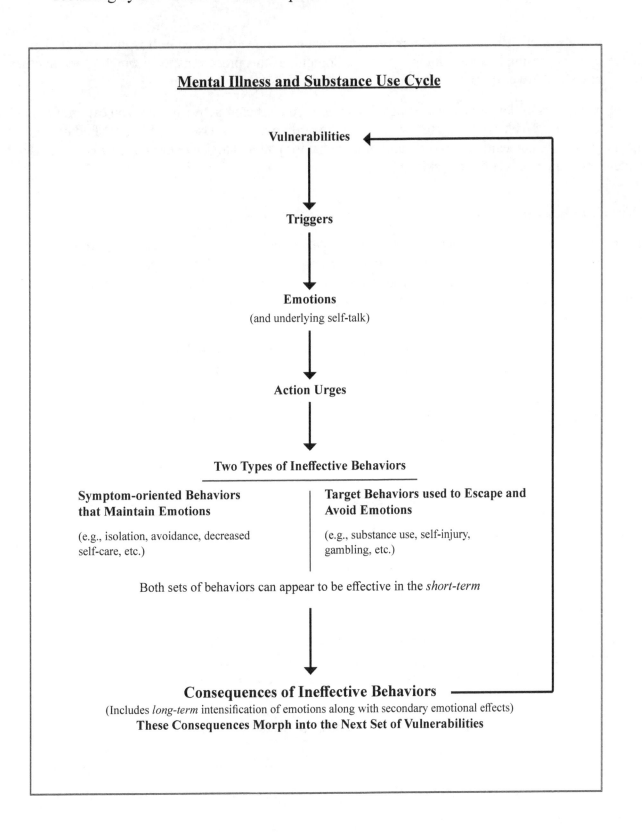

Mental Illness and Substance Use Cycle

Vulnerabilities

↓

Triggers

↓

Emotions
(and underlying self-talk)

↓

Action Urges

↓

Two Types of Ineffective Behaviors

Symptom-oriented Behaviors that Maintain Emotions

(e.g., isolation, avoidance, decreased self-care, etc.)

Target Behaviors used to Escape and Avoid Emotions

(e.g., substance use, self-injury, gambling, etc.)

Both sets of behaviors can appear to be effective in the *short-term*

↓

Consequences of Ineffective Behaviors
(Includes *long-term* intensification of emotions along with secondary emotional effects)
These Consequences Morph into the Next Set of Vulnerabilities

Observing and Describing a Process of Relapse

■ *CORE CONCEPT:* Similar to symptoms of mental illness and addictive behavior, relapse often follows a predictable cycle.

The following exercise discusses common elements that contribute to a relapse. It is important to know that a relapse is not simply an event but a process. Sometimes this process happens quickly, and at other times it may unfold over days, months, or even longer.

Gaining awareness of how this process unfolds can help you to be proactive in how you can minimize risk and maximize effective coping to stay on track toward your goals. Use your history of addictive behavior, your mental health symptoms, and other behavior patterns to discover your relapse process and transfer what you discover to your skills plans.

1. Vulnerabilities thrive

Vulnerabilities frequently begin with a lack of adequate self-care. When people are not getting enough sleep, exercise, or nutrition, it is difficult to be emotionally regulated. If you have cut down or eliminated your addictive behavior, the discomfort that comes with withdrawal symptoms is a set-up to relapse without careful attention to helping your body and mind recover (this occasionally happens after a long, sustained period of abstinence too).

Inadequate self-care paired with too much stress (e.g., work, school, financial, housing issues, isolation, and/or other relationship problems) can make it especially hard to resist addictive behavior.

Additionally, not actively working on creating a satisfying life without your addictive behavior leaves a lot of opportunities to fall into old behavioral patterns, as does unnecessarily exposing yourself to people, places, situations, and things that are high risk when vulnerabilities are strong.

Describe the vulnerabilities that apply to you, including additional vulnerabilities not listed:

_____

Describe the skills you need to practice to address these vulnerabilities:

_____

2. Strong feelings, cravings, and urges build

Unchecked vulnerabilities feed strong emotions, especially when people are predisposed to anxiety, depression, anger, or another type of emotion dysregulation. Vulnerabilities also lead to strong cravings and urges, especially if your addictive behavior had short-term benefits in the past. In an emotional moment, urges can seem like they last forever.

Describe the feelings, cravings, and urges that can be difficult to manage:

_____

Describe the skills you need to practice to address these feelings, cravings, and urges:

_____

3. Thinking about the addictive behavior becomes a preoccupation

You become preoccupied with your addictive behavior, and you may minimize or rationalize engaging in it or get into another type of "stuck thinking" that will not work for you. You may convince yourself that the behavior will work and not be any big deal, "just this time." Or you may tell yourself that it is hopeless and does not matter anyway.

Describe what you have told yourself in your mind (i.e., your self-talk) about substance use before a relapse happens. Also describe how your self-talk at those times appears to you in retrospect:

_____

Describe the skills you need to practice to address this self-talk:

_____

4. Planning a relapse in your mind

At some point thinking shifts into planning. What are you going to do, where will it happen, who will you be with, or how will you plan the time you need to do it alone? How will you keep it secret or minimize it to others? At this point you are practicing in your mind what does not work in your life.

Describe how your planning at those times appears to you in retrospect:

_____

Describe the skills you need to practice to address mental planning:

_____

5. Putting your plans into motion

At this point you are taking active steps to engage in your addictive behavior, and you start to take the behavioral steps that put your plan into motion. While each of these steps is an opportunity to change course and make a u-turn, the further you go down this road, the more difficult it is to avoid a SLIP (see point six below).

At this stage you are in Emotion and Addiction Mind and need to work toward Wise and Clear Mind.

Describe how putting your plans into motion at those times appears to you in retrospect:

_____

Describe the skills you need to practice to address behavioral steps toward use:

_____

6. Having a SLIP

A SLIP (**S**kills **L**earning **I**mproves **P**rogress) is the final destination in this process: This is actual engagement in the addictive behavior. The task now is to revisit dialectical abstinence as soon as possible, to quickly repair the mistake, and to learn from it as you recommit to your goals. A step in a different, skillful direction in needed.

Describe what you have learned from your SLIPs and how it can improve your progress:

_____

Describe the skills you need to practice to minimize and/or avoid SLIPs:

_____

Opposite to Emotion With Urges for Addictive Behavior: U-Turn

■ *CORE CONCEPT:* Any moment is an opportunity to turn around harmful behavior.

A u-turn consists of making a complete change of direction. Sometimes urges for addictive behaviors lead us to take steps to make those behaviors happen, leading to a relapse. Imagine a continuum where one direction leads to greater health and well-being and the other direction leads to diminished health and well-being. Sometimes we get moving in an ineffective direction, either accidently or by choice, but, once we realize we are moving further away from our goals, we can make an abrupt change and head in the other direction.

Think about times when you have been driving or been a passenger in a car that has taken a wrong turn and is moving away from the destination. How does it feel to willfully stay on this route in spite of increasing indications that the direction is leading to a place you do not want to go? The reality is that it is possible to stop, reassess the situation, and make a u-turn if needed, and that many opportunities to turn around usually exist until we have actually acted on an urge. Even if you have a lapse, there is still an opportunity to turn it around by recognizing the mistake, quickly repairing it, and reversing course before a full-blown relapse happens.

When we understand the vulnerabilities and triggers that lead to substance use, we can identify many intersections at which to make a u-turn and avoid being in a place that we want to avoid. The next time you notice urges and behaviors that move you toward relapse, take the wheel and make a u-turn.

Addictions 5: Opposite to Emotion and the U-Turn

CORE CONCEPT: Use this worksheet to see the outcomes of your addictive behavior versus making a u-turn.

Event ⟶ **Emotion** ⟶ **Natural Response**

Followed Natural Response?

YES   **NO**

Action   **Opposite Action**

Outcomes   **Outcomes**

Using DEAR MAN to Refuse Addictive Behaviors

■ *CORE CONCEPT:* Assertiveness is required to refuse engaging in addictive behavior.

When people give up an addictive behavior (or are working to do so), it is common to encounter pressures, both subtle and obvious, to take it up again. You may find yourself in situations where others are engaging in an addictive behavior and where it seems to be part of the norm. In these situations you may find that others encourage you to engage in the behavior, sometimes in seemingly friendly ways and sometimes in pushy ways. Sometimes the encouragement is subtle, being passive and implied.

In situations where you are invited to engage in your addictive behavior, or anything else that is unwanted, you can simply say "no" without any additional information or justifications. However, saying no is difficult for many people. For this reason, it is important to do behavior rehearsal, having your therapist, a fellow program member, or someone else "pressure" you to engage in the behavior while you practice setting a limit. Have your behavior rehearsal partner continue to challenge you in increasingly intense ways while you continue to use the broken record technique (see DEAR MAN in Module 5: Interpersonal Effectiveness). Note that you can also rehearse other ways of refusing if you find them to be useful.

As you rehearse this skill, remember to practice various scenarios (e.g., being at a social event, having someone bring substances to your home, having your partner or spouse encourage you to engage in a harmful behavior with him/her) with various people (e.g., strangers, a close friend, a family member), making the rehearsal as real as possible. It helps to have people share actual events with each other to increase the realism of the rehearsal. Having one or more observers give feedback and "jump into" the rehearsal to model skills when you get stuck increases the effectiveness of this exercise. Writing a script to follow can assist those who are in the process of learning how to speak more spontaneously.

Remember that you have worked hard for your successes, and people who would ridicule, criticize, or pressure someone who has worked to improve have their own issues. Try not to personalize, and remember that you can simply leave the situation if necessary. Use your Wise and Clear Mind to guide you.

Using Interpersonal Effectiveness to Address Resentments

■ *CORE CONCEPT*: Addressing resentments can be an important part of recovery.

Resentments contribute to painful emotions, addictive behaviors, and other ineffective behaviors. Start by Observing and Describing the role resentments have had in your life with your therapist and/or program members. We can be surprised how much resentment we have once we begin to talk about it. In these discussions, be straightforward in how you have played a role in and participated in resentments.

Resentments can then be divided into categories. One category is for resentments that you decide to accept and release without addressing them with other people, essentially beginning a process of unburdening yourself. It is helpful to share your desire to release these resentments with someone else, and you may find that you need to revisit this process of acceptance from time to time.

The other category is for resentments that need to be addressed with other people, directly or symbolically. Begin by talking about these resentments in greater detail with impartial others to better understand the nature of the resentments and what you need to say. Try to discuss resentments descriptively and nonjudgmentally, and allow yourself to feel the pain attached to them. Do not amplify your emotions, but also do not attempt to minimize their impacts on you. You may consider journaling as an alternative to or as an initial step toward talking with someone. If expressing the resentments will likely overwhelm you, make sure you are in a safe environment and in Wise and Clear Mind.

After journaling and/or discussing resentments, choose one that you may want to address. Take on resentments one at a time. Specifically decide what you want to say to the person or people relative to your chosen resentment. Remember your FAST skills, especially being fair and grounded in values, and how you can use GIVE along with what will essentially be a DEAR MAN. Write a script and rehearse it with someone. Anticipate how your DEAR MAN, even done skillfully with GIVE, will be received. *Remember to own your contributions to the situations that caused the resentment and include that aspect in the script.*

After you finish this preparation, make a final decision about whether you want to address the resentment directly. Discussing resentments with the people involved works when you anticipate that they will be receptive. *In general, avoid directly discussing resentments with people who would likely react in a way that harms you and with people who would likely be harmed by the discussion.* In these situations, writing a letter that you will not mail, journaling, or talking to an open chair can be a healing outlet.

When you have clear interpersonal and distress tolerance plans along with sufficient behavioral rehearsal, reach out to set up a time to talk. Consider the timing and other factors to set the discussion up for success. Keep in mind the qualities of being assertive: Your goal is to skillfully discuss the resentment.

The ultimate goal of addressing resentments in one way or another is acceptance and forgiveness, so you can be free to move forward. The preparation and conversation can be stressful, but the reward will likely be worth it.

Addictions 6: Resentments

CORE CONCEPT: Use this worksheet to work through resentments that hinder recovery.

Use this exercise to learn more about your resentments and to begin the process of addressing them.

Describe a resentment related to another person in detail and in nonjudgmental language:

_____

_____

Describe your behaviors that contributed to the resentment:

_____

_____

Describe your goal(s) for addressing the resentment (if you choose to do so):

_____

_____

Describe what you would like to say to the other person using GIVE and DEAR MAN (use another sheet of paper if necessary):

_____

_____

Describe in more detail your plan for addressing this resentment (if you choose to do so), including the skills you will need to practice:

_____

_____

Using Interpersonal Effectiveness to Make Amends

■ *CORE CONCEPT:* Similar to addressing resentments, making amends can be an important part of recovery.

Addictive behaviors and other ineffective behaviors can result in harm to other people in both direct and indirect ways. The pain and suffering you may have caused others through your actions (and inactions) may create pain and suffering for you as well. The guilt and shame that result from harming others can directly keep people in the cycle of addiction or make them vulnerable to relapse by allowing for escape and avoidance of these emotions.

Not addressing the harm caused to others also interferes with recovery. For example, you may think you need to continue to avoid those you have hurt, closing your world rather than opening it. Additionally, ignoring the need to make amends allows you to ignore the negative effects of the addictive behavior (or other behavior), creating another barrier to your recovery.

Making amends begins with openly acknowledging the behaviors that harmed other people. What did you do, and who did it affect? With this acknowledgment comes emotion, and you need to experience it without amplifying it or minimizing it. The emotion honors the relative seriousness of what was done. Balance experiencing any intense emotion with distress tolerance skills, and consider whether you need to do this work in a safe environment.

One part of making amends is apologizing for the specific actions that affected others, clearly recognizing the impacts of those actions. If a direct apology cannot be made (i.e., if it would cause further harm), writing a letter that you will not mail, journaling, or talking to an open chair can be helpful.

However, amends go far beyond an apology. An important part of making amends is repairing the situation to the best of your ability. For example, if you stole money or property, you would pay it back or return it. Justice is restored through restitution that honors the pain and loss that resulted from your actions. If you cannot make amends for a practical reason (e.g., you cannot or should not contact the affected person or you literally do not have the means to restore the situation), then you may have to make symbolic amends, often through committing to touch the lives of others in positive ways. Dialectically, this makes meaning out of something that was terrible.

Truly making amends is about changing your life so that you no longer fall into making the mistakes that previously caused others harm; it is about pursuing health, wellness, and recovery. It is about using skills to live a life grounded in values and your true intentions.

Although the process of making amends is focused on and for others, you can enjoy the freedom that ultimately comes from sincere efforts.

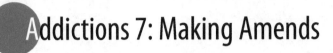

Addictions 7: Making Amends

CORE CONCEPT: Use this worksheet to make amends for situations that hinder recovery.

Use this exercise to begin the process of making amends with people who have been harmed by your addictive behavior.

Describe in detail and in nonjudgmental language the behavior that harmed someone else and who that person is:

_____

_____

Describe in detail and in nonjudgmental language how you believe that person was affected by your behavior, including the emotional impact:

_____

_____

Describe the apology you would like to make, taking responsibility for your behavior and making no excuses:

_____

_____

Describe how you plan to repair the situation, in real and symbolic ways:

_____

_____

Describe your commitment to implementing changes in your life to avoid making the same mistake again:

_____

_____

Module 9

Building a Satisfying Life

Introduction to Building a Satisfying Life

■ **CORE CONCEPT:** Routines and structure lead to a satisfying life.

Every life is worth living, but many of us find our lives unsatisfying, unenjoyable, or even miserable at times. Life is more satisfying when we develop routines that include predictable and enjoyable relaxation and fun balanced with responsibilities.

Routines do not need to be complicated. In fact, most of us benefit from mindful simplicity in life. Mindful simplicity means connecting to and experiencing the routines that define and structure our days.

Consider that the Dalai Lama (2009) describes a daily routine that includes meals, meditation, studying scripture, mending watches, gardening, working, and watching a little TV before bed. Our routines do not have to be spectacular. Peace and enjoyment can come with predictability.

Also consider that what works for children generally works for adults. Many of us make the mistake of believing that we no longer need the structure and predictability that children do. In some cases, we never had structure or predictability as children, so we never had the opportunity to continue having it in adolescence or adulthood.

One of the first tasks of building a satisfying life is establishing a routine. Before beginning, consider the following dialectic: *want to* versus *have to*. Our routines need balance between what we want to do and what we have to do, and we need to have a middle ground between enjoyable activities and responsibilities. Dialectically speaking, going too far in either direction creates the need for balance with the opposite. We need to rework our routine when we are stuck on one side or the other.

Two other dialectics to consider are *structure* versus *flexibility* and *predictability* versus *novelty*. Remember that structured routines benefit us, but, if they become too rigid, we may feel trapped by them. Obviously, the other extreme of excessive flexibility may result in too much unpredictability or chaos, which stands in the way of developing a satisfying life.

Too much flexibility leaves us unsure about what we need to be doing, and that causes distress. The middle ground is creating a routine that is solid but includes opportunity for change and flexibility based on the demands of the day.

A predictable routine allows us to feel settled and safe and to have a "home base" from which to operate. At the same time, too much predictability leads to feeling stifled. We also need to experience novelty and change in our routines. Every day does not need to be the same. Planning open times and free days can be part of establishing the balance.

Remember that building a routine will take time but will reap great rewards.

Using ROUTINE (RO)

■ *CORE CONCEPT:* Develop a schedule to get your life on track.

Use the acronym ROUTINE to remember the building blocks (**R**esponsibilities, **O**ngoing structure, **U**se of skills, **T**raditions, **I**nterests included, **N**ovelty, **E**nvision a satisfying life) of this skill. These building blocks are described in further detail in the paragraphs that follow.

Responsibilities

We get overwhelmed when our responsibilities are not taken care of daily. Break bigger responsibilities down into daily steps. Make a list of both major and minor responsibilities and fill them into the My Routines and Schedule worksheet (below).

Ongoing structure

Routines are about structure that is ongoing, predictable, and repeating. Structure keeps us from getting stuck in symptoms and is the foundation for building a satisfying life. Use the My Routines and Schedule worksheet (below) to structure your days, and be sure to follow it.

Use of skills

Remember that you need to learn and practice all of your skills as a part of your routine, just like someone in school or college does daily homework. Include reminders for the skills you specifically want to practice on a given day. Also remember that other skills might be needed to follow your routine, such as Opposite to Emotion.

Traditions

Traditions give meaning to our lives and those of others. Part of a satisfying life is developing traditions that you and the people around you enjoy.

Many of us think of traditions as being tied to seasons and holidays, and those can be fun to establish, but traditions can also be as simple as a family bowling night, a specific dinner on a certain night, or celebrating accomplishments (yours or others') with something special. You can get back into traditions you have valued or use your imagination to create new traditions for yourself and your loved ones.

Interests included

Routines that do not include our personal interests are difficult to maintain. Be sure to build in what you like to do. If you are unsure what you are interested in, pick some options from the Activities List (see below) and plug them into your schedule. Remember to approach a new interest or activity with a Nonjudgmental Stance.

Novelty

Be careful not to build too much structure into your routine. Routines also need space for flexibility and novelty. Make sure you explicitly leave space to try new activities or be spontaneous. Consider scheduling a free morning, afternoon, evening, or day into your routine.

Envision a satisfying life

Routines, schedules, and structure take time to get established. Remember not to give up on building habits toward living a more satisfying life. Stay mindful of how your routine will help you with your priorities, goals, and values. Do not give up!

Everyday Care

■ *CORE CONCEPT:* Basic physical and mental self-care need to be part of a daily routine.

Basic physical and mental self-care are needed every day to establish a foundation on which to build. As we learn more skills, we might develop (or you may already have developed) more elaborate and effective self-care. For most of us, we need to revisit the basics at least occasionally, and all of us need to have these basics be part of our daily routine.

Refer to the lists that follow and then describe the other tasks you would like to attend to each day.

Routine physical self-care

Brush teeth

Wash face and/or bathe or shower

Put on clean clothes

Take medications, vitamins, etc.

Eat a balanced meal at least three times a day plus healthy snacks

Move around, stretch, and exercise

Have a bedtime routine

Describe other routine **physical** self-care tasks you need daily:

_____

Routine mental self-care

Mindfulness (breathing or relaxation)

Identify positives and gratefulness

Encourage yourself

Plan positive activities

Connect with family, friends, and support

Nurture your spirit

Describe other routine **mental** self-care tasks you need daily:

_____

Describe how your life will be different when you effectively practice physical and mental self-care:

_____

Building a Satisfying Life 1: Activities List

CORE CONCEPT: Use this list to plan activities in your schedule.

We need to have pleasant activities scheduled every day. Below is a list of pleasant activities, many of which are free. Add pleasant activities that you enjoy to the list. Make sure to schedule at least three pleasant activities each day. Also, remember to use mindfulness skills with each experience.

1. Dress up or down.
2. Play board games.
3. Have a snack mindfully.
4. Appreciate a favorite actor or act yourself.
5. Read a text of your religion.
6. Advocate for the National Alliance on Mental Illness, a political cause, or the environment.
7. Stargaze, find constellations, or wonder about the universe.
8. Read about animals or visit the zoo.
9. Appreciate the arts or create your own artworks.
10. Play badminton.
11. Redecorate or rearrange your house.
12. Join a group.
13. Have a conversation with a friend or a stranger.
14. Watch or play baseball or softball.
15. Make crafts.
16. Watch, read about, or fly an airplane or build a model.
17. Watch or play basketball or play HORSE.
18. Bathe or shower mindfully.
19. Relax at (or imagine being at) the beach; look for shells or clean the beach up.
20. Do beadwork.
21. Beatbox, rap, or sing.
22. Ring a bell.
23. Breathe mindfully.
24. Write a short story.
25. Bike.
26. Feed or watch birds.
27. Blog or visit blogs.
28. Boat.
29. Bowl.
30. Bet a small amount of money.
31. Start a fantasy football league (or join one).
32. Play checkers.
33. Help the disabled.
34. Contribute at a food pantry.
35. Bake a cake and decorate it.
36. Go geocaching.
37. Do calligraphy.
38. Camp.

39. Make candles or ice candles.

40. Canoe.

41. Have a picnic in your home.

42. Read about cars or go for a drive.

43. Do some cheerleading.

44. Take a nap.

45. Watch one TV show mindfully.

46. Window-shop (without spending).

47. Play chess.

48. Go to a place of worship or engage in associated activities.

49. Watch clouds.

50. Make a sand castle.

51. Collect coins.

52. Go to an antique shop to browse.

53. Collect artwork.

54. Collect vinyl or CDs or look at and listen to old ones.

55. Compose music or lyrics.

56. Look at architecture in magazines or around town.

57. Enjoy perfume or cologne.

58. Do computer activities.

59. Cook.

60. Crochet.

61. Cross-stitch.

62. Do a crossword puzzle.

63. Dance anywhere.

64. Play darts (not lawn darts).

65. Look at your collectibles.

66. Bowl with friends or in a league.

67. Daydream.

68. Juggle.

69. Play dominoes or set them up to let them fall.

70. Draw.

71. Eat out or fix a special meal at home.

72. Take a community education course or educate yourself on a new topic.

73. Tinker with electronics.

74. Do embroidery.

75. Entertain others.

76. Exercise: aerobics, weights, yoga.

77. Go fishing.

78. Watch or play football.

79. Take a hot or cool shower.

80. Tell jokes and laugh.

81. Go four-wheeling.

82. Paint a wall.

83. Enjoy or maintain an aquarium.

84. Play Frisbee or disc golf.

85. Mend clothes.

86. Have a spirited debate (without needing to be right).

87. Join a club.

88. Play games.

89. Garden.

90. Swim.

91. Keep a dream journal.

92. Hug a friend or family member.

93. Visit garage sales.

94. Be intimate with a loved one.

95. Be a mentor.

96. Build a bird house.

97. Do genealogy.

98. Walk your (or a neighbor's) dog.

99. Visit an art museum.

100. Go to the movies or watch a favorite movie.

101. Golf.

102. Practice putting.

103. Give yourself a facial.

104. Paint a picture or finger-paint.

105. Watch funny YouTube videos (or post one).

106. Find an activity listed more than once on this list.

107. Go go-kart racing.

108. Play Texas Hold'em.

109. Volunteer at an animal protection organization.

110. Write a letter to an editor.

111. Light a candle and enjoy the smell or the flame.

112. Play video games.

113. Scrapbook.

114. Become a pen pal.

115. Support any cause.

116. Play guitar.

117. Write a handwritten letter.

118. Hike.

119. Do home repair.

120. Breathe in fresh air.

121. Build a home theater system.

122. Record your favorite shows and watch them back to back.

123. Air drum or air guitar to a cool song.

124. Ride a horse.

125. Write a thank-you letter.

126. Hunt.

127. Surf the internet.

128. Fix a bike.

129. Make jewelry.

130. Browse your favorite store.

131. Put together a jigsaw puzzle.

132. Build a fort with your kids.

133. Journal.

134. Juggle.

135. Kayak.

136. See life like a young child.

137. Say a prayer.

138. Build or fly kites.

139. Knit.

140. Tie knots.

141. Sing a silly song.

142. Pick flowers.

143. Learn anything new.

144. Learn a foreign language.

145. Practice telling a joke.

146. Learn an instrument.

147. Listen to music.

148. Macramé.

149. Color with kids (or without).

150. Smile at someone.

151. Be affectionate.

152. Do a magic trick.

153. Meditate.

154. Use a metal detector.

155. Teach a child something.

156. Build models.

157. Ride or look at motorcycles.

158. Play with children.

159. Go mountain biking.

160. Work with a team.

161. Plant an herb garden.

162. Go to a community center.

163. Grow a Chia pet.

164. Climb a mountain.

165. Make a root beer float.

166. Lie in the grass.

167. Scrapbook.

168. Practice a musical instrument.

169. Make an item of clothing.

170. Read reviews on a topic of interest.

171 Do origami.

172. Play Trivial Pursuit or any trivia game.

173. Clean out a closet and donate unneeded items.

174. Plan a movie marathon.

175. Look at StumbleUpon.com.

176. Join a chat room.

177. Play paintball.

178. Go to a water park.

179. Pass on something thoughtful found on the internet.

180. Go to a video arcade.

181. Indulge in a guilty pleasure.

182. Email friends and family.

183. Join a drum circle.

184. Rollerblade.

185. Swing at a playground.

186. Go to the mall to walk or browse (without spending).

187. Water your plants.

188. Make a collage.

189. Hang with a friend.

190. Listen to music and read the lyrics.

191. Try a new recipe.

192. Paint your nails.

193. Sit by any body of water.

194. Go to the library.

195. Organize a neighborhood garden.

196. Groom a pet.

197. Watch a sunrise or sunset.

200. Go to a coffee shop.

198. Take a walk.

199. Go to a health club or YMCA.

List the activities you like (or have liked) to do:

_____

_____

_____

Circle at least 10 new activities from the list that you are willing to try.

Describe how your life will be different when you schedule and involve yourself in activities:

_____

_____

_____

Building a Satisfying Life 2: My Routines and Schedule

CORE CONCEPT: Develop your routines and daily schedule.

Get a calendar or an appointment book and commit to a routine by filling out a weekly schedule. Begin by scheduling regular wake and sleep times and fill in the hours in between starting with your non-negotiable appointments and obligations. Then, fill in times for self-care and positive activities.

Use ROUTINE, the Everyday Care section (above), and the Activities List (above) to outline the days in a typical week for you. Also, consult the Small Routines worksheet (below) for other ideas.

Follow your schedule and fine-tune it weekly based on what works and what needs change. Remember that mindfully following a balanced and predictable routine will be a huge step toward building a satisfying life.

Day of The Week: _____

Time	Activity

Building a Satisfying Life 3: Small Routines

CORE CONCEPT: Develop small routines that reap big benefits.

Start to develop small routines in life and be consistent with what works. Note the examples, but be sure to individualize your routines. Be sure you make time for these small routines in your daily schedule above. Also remember to practice mindfulness with your routines.

Describe your morning routine (e.g., get up, take medications, use bathroom, make tea, eat breakfast, shower/bathe, journal, meditate/relax, prepare to leave or transition to next routine):

_____

Describe your work (or school, volunteering, etc.) routine (e.g., arrive, get organized, listen to voicemail and check emails, check in with coworkers, set goals for the day, get started):

_____

Describe your evening routine (e.g., check mail and complete tasks, make dinner and eat, clean up kitchen, socialize, read, watch TV, relax):

_____

Describe your bedtime routine (e.g., brush teeth, wash face, put on pajamas, lay out clothes for tomorrow, write down positives and gratefulness and goals for tomorrow, practice mindfulness and relaxation):

_____

Describe other small routines (e.g., leisure, relaxation) that are important to you:

_____

Describe how your life will be different when you effectively and mindfully follow routines and schedules:

_____

Module 10

Social Media

Introduction to Social Media

■ *CORE CONCEPT:* Be mindful and effective when using technology-based communication and social media.

Technology-based communication and social media have become an inevitable and almost unavoidable part of interpersonal communication and relationships. Emails, texting, Facebook, Twitter, and the myriad other formats in which people communicate are here to stay and will likely only grow in popularity. Like any tool, these forms of communication are neither good nor bad in and of themselves, but their use (or misuse) has the ability to either add to or detract from relationships.

Communication is much more complicated than words spoken or typed. Researchers note that up to 70% of communication is nonverbal, including facial expressions, gestures, and other body language. Further, spoken words communicate differently based on verbal variations in rate, tone, pitch, volume, and speaking styles. Because so much of what is communicated goes beyond mere words, users of technology-based communication and social media need to consider what might be lost in those formats as opposed to if the same communication happened in person. The takeaways are to proceed with and to interpret others' communications with caution.

This module sets forth guidelines to promote responsible behaviors for using communication technology and social media so they can be an asset and not a liability to having satisfying relationships.

MEDIA (ME)

■ *CORE CONCEPT:* Communicate responsibly and with care when using technology.

General concepts and guidelines will go a long way toward the effective use of tech communication and social media.

Use the acronym MEDIA (**M**oments can live on, **E**veryone could possibly see the communication, **D**o not send or post in Emotion Mind, **I**magine possible outcomes, **A**dd to communications and the social network) to remember the building blocks of this skill. These building blocks are described in further detail in the paragraphs that follow.

<u>M</u>oments can live on

With face-to-face communication, thoughtless words decay into silence and are gone. Although verbal words can be remembered and have lasting effects, they cannot be passed on and on to an increasingly larger audience. Further, once a communication is sent, it is likely to be saved somewhere, so it may be found again. Think about the lasting effects before sending or posting comments or pictures.

<u>E</u>veryone could possibly see the communication

Tech-based communications should never be assumed to be private, and some are designed to be public. Do you want your all your friends, neighbors, and/or coworkers to receive the communication? How about your parents, teachers, employer, or religious leader? Consider that people whom you would not want to receive your communication very well might.

<u>D</u>on't send or post in Emotion Mind (or under the influence of substances)

Intense emotions and substances distort communication, and what seems like a good idea now may not be when you are in Wise Mind. If you feel intense, disinhibited, or impulsive, the communication needs to wait.

<u>I</u>magine possible outcomes

Thoughts and opinions do not need to be broadcast, especially on impulse. Could someone be hurt? Might you be embarrassed later or suffer a consequence? Think through your communications and actions.

<u>A</u>dd to communications and the social network

Tech-based communications and social media can be fun, informative, thought-provoking, and supportive and can build community. Be a steward for the best possibilities for these evolving ways to connect and communicate. Ask yourself:

- Is my communication respectful and thoughtful, and does it add to a dialogue?
- Does it represent my values?

- Does it stick to facts and what I know and can prove?

- Am I building relationships and community?

Other Suggestions

In addition to following the MEDIA acronym, consider the following suggestions:

- Do not share others' personal information or pictures (especially if they are unflattering or too personal or intimate) without consent. We all have different boundaries, and other people may not want their information to be public. When in doubt, err on the safe side or obtain permission from the other person(s).

- Similarly, be aware of confidentiality concerns related to connecting online with people you know through treatment services.

- Share major announcements face to face or by telephone first. Life events such as engagements, pregnancies or the birth of a child, job promotions, and the such should be shared with the most important people in your life before being put in a public forum.

- Be careful not to overshare, vent, or communicate in other ways that might be regretted later. Consider how your communications might be (mis)interpreted. Read what you have written out loud (and maybe wait) before sending.

- Many social media outlets such as Facebook have guidelines for respectful use, and specific communities of users have established their own social norms for engaging in those communities. Spend some time on the internet and read up on the responsible use of these platforms.

Unfortunately, some people will not adhere to respectful behavior and will use tech-based communication and social media as an opportunity to hurt people from a distance. If you are or have been the target of hurtful or untrue statements from others or otherwise bullied over social media, the embarrassment, humiliation, anger, and other painful emotions that you feel are real, and the bullying can have serious impacts on your emotional health and functioning at home, with other people, at school or work, and in other areas. You may also feel extremely exposed and all alone.

Fortunately, you are not alone. Seek the support and guidance of friends, family, and/or your therapist or another professional if you are the target of harassment or bullying. Further, some of these issues may warrant the involvement of your school, employer, and even the police. Do not respond to or forward the statements, but instead keep a record and seek the advice of others. More information can be found at www.stopbullying.gov. Although this site is especially oriented toward young people, the information this and similar sites have on bullying and cyber-bullying applies to all ages.

One final, important note. When you are with other people or doing any other behavior (e.g., eating, walking, attending an event), consider putting down your mobile device to be One-Mindful and present with people and/or activities. Do not let tech-based communication, social media, or other online use of your mobile device or computer detract from opportunities to engage, become a substitute for face-to-face communication, or become a means of avoiding relationships or otherwise being in the moment.

Therapist and Program Resources

Teaching DBT Skills: Methods and Styles

Many therapists have practical questions in regard to teaching DBT skills. These questions concern what service format to use for skills training, what to include in a skills curriculum, how long it takes to go through the curriculum, and when clients can join a skills group. Therapists also have stylistic questions in regard to teaching the skills. This section is not intended to answer every question that may come up in your program or practice, but it will get you headed in the right direction.

Formats and curriculums

DBT skills can be taught in individual sessions, in group formats, or both. That said, therapists most often think about teaching skills in a group format because that is how it is done in standard DBT and many other DBT programs. Further, it tends to be efficient to teach skills to groups of people, and clients who have significant treatment needs usually benefit from having dedicated skills training time (i.e., there is not usually time to teach skills to high-need clients in individual therapy only).

In standard DBT the skills group meets once a week for 2.5 hours. Other DBT programs have skills groups that vary in frequency and length. Most often skills groups tend to be psychoeducational without a group therapy process, although some programs conducted in a group service delivery also include a DBT group therapy process in addition to skills training time. This process time provides an opportunity for validation and problem-solving using the skills. Most skills groups will also allot some time to check in on skills practice and homework.

The most effective way to do a DBT skills group—be it skills group only, skills group plus individual therapy, skills group in a standard DBT format, skills group plus DBT group therapy, or skills group combined with other treatment services—will depend on your setting and the needs of your clients. The same can be said in regard to how often your skills group meets, for how long, and for what length of time. A more complete discussion of treatment structure and options can be found in Pederson (2015).

Lower-intensity clients may not need a skills group, and they can be taught skills using bibliotherapy or by taking 5 to 10 minutes of each session to teach skills. Of course, individual therapists also teach skills on the fly and in the moment to clients as needed, even if their clients are also in a skills group.

Occasionally high-intensity clients will be taught skills in individual sessions because they have issues that make attending a skills group too difficult, such as having a learning disability, a traumatic brain injury, or a clinical disorder that will not mix with the regular client population. In these cases skills training can be integrated into every session or one-to-one skills training sessions can alternate with regular therapy sessions.

Therapists also often wonder what order the skills modules should be taught in and whether skills need to be taught in a particular sequence. They also wonder how much time should be dedicated to each skill or module. The modules in this book and the skills in the modules are laid out in a suggested order. Dialectics come first, followed by the four original DBT modules: mindfulness, distress tolerance, emotion regulation, and interpersonal effectiveness. However, many skills curriculums often have a brief review of mindfulness between the other modules, and a common order may be:

- Dialectics

- Mindfulness

- Distress tolerance

- Mindfulness review

- Emotion regulation

- Mindfulness review

- Interpersonal effectiveness

- Mindfulness review

- (Repeat)

If you follow this curriculum, you can expect to teach these modules and their component skills within the range of 30 to 40 hours. This estimate assumes that, in addition to lecture, the members of the skills group have time for discussion and experiential practice. To get an estimate of how many sessions it will take to cover these modules and skills in your skills group or program, simply divide both 30 and 40 by the number of hours dedicated to skills training each session. You can then calculate how many weeks it will take by accounting for the number of skills training sessions you hold each week. With the rough parameters you establish, you can then go through the component skills from each module and create a schedule.

If you run a closed skills group (i.e., there is a defined end to it; for example, you have 12-week-long skills program), you have to stick closely to your schedule. However, if you run an open skills group (i.e., members come and go and there is no defined end to the group), you have more flexibility as the curriculum continues to roll around.

With experience you will find your teaching "groove," and the topics and timing will fall into place. Via teaching from several DBT manuals for many years, both authors found an individualized "flow" to presenting the skills that did not always follow the suggested order of skills. Dialectically, you should approach skills teaching with a plan that takes into account the needs and energy of the group; sometimes you may go through a skill quickly or simply review it, and at other times you may spend a long time on a skill if it is particularly interesting or relevant to the needs of the individual or group. Further, you may sometimes choose to insert a skill from another module if it helps clients make connections, you may revisit a skill spontaneously if it is needed, or you may even bring in a completely novel skill from another source.

Remember that any suggested curriculum is just that, a suggestion. What you teach and how you teach has to work in your setting for your clients. Regardless of what skills you teach, the takeaway is balancing a structured, planned, and predictable curriculum with sufficient flexibility.

Of course, the time parameters of the schedule above work well if you do not add in extra modules or skills. However, it stands to reason that anything you add in will take some extra time to teach, assuming that you do not cut out other content. If you use the supplemental modules and skills in this book, simply budget extra time for these additions to the curriculum. There is no established order for supplemental modules and/or skills, so they can be taught in any order, interwoven into the four main modules as needed, assigned via bibliotherapy, or left out completely.

In some settings (e.g., a short-term hospital setting), there will not be time to teach all of the skills, even from the four original modules, so certain skills will have to be prioritized and others will be left out. In these cases therapists can adapt the order and pick and choose modules and skills based on programmatic and client needs. Often hospital settings focus more on the distress tolerance skills and on having patients create a skills plan prior to discharge.

In regard to when clients can join a skills group, many programs wait for the start of a module (e.g., mindfulness) before new clients are allowed to join the group. We disagree with this guideline and believe it is not necessary. Clients will pick up the skills eventually, and we believe it is more important to start clients who need therapy as soon as possible than to wait for an arbitrary time.

Last, if you are an individual therapist who has a different theoretical orientation and you have no designs to become a DBT therapist or to establish a group or program, then you can simply use this book as a resource to pick and choose skills for clients as needed. In individual therapy, skills most relevant to current difficulties can be prioritized over following a curriculum.

Teaching styles

While therapists may be acquainted with the following teaching methods, it is also true that we often default to the style that is familiar and/or comfortable to us. In DBT, we ask clients to practice difficult and unfamiliar skills. Our professional growth, which also benefits clients, comes from our practice of various teaching styles. To become a well-rounded skills trainer, practice the styles that feel unfamiliar and awkward until you gain mastery in them.

Interactive lecture

Present the topics and expand on the written explanations and examples. Generate discussion and expect your clients to participate and share questions, thoughts, and examples. Leave space for clients to think and jump in rather than generating all of the material or dominating the lecture. Do not instantly jump in to fill silence.

Use Socratic questioning

Socratic questioning is a method that draws clients to answer their own questions. You can question assumptions, views, reasons, consequences, and the questions themselves. This process helps clients to think critically and own the resulting conclusions. Socratic questioning is dialectical in nature, in that the questions move clients to conclusions that may exist at a different "place" on the dialectic from where they started.

Group presentation and discussion

In group therapy, assign skills or sections of skills to each client to teach the others. Assigning skills to dyads or triads also works well. Not only do clients integrate the skills through teaching but this approach also challenges clients to practice distress tolerance and interpersonal effectiveness, among other skills.

In-group experiential learning

Experiential learning has clients practice skills in session with support, feedback, and coaching. Experiential learning also exposes clients to barriers so problem-solving can occur.

Be creative with your ideas to make the skills real and behaviorally based for clients. Using arts and crafts can be a great way to learn and practice skills. Most clients greatly enjoy experiential teaching, and often it is the most impactful way of connecting clients to skills.

Beginning and ending sessions with mindfulness is a wonderful example of experiential learning.

Role-plays

Role-plays are a specialized type of experiential learning that can be used to work on interpersonal skills. Clients (and therapists) often need to use Nonjudgmental Stance to engage in role-plays.

Frequent role-plays become part of the norm in therapy. Make role-plays relevant but have fun with them, too.

Modeling

Role-plays are effective partly due to modeling. Remember that nearly every interaction is an opportunity to model skills. Also point out when peers or others are modeling a skill and be sure to name it. Modeling is a powerful form of learning, as captured in the idiom "monkey see, monkey do." Be sure to reinforce desired new behaviors when clients imitate them.

Mix in audio, video, and other media

Make skills relevant by connecting to songs, movies, and other media that hold your clients' attention and interest. These connections can explain concepts in unexpected ways. Be on the lookout for opportunities to use these stimulating tools to position skills. Adolescents especially tend to enjoy this approach to teaching skills.

Behavioral homework

Homework focused on practicing skills is essential to effective outcomes. Orient clients to the idea of homework and explain why it is important. (Or, better yet, use Socratic questioning to get to that conclusion!)

Clients become accustomed to homework when it is assigned each session and is part of the therapy milieu. Be sure to follow up on assignments and treat resistance and lack of follow-through as therapy-interfering behavior. Homework should be individualized to each client's unique problems and opportunities and relevant to his or her treatment goals and objectives.

Remember that each style has a purpose, and mixing up styles keeps skills training stimulating for clients, and you!

Developing Skills in the Face of Barriers

The following ideas will fine-tune skills training while addressing common barriers. Use these ideas to keep skills training on track and effective.

Make learning skills client driven

Barriers develop when clients do not connect skills teaching to their personal priorities, goals, and values. Therapists must explicitly help clients to see how each skill relates to the client's Life Vision and what the client wants from therapy.

When clients can connect to the "why," they can overcome barriers to figure out the "how" with skills. Continually show clients the "carrot" that matters to and motivates them.

Identify stuck points

Use behavior and solution analysis to figure out where clients get stuck and then use Socratic questioning to have clients explore how various skills might make a difference.

Recognize what worked

Clients (and therapists) often think about skills in terms of success and failure. Dialectically, something about a skill has probably been effective on some level. Therapists must recognize the effective part of efforts to shape and reinforce behaviors. When clients receive reinforcement for the part of a behavior that was effective, they are more likely to be open to coaching and correcting the ineffective part(s).

Prescribe the missing skill

Clients need to "use skills to use skills." Often mindfulness is the missing skill. Use your knowledge of the connections between skills to direct clients when they cannot find the missing skill or skills themselves. This approach works well when balanced with the previous two approaches.

Catch and label skill use

Therapists can get caught addressing deficits rather than building strengths. Instead of or in addition to attending to the problem, it is frequently more effective to be ready to reinforce the behaviors (skills) that exist in the absence of problem behaviors.

Clients rarely emit problem behaviors continuously, and all clients continuously engage in skills without awareness (theirs and the therapist's). Actively use Observe and Describe to recognize skills in action and label them so they can be used with intention next time.

"Coach up" and cheerlead clients' efforts

Great coaches can inspire their players to give maximal effort, which can lead them to perform seemingly beyond their abilities. This phenomenon highlights the power of belief and expectancy, which research shows is an essential part of effective treatment. Be a great coach. Be a great cheerleader.

Reinforce efforts and accomplishments

Clients will increase their efforts and practice more skills when reinforced. Continuous reinforcement establishes new behaviors, and intermittent reinforcement maintains them. Once a client starts to perform a skill, the behavior must be maintained or it will diminish and may be unintentionally extinguished.

Therapists can overlook opportunities to reinforce, especially when they get too focused on deficits. When we extinguish old behaviors, we need to reinforce replacement skills. Make sure clients' support systems and environments reinforce skill use (and avoid punishing it) too.

Remember that clients engage in many more positive than negative behaviors. Noticing and reinforcing positive behaviors that happen in the absence of problem behaviors is essential when working to help clients change.

Other Skills Training Tips

Here are some additional tips for therapists conducting a skills group. These tips were compiled from some of the most frequent questions that come up in DBT training.

- Compile all of the handouts and worksheets you intend to use in your skills group into a program binder for clients. What you include might come from one manual (such as this one) or can be compiled from many manuals and sources. Also include your orientation information, clinical policies and program rules, practical information (e.g., contact information for the therapists and clinic, when the clinic may close due to weather, the FAQs), and extras of frequently used forms such as diary cards and behavior and solution analyses. Expect clients to bring their binders to session, and keep a couple of extras on hand for clients who forget their binders.

- Revise the program binder at least annually, adding new content and deleting content that has been less impactful.

- Customize the manual to your population. Most manuals are written generally because publishers want to sell to a large market. Edit and change manuals to make them more user friendly for your clients. For example, change pronouns or add examples that are typical of your clients' lives. Alternatively, author your own manual and/or worksheets for your program. While the words in published manuals are copyrighted, the modules and skills themselves do not enjoy copyright protection since they are part of a scientific theory and method. Hence, you are free to write your own manual if one on the market does not suit your needs.

- Use a whiteboard to write down key words and make diagrams as you explain skills. Using a whiteboard especially helps visual learners. A whiteboard can be used in individual sessions, too, and sometimes during clients' processing and problem-solving time.

- Design posters featuring the skills to hang on the walls, or have clients create the posters using poster board and art supplies. Clients who create their own posters take more ownership of their program space and of using the skills.

- Go beyond the material in manuals to bring authenticity to teaching skills. Bring yourself and your own ideas to skills training sessions.

- Sit in on other therapists' skills training sessions to pick up fresh ideas, and dedicate some consultation time to talking about DBT skills and teaching them. Therapists new to DBT can have difficulty with the concepts, and experienced DBT therapists can become unimaginative in their teaching. New and tenured therapists can help each other by working together.

- Finally, use clients' wisdom in skills teaching. Create space for clients to participate and educate each other (and you!). Clients can be the best inspiration for going beyond the manual to make skills training sessions extra-impactful.

Clinical Policies, Contingencies, and Related Forms

This section contains brief explanations of important policies and contingencies that bring structure to your DBT program and/or individual therapy. Commonly used client forms are included, but these materials are simply examples and are not intended to serve everybody. Many of the forms included were developed by people across several programs and settings over a period of many years. The forms were then revised again for this book. All of these are "living" documents. Thus, it is recommended that you change the forms as needed to better fit your population and setting.

Remember that structure, rules, and expectations constitute important facets of all skills groups, programs, and individual therapy. Clients need structure to thrive, and clients rise to expectations or fall in the absence of them. Therapists similarly need the direction that comes from these and similar policies to keep their programs and their clients on track. Consult Pederson (2015) and other DBT authors for more clinical information related to applying these concepts.

Last, this section includes basic information on monitoring clinical outcomes. The information provided is not intended to be comprehensive, but it should get you thinking about how you can evaluate clinical outcomes in your setting with your clients. Explore options and commit to the collection of outcome data so you can monitor and adjust therapy consistent with evidence-based practice. Consult Pederson (2015) for a complete discussion of using clinical outcome data in your practice.

Commitment agreements

DBT can be a long-term commitment for clients. Consider stages of change (Prochaska et al., 2007) when you discuss commitment with clients and try to meet clients at their stage. Stages of change can swing rapidly based on unforeseen influences within and outside therapy. Premature judgments and ruling out clients struggling to attach to therapy can result in lost opportunities. "Perfect" candidates for therapy are the stuff of random clinical trials and not real life.

To obtain commitment, it is important to orient clients to the expected course of treatment required to achieve significant clinical change and improvement in functioning. Outcome data and your clinical expertise can assist in determining the course of treatment for individual clients.

Many DBT programs require a significant time commitment—up to a year—with the opportunity to recommit to further therapy following the initial contract. Even when a long-term commitment is indicated, many clients have reservations about investing in something new and uncertain for the long haul. (Can you blame them?)

A middle-ground option is a good faith commitment to try the DBT program or individual therapy for a shorter length of time or a number of sessions that will provide a realistic evaluation from both sides. That level of commitment may vary by client and is based on the expected time required to connect and experience benefits; if applicable, try to balance this commitment with the expectations and structure of your program. The most important piece is that you and the client agree on a timeline, expectations, and how the mutual investment will be evaluated.

Commitment agreements, whether standard to your program or individualized, need to be discussed up front and preferably put in writing. Remember that commitment has to do with length of time or number of sessions, *not* with changing program or individual rules and expectations or with taking an "à la carte" approach to an otherwise comprehensive program.

See Pederson (2015) for a discussion of orienting clients to DBT and the use of commitment strategies.

Commitment Agreement Form

The following information has been explained to me and I have been given an opportunity to ask questions for clarification:

- My diagnosis

- My expected course of treatment

- My individualized treatment plan with initial goals

- The program and/or individual rules and expectations

- The program and/or individual attendance policy

- The cost and my financial responsibility (e.g., copays, deductibles, payment agreements)

- Other important information.

I agree to make a good faith investment in the program and/or individual therapy with my willing participation for a period of _____ or _____ sessions. As a part of this commitment, I agree to follow the program and/or individual rules, expectations, and the attendance policy. At the conclusion of this commitment period, my therapist(s) and I will evaluate the course of treatment and decide among the following options:

- Continue the program and/or individual therapy with a new commitment agreement

- Make an appropriate referral

- Other arrangements.

Signed by client: _____ Date: _____

Signed by therapist: _____ Date: _____

Original to client; copy to chart

Skills group, program, and individual therapy rules and expectations

DBT skills groups, programs, and individual therapy require rules and expectations. Rules and expectations keep clients safe and let them know what is expected. Think about times when you have been in unclear situations (e.g., when you had a laissez-faire boss or a teacher without a grading system or syllabus) and how uncomfortable, anxiety provoking, or frustrating those times were. Now think about clients who have dysregulated emotions and chaotic behaviors. These clients desperately need structure and containment to learn new skills and thrive. Not being clear about what is expected is unfair and puts clients in unneeded distress.

Sometimes we have clients who resist rules, expectations, and structure, and our approach can cause behavioral outbursts that buck the system. These reactions can tempt us to abandon ship and allow for greater flexibility and a lack of accountability. As a rule, if you abandon your structure or change your rules for a client, you are participating in therapy-interfering behavior with the client. Clients do not always need to agree to rules and expectations, but they need to respect them. Sticking to rules and expectations is difficult for both clients and therapists, but it models what happens in real life. If you have difficulties holding clients accountable, seek consultation.

It is compassionate to have rules and expectations and to stick to them, even if the consequence is discharging a client from the program. Be clear and consistent; say what you do and do what you say. To do otherwise recreates the type of environment that may have created the client's problems in the first place.

Rules and expectations need to be discussed and acknowledged up front during orientation as clients need to know the rules and expectations to be accountable to them. Consider the use of a behavior contract for clients who require additional accountability.

When presenting rules and expectations, have clients tell you the rationale for each one instead of explaining it to them. This type of presentation lets clients "own" the rules and expectations. Be sure to clearly post rules and expectations in program areas.

Remember, the forms that follow are intended to be examples. Revise as needed.

DBT Skills Group and Program Expectations

- Members are expected to attend all scheduled sessions. All absences must be planned with therapists prior to the absence by phone or in person. Documentation of absences may be requested. Three consecutive absences without approval will be grounds for discharge.

- Members are accountable to the attendance policies and may be discharged for violation of these policies.

- Members are to maintain confidentiality. Group issues are not to be discussed outside group or during break. Violating confidentiality may be grounds for discharge.

- Members are expected to participate in skills teaching, to complete assignments, to present diary cards, and to give validation, support, and suggestions to peers.

- Members are expected to take time to problem-solve and practice skills whenever significant distress is reported.

- Members are expected to complete homework and change analyses as assigned.

- Members are not to engage in suicide ideation (SI), self-injurious behavior (SIB), or therapy-interfering behavior (TIB) when on premises. These behaviors on premises will be grounds for immediate discharge.

- Members are not to come to group under the influence of drugs or alcohol.

- Members' feedback and behavior are expected to be respectful at all times. Anyone giving disrespectful feedback or engaging in disrespectful behavior may be asked to leave.

- Members are encouraged to form friendships with others in group. However, members are expected to be clear about their personal boundaries and be respectful of others' personal boundaries.

- Romantic or intimate relationships are not allowed between group members.

- Friendships with others in group may not be private and must remain skillful.

- Members are not allowed to use alcohol or drugs or to engage in unskillful behaviors together.

- Members are not allowed to share medications.

- Members are not allowed to keep secrets regarding other group members' harmful behaviors.

- Members are encouraged to use other members for support outside of group. However, members are not obligated to be available to others outside of group. Again, members are expected to be clear about their boundaries and respectful of others' boundaries.

- Members may not call other members after they have been engaged in SI, SIB, or TIB.

- Members are expected to attend all scheduled professional appointments and comply with prescribed medications.

- Members are expected to honor payment agreements for copays, deductibles, and uncovered services.

- Violation of group rules may result in consequences including homework, behavior and solution analysis, suspension, and/or discharge.

- Clients are expected to follow other rules and policies.

DBT Individual Therapy Expectations

- Clients must attend all scheduled sessions. Cancelled or missed sessions will be treated as TIB unless negotiated up front and cleared by the therapist.

- Clients in the DBT program who miss sessions will be accountable to the attendance policy of the program (i.e., 90% attendance of all DBT sessions).

- Clients not in the DBT program will be accountable for attending 90% of all scheduled individual sessions. Two no-shows (not coming to session and not calling ahead to cancel) to individual therapy will result in discharge.

- Clients are expected to be on time for sessions.

- Clients are expected to complete homework and change analysis as assigned.

- Clients are expected to participate in safety assessments and safety planning. Being unable to commit to safety or being unwilling to engage in safety commitments and planning will result in hospitalization.

- Clients are expected to honor payment agreements for copays, deductibles, and uncovered services.

- Clients are expected to follow other rules and policies.

Attendance policy and contracts

DBT skills groups, programs, and individual therapists need to be clear about attendance policies for clients. A clear and up-front policy is an important way to instill expectations and to avoid becoming a crisis drop-in center.

Attendance is required in school, college, work, and relationships, making it a primary life skill. Have your clients practice this life skill by expecting their presence at all appointments.

The attendance policy and contracts that follow are examples of how attendance expectations can be addressed. The intention of attendance contracts is to keep clients engaged in skills training and/or therapy. Therapists need to decide what type of attendance policy and contracts work for their unique populations and settings and design their own if needed. The specific policy is less important than making clear what the policy entails, how clients are expected to be accountable, and, most importantly, how the policy will be enforced. Following an attendance policy and using contracts like the examples in this book usually results in consistent attendance and retaining clients.

Along with attendance, also expect clients to be on time (and be on time yourself). Lateness by the client (or you) is therapy-interfering behavior and needs to be addressed as such. If a client has a pattern of being significantly late (e.g., 15 minutes), consider counting future lateness toward the attendance policy (i.e., treating it in the same way as an absence). Of course, let clients know up front how you intend to address lateness and what the potential consequences may be.

DBT Skills Group and Program Attendance Policy

Consistent attendance at your DBT program is essential for it to be effective for you and other program members. Attendance, timeliness, and consistency are also important life skills.

It is expected that program members will attend appointments at or above 90% of all scheduled sessions (individual and group). Please schedule other appointments around your DBT program.

If you fall below 90% attendance, you will be put on an attendance contract and your treatment team will be contacted. The contract is for 10 sessions; you must attend 9 out of 10 of these sessions to complete and go off of the attendance contract. If you miss more than 1 of these 10 sessions, you will be put on a discharge contract and your team will be contacted again.

The discharge contract is also for 10 sessions. As with the attendance contract, you must attend 9 out of 10 of these sessions to complete and go off of the discharge contract. If you miss more than 1 of these 10 sessions, you will be discharged from the program and **cannot reapply for 3 months**.

Excused absences are at the discretion of your therapist(s) and may or may not be negotiable. Documentation may be required.

You are responsible for keeping your therapist(s) informed if you have to miss a session. Always call before the session if you will be absent. An absence without a call before the session will most likely not be excused.

Three consecutive no-shows (not coming and not calling ahead to cancel) to the program may result in discharge.

A leave of absence (LOA) may be granted in some cases at the discretion of the therapist(s) and/or the treatment team. LOAs must be planned with a clear time limit. It is your responsibility to keep your therapist(s) and team informed during an LOA. Documentation of an LOA may be required.

Signed by client: _____ Date: _____

Original to client; copy to file

Attendance Contract

My attendance to scheduled DBT sessions has dropped below 90%.

I am on this attendance contract to get my required attendance to 90% or above of scheduled sessions.

I must attend 9 out of the next 10 scheduled sessions to complete this contract.

If I miss more than 1 of the next 10 sessions, I will move to a discharge contract.

All absences on this contract will be considered unexcused unless negotiated with my therapist before the absence. Excused absences will be granted only in extreme circumstances as approved by my therapist.

Signed by client: _____ Date: _____

Signed by therapist: _____ Date: _____

Original to client; copy to file

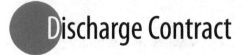

Discharge Contract

My attendance to scheduled DBT sessions has dropped below 90%, and I have not completed the assigned attendance contract.

I am on this discharge contract to get my required attendance to 90% or above of scheduled sessions.

I must attend 9 of the next 10 scheduled sessions to complete this contract.

If I miss more than 1 of the next 10 sessions, I will be discharged and given referrals to other treatment options.

All absences on this contract will be considered unexcused unless negotiated with my therapist before the absence. Excused absences will be granted only in extreme circumstances as approved by my therapist.

Signed by client: _____ Date: _____

Signed by therapist: _____ Date: _____

Original to client; copy to file

Safety plans and contracts

Identify clients with a history of suicidal ideation and/or self-injurious behavior at the initial intake assessment. All of these clients need a safety plan that is proactively created as a primary goal of therapy.

Most clients already have "safety skills," but they may not be able to label or name them. The lack of a name for such skills, along with the lack of a plan, makes it difficult for clients to use these skills consistently and effectively. Careful questioning will reveal clients' ways of staying safe and other strengths and resources to build on.

Check safety early in each session via the diary card and dedicate some time to reviewing and building on the safety plan. Rehearse safety contingencies in sessions (e.g., what skills would you use if your spouse stormed out? What if no one is home and you're scared? What skills can you use in the event of a crisis?).

Make sure clients practice the skills in their plan so they develop the competency to use them in crisis. As clients build skills, have them further expand their safety plan. A safety plan is a "living" document, both metaphorically and literally.

Mindfully and consistently reinforce safety behaviors, as clients are typically "safe" more than they are "unsafe," and create safety homework for crisis behaviors and unhealthy coping. The requirement of a behavior and solution analysis and active work on the safety plan are reasonable consequences and are also needed for clients to reach their goals.

Remember that safety is one of the few either–or issues in treatment, with clear "yes" and "no" answers required to questions about safety. An unclear safety commitment and/or lack of willingness to use the safety plan indicates that hospitalization is needed if the client is imminently suicidal.

See the following examples of safety expectations, plans, and contracts. Like most forms in this book, adapt them as needed for your clients.

Safety Expectations

Safety will be assessed each session. Identify all safety concerns on your diary card. Clients with a history of safety issues will also be asked about safety and reinforced for effective safety behaviors.

Please refer to the following safety expectations:

- All clients will accurately report safety issues on the diary card.

- All clients with current or a history of safety issues will develop a safety plan. The safety plan will be practiced, updated, and reviewed regularly.

- Clients will willingly participate in safety assessments in the time allotted. Clients unwilling to cooperate will be hospitalized.

- All safety assessments and safety planning must be completed in the allotted time and by the end of the session. Clients without a safety commitment by the end of the session will be hospitalized.

- All clients with safety issues will be asked to commit to safety. A safety commitment is a "yes" or "no" regarding willingness to use the safety plan. Clients without a clear commitment to safety who are suicidal will be hospitalized.

- Clients will be sent to hospital only by ambulance or police.

- Hospitalized clients will be sent with a change analysis to work on and a safety plan to update. These assignments will be completed during the hospital stay and/or before returning to the program/individual therapy.

Signed by client: _____ Date: _____

*Original to client; copy to file**

Safety Contract and Plan

I, _____, contract for my safety. This means that I will not act on my plan to commit suicide. I will use the skills listed below to assist with my safety and call the people in my support system as needed. I will call 911 or admit myself to hospital if unsafe and before acting on urges.

DBT skills I will use to maintain my safety:

1.

2.

3.

4.

5.

6.

7.

Team members and other people in my support system I can call for help in crisis and before acting on urges:

1.   Phone number:

2.   Phone number:

3.   Phone number:

4. Crisis resource(s):   Phone number(s):

5. Emergency: 911

Signed by client: _____ Date: _____

Signed by therapist: _____ Date: _____

Original to client; copy to file

Crisis Safety Plan

Name:

Crisis behavior:

Warning signs and triggers:

Plan to maintain safety until next session (list specific skills and behaviors under each section):

Mindfulness skills:

Interpersonal skills:

Emotion regulation skills:

Distress tolerance skills:

Skills from other modules:

Diagnoses and symptoms:

Medications:

1.   Dosage:

2.   Dosage:

3.   Dosage:

4.   Dosage:

5.   Dosage:

6.   Dosage:

Medical alerts (allergies, etc.):

Contacts (people to call for support):

Therapist: Phone number:

Psychiatrist: Phone number:

Case manager: Phone number:

Family: Phone number:

Friends: Phone number:

Other: Phone number:

If you have a plan and intent to act on your urges, call 911 or go to your nearest emergency room.

Signed by client: _____ Date: _____

Signed by therapist: _____ Date: _____

Original to client; copy to chart

Safety Contract

I, _____, contract for my safety. This means I will not act on any plan to commit suicide. I will use my skills to assist with my safety and will call my team members, crisis resources, and/or people in my support system before acting on urges. I will call 911 and/or admit myself to hospital if needed.

As a part of my safety contract, I will also attend all scheduled appointments and my DBT program.

Not attending group or other appointments as planned will be considered a violation of my willingness to commit to safety and will be treated as therapy-interfering behavior.

Signed by client: _____ Date: _____

Signed by therapist: _____ Date: _____

Original to client; copy to chart

Behavior contracts

Behavior contracts increase accountability by specifically defining problem behaviors and consequences. These contracts are useful when routine interventions for disruptive behaviors have not worked and when these behaviors have been ongoing in nature.

It is helpful to get clients' team members onboard with a behavior contract and to frame this as an effort to get clients on track and progressing in therapy. Clients may experience behavior contracts as punishment, so remember to validate the experience *and* indicate that a client's accountability to a behavior contract is in his or her best interest. Holding clients accountable for difficult behaviors shows caring and respect.

Keep in mind that clients rarely engage in problem behaviors all of the time. Behavior contracts will be as successful as therapists' efforts to continuously look for and reinforce nonproblematic behaviors. Trying to extinguish a difficult behavior without reinforcing other effective behaviors is unfair to clients and ineffective in therapy.

Below are examples of behavior contracts. One is a general behavior contract and the second is a GIVE contract for clients who struggle with respectful behaviors in program and/or in relationships.

Behavior Contract

The following behaviors have become disruptive to your therapy, your group, or the clinic:

1.

2.

3.

4.

The purpose of this behavior contract is to help you change these difficult behaviors so you can reach your treatment goals.

These behaviors will result in homework and/or behavior and solution analysis. If you engage in these behaviors, your therapist and/or group members will respectfully Observe and Describe the presence of the behaviors, and you will have an opportunity to redirect the behaviors and practice skills.

If you choose not to redirect the behaviors or practice skills, you will be asked to leave for the day and the session will be counted as an absence. The absence will count toward the attendance policy.

If you are asked to leave, you may be suspended pending a team meeting. The team meeting may involve further problem-solving or a decision to discharge you with referrals.

As part of this contract, your therapist and/or group members agree to notice and reinforce your efforts, positive behaviors, and skill use.

Signed by client: _____ Date: _____

Signed by therapist: _____ Date: _____

Original to client; copy to client

Give Contract

Due to ongoing interpersonal difficulties in group, your immediate focus in treatment will be to learn and use **GIVE** skills.

Until you can demonstrate the consistent use of GIVE, you will be expected to be **G**enuine, **I**nterested, and **V**alidating and to use an **E**asy manner with others as your primary way of relating.

During your interactions in the program, you are to focus on the validation and encouragement of others.

Disrespect of your therapist(s) and program members will be addressed and not tolerated.

You are to take responsibility for yourself and help others to see the positives in you.

If your therapist and/or program members decide that you are not following these expectations, the following will occur during the course of a session:

- You will be given a warning on the first occurrence.

- You will be assigned a behavior and solution analysis on the second occurrence. Your behavior and solution analysis must focus on your behavior, not the behavior of others, and it must be completed prior to your return to the next session. Your change analysis will be reviewed by your therapist prior to your presenting it.

- You will be asked to leave on the third occurrence. The absence will be subject to attendance policy expectations.

As part of this contract, your therapist and/or group members agree to notice and reinforce your efforts, positive behaviors, and skill use.

Signed by client: _____ Date: _____

Signed by therapist: _____ Date: _____

Original to client; copy to client

Phone coaching

The primary function of phone coaching is to help clients generalize skills to everyday life between sessions. To meet this function, coaching calls are brief, around 5 to 10 minutes, and focused on skills. As a phone coach, do not participate in "venting" calls or calls that turn into therapy sessions. To keep calls focused on skill use, it is recommended that clients fill out the phone coaching form (below) before calling. In addition to phone coaching, and perhaps as a substitute, also consider the use of the skills generalization form (below) included in this section.

Standard DBT requires individual therapists to provide phone coaching availability to clients 24 hours a day, 7 days week. In standard DBT, this availability is balanced with limits, meaning that contingencies are established that keep clients from pushing the boundaries of therapists. If clients call too much or too often, it is treated as therapy-interfering behavior. Therapists who do not observe limits with phone coaching might be practicing obtuse and unskillful limits or boundaries.

Phone coaching 24/7 is *not* proven to be a necessary component of effective DBT treatment. In fact, dialectical therapists find that there are both upsides and downsides to this level of availability. Clients who do not have therapists with 24/7 availability learn that most life problems do not have immediate support and solutions and therefore practice their distress tolerance skills. These clients learn to rely on skills and other people in their support networks and learn to access support proactively with the knowledge that there are times when phone coaching is not available. Further, therapists who choose to set limits on their availability model effective self-care and limits, and they also teach clients about individual differences with boundaries.

All therapists who provide phone coaching (whether it is 24/7 or following an adapted plan) need to establish expectations for phone coaching up front. See the following form for phone coaching expectations that can be applied across settings.

Last, clients are not allowed to use phone coaching for 24 hours after the use of self-injurious behavior (SIB) or therapy-interfering behavior (TIB) to avoid the unintentional reinforcement of those behaviors. Clients are expected to call *before* acting on urges. If clients are reliant on your phone contact to stay out of danger and stay alive, they need a higher level of care.

Phone Coaching Expectations

Phone coaching is available to help you practice skills between sessions. Please follow these expectations:

- Phone coaching is for the generalization of skills.

- I cannot use phone coaching for 24 hours after I have engaged in SIB or TIB. I am expected to call before acting on urges.

- A phone coaching worksheet must be completed before the call.

- Phone coaching will focus on skills and not be therapy oriented.

- Phone coaching will be limited to 3 to 5 minutes.

- Not respecting the limits of phone coaching will be treated as TIB.

- Phone coaching availability and limits are established and negotiated up front by therapists and clients.

My therapist's availability, limits, and rules for phone coaching:

Signed by client: _____ Date: _____

Signed by therapist: _____ Date: _____

Original to client; copy to chart

Phone Coaching Worksheet

Please complete this worksheet prior to calling for coaching.

Describe the problem or difficulty:

Describe the skills you have already used:

Describe what specific skills you need help with:

Describe what other skills or supports you can use if your therapist is not immediately available:

Specific expectations:

- The call will focus on skills and last no more than 5 minutes.

- I will be willing to be coached and practice the specific skills.

- I will be respectful of my therapist's availability and limits.

- I understand that I will be hospitalized if I am unclear about safety issues.

Signed by client: _____ Date: _____

Signed by therapist: _____ Date: _____

Original to client; copy to chart

Skills Generalization Plan

Use to supplement or replace phone coaching.

Name:

Crisis behavior:

List situational factors, feelings, thoughts, physical sensations, and behaviors typically associated with the crisis at each level of intensity.

0: No crisis

Typical situational factors:

Typical feelings:

Typical thoughts:

Typical physical sensations:

Typical behaviors:

Skills in use:

1–2: Early warning signs

Typical situational factors:

Typical feelings:

Typical thoughts:

Typical physical sensations:

Typical behaviors:

Skills to use:

3–4: Some distress

Typical situational factors:

Typical feelings:

Typical thoughts:

Typical physical sensations:

Typical behaviors:

Skills to use:

5–6: Increased distress

Typical situational factors:

Typical feelings:

Typical thoughts:

Typical physical sensations:

Typical behaviors:

Skills to use:

7–8: Intense distress

Typical situational factors:

Typical feelings:

Typical thoughts:

Typical physical sensations:

Typical behaviors:

Skills to use:

9–10: Crisis point

Typical situational factors:

Typical feelings:

Typical thoughts:

Typical physical sensations:

Typical behaviors:

Skills to use:

Diagnoses and symptoms:

Medications:

1.   Dosage:

2.   Dosage:

3.   Dosage:

4.   Dosage:

5.   Dosage:

6.   Dosage:

7.   Dosage:

Medical alerts (allergies, etc.):

Contacts (people to call for support):

Therapist: Phone number:

Psychiatrist: Phone number:

Case manager: Phone number:

Family: Phone number:

Friends: Phone number:

Other: Phone number:

In case of emergency: Call 911 or go to your nearest emergency room.

Program graduations and transitions

The reality of most programs is that clients can only be seen for a finite period of time within respective levels of care. Program graduations recognize clients who have met certain benchmarks and goals that signal the transition from your program to a lower level of care. Particular benchmarks and goals will be unique to your population and program and should be decided carefully in consultation between clients and therapists. The example given here might apply to an intensive program. In addition to these criteria, clinically significant change as measured by an outcome measure may be important to determine a transition to a lower level of care.

Not all clients graduate, and some clients will simply transition to other providers or to the community. Their hard work and accomplishments can still be recognized. Many people attend college classes, but not everyone completes a degree and graduates. Similarly, not all clients may meet your program's graduation standards, but the experience can still be valuable.

Client graduations and transitions require careful thought and planning to make sure therapeutic gains are consolidated and to minimize relapse. As with the entire course of DBT treatment, remember to sufficiently structure graduations and transitions.

When clients have progressed and are ready to move on, recognize their hard work and create a ceremony around the change in treatment or greater movement into the community. In addition to the graduation examples given here, traditional relapse prevention plans can be useful.

Graduation Criteria For An Intensive Program

- Average distress levels on diary cards at 3/10 or below for at least 3 months

- No hospitalizations for a psychological reason for at least 6 months

- No suicidal behavior for at least 6 months

- No self-injurious behavior for at least 3 months

- No therapy-interfering behavior for at least 2 months

- Completion of revised safety/crisis plan and skills generalization plan

- Completion of graduation/transition discharge plan

- Clearly identified social support

- Agreed-on transition plan to another level of care or to structure in the community.

Graduation Discharge Plan

Describe the DBT skills that help when you're doing well:

Describe the DBT skills that decrease vulnerability to intense emotions:

Describe the DBT skills that help when you are in distress:

Describe the DBT skills that help when you are in crisis:

Describe your barriers to using DBT skills and skills to address those barriers:

Describe the DBT skills that will help when you experience setbacks:

Describe how your life is different from when you started the DBT program:

Attach the following:

1. Revised routine/schedule
2. Revised safety/crisis plan
3. Revised skills generalization plan
4. Revised Life Vision
5. List of social support with phone numbers.

Original to client; copy to chart

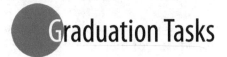

Graduation Tasks

Verify with your therapist(s) that you meet the objective criteria for graduation. Then carry out the following:

- Negotiate a graduation date with your therapist(s) and group.

- Complete the graduation discharge plan.

- Revise your routine/schedule, safety/crisis plan, skills generalization plan, and Life Vision at least 2 weeks prior to the graduation date.

- Present the items in numbers 2 and 3 to your therapist(s) and/or group at least 2 weeks prior to graduation (to incorporate feedback).

- Discuss your graduation plans with therapist(s), psychiatrist, team members, family, friends, and other supports.

- Plan a graduation ceremony with your therapist(s) and/or group.

- Proactively discuss problems and barriers to graduation with your therapist(s) and/or group.

On your graduation day:

- Have a summary of your progress to share with your group.

- Say your goodbyes to peers, staff, and others. Prepare something memorable to share with each group member. Expect to hear from your therapist(s) and each group member. Grateful acceptance of compliments and positives indicates that you are ready to graduate.

Consultation group

Consultation group is an essential element of DBT and is a best practice regardless of therapy approach or model. The function of consultation is to enhance the motivation and skill of therapists so that clients can receive the best possible therapy.

Consultation group follows DBT philosophies, which include a nonjudgmental approach to clients and to each other so that members feel supported when discussing problems, mistakes, and clinical shortcomings. The recognition that we all need support and that we are all fallible is central to effective consultation. Members are expected to be active, mindful, involved, and reciprocally humble and vulnerable.

Active, supportive, and accountable consultation groups reduce therapist burnout and build effective therapeutic responses. This approach helps us minimize harmful iatrogenic responses that complicate our clients' difficulties and cause setbacks. Some examples of harmful iatrogenic behaviors include lack of structure and accountability, extreme responses (e.g., too nurturing versus too strict), and causing or participating in boundary violations.

Most consultation groups have weekly readings and homework to stay current with DBT teachings, philosophies, and related topics. Some time spent reviewing and expanding the approach helps prevent "drift," in which therapists move too far away from the core approach.

Consultation group members generally sign an agreement and may be prescribed DBT "treatment," such as being asked to use a certain skill or asked to complete a behavior and solution analysis about a client issue.

Most consultation groups meet weekly for 60–90 minutes. If you have a DBT program, it is encouraged that you have a consultative milieu within your program and clinic in which therapists can consistently seek out support and guidance.

It could be argued that consultation group is one of the most effective aspects of DBT since it directly benefits the therapeutic alliance. If you are unable to find or create a DBT consultation group, seek consultation from someone who values your clients and their outcomes over proving that their model or approach is better than yours (and show similar respect).

For a complete discussion of consultation, see Pederson (2015).

Consultation Group Agreement

This consultation group is a collective of therapists and providers working together to benefit all of our clients. We meet weekly for 90 minutes, and members can also consult by phone and secure email between consultation groups. Participation in this consultation group follows these guidelines:

- Members agree to 90% attendance of all consultation group meetings.

- Consultation group members will maintain a Nonjudgmental Stance toward clients and each other. We understand that clients and therapists are doing the best but that they can and need to do better. To do better, we need the regular support and guidance of consultation group members.

- Consultation group members will follow basic DBT philosophies and balance validation and change strategies with each other.

- Consultation group members will be active and mindful, present on clients, and give feedback to each other. Feedback is reciprocal and involves validation, encouragement, and suggested interventions.

- Consultation group members will come prepared with cases and will have completed agreed-on readings, assignments, and homework.

- Consultation group members will promote DBT in a positive manner that respects other providers and approaches.

I agree to be accountable to myself, to the other consultation group members, and to my clients.

Signed by therapist: _____ Date: _____

Monitoring clinical outcomes

The evidence-based practice of DBT (and therapy in general) requires the collection of clinical outcomes. Clinical outcomes can be used to monitor and adjust therapy for each individual and assess the overall effectiveness of your DBT program or services. Clinical outcomes demonstrate accountability to clients and other stakeholders, and successful outcomes give clients and their therapists confidence in the services provided.

Do not be afraid of clinical outcomes. The information they give allows you to fine-tune individual goals and objectives and to make quality improvements in your programming. Data happens whether or not you track it, so make a commitment to monitor outcomes to deliver the best possible services.

Below are some suggested outcome measures, behaviors to track, and resources to get you started. Visit the suggested websites for more comprehensive information, consult with a professional with a competency in tracking outcomes for additional guidance, and investigate options that fit your population and setting. For a complete discussion of using clinical outcomes in a DBT setting, see Pederson (2015).

- Comprehensive measures such as the Symptom Checklist 90 (SCL-90), the Brief Symptom Inventory (BSI), and the Treatment Outcome Package (TOP) track symptoms and functioning across multiple domains. These measures work well for heterogeneous populations. Administer these measures at intake, every 3 months, and at discharge or as otherwise indicated based on the needs of your population. The SCL-90 and BSI are available from Pearson Assessments at www.pearsonassessments.com, and the TOP is available from Behavioral Health Laboratories at www.bhealthlabs.com.

- Targeted and brief measures such as the Beck Depression Inventory (BDI) and the Beck Anxiety Inventory (BAI) can be useful. The Beck inventories are available from Pearson Assessments at www.pearsonassessments.com.

- Another highly recommended method of tracking outcomes is the Partners in Change Outcome Management System (PCOMS), which includes the Outcome Rating Scale (ORS) and Session Rating Scale (SRS). PCOMS gives real-time feedback on clients' functioning and their view of the treatment alliance so that adjustments to the therapy can be made to better serve them. PCOMS is also listed as an evidence-based practice by the Substance Abuse and Mental Health Services Administration (SAMHSA). For more information on PCOMS visit www.heartandsoulofchange.com.

- Data on hospitalization rates before, during, and after treatment for populations known to have frequent hospitalizations (e.g., those with borderline personality disorder) can demonstrate stabilization at a lower level of care and cost savings. Record both number of hospitalizations and number of days in the hospital for each incident.

- Data on suicide attempts and self-injurious behavior rates before, during, and after treatment for populations known for these behaviors can demonstrate stabilization, safety, and (potentially) cost savings.

- Quantifiable data on functional improvements that demonstrate clinically significant change or progress can be useful. Examples include decreased rates of alcohol or drug use; decreased rates of any specifically defined behavior problem; and increases in activities of daily living, work or school attendance and performance, social contacts, or any specifically defined positive behavior. Make sure to clearly define targets to measure and to get accurate baselines for comparisons.

Master Skills List

Life Vision (LV): To focus on the life you are working toward

Wise Mind (WM): To dialectically balance emotion and reason so you can respond rather than react

Observe (OB): To just notice experience

Describe (DE): To put words on experience

Participate (P): To get into your experience

Nonjudgmental Stance (NJS): To not attach strong opinions or labels to experience

One-mindfulness (OM): To focus your attention on one thing

Effectiveness (EF): To focus on what works

Teflon Mind (TM): To not let things "stick to" you

ACCEPTS

> **Activities (AC):** To keep busy and involved
> **Contributing (CON):** To do something for others
> **Comparisons (COM):** To see that others struggle too
> **Emotions (EM):** To do something that creates other emotions
> **Push Away (PA):** To shelve your problem for later
> **Thoughts (T):** To think about something other than your distress
> **Sensations (S):** To do something physically engaging

Self-Soothe (SS): To relax yourself through the senses

Urge-Surfing (US): To ride the ebbs and flows of emotions and urges without reacting

Bridge-Burning (BB): To remove the means to act on harmful urges

IMPROVE the Moment

> **Imagery (IM):** To relax or practice skills visually in your mind
> **Meaning (ME):** To find the "why" to tolerate a difficult time
> **Prayer (PR):** To seek connection and guidance from a higher power
> **Relaxation (RE):** To calm the mind and body
> **One Thing or Step at a Time (OT):** To focus on one thing or one step when life is overwhelming
> **Vacation (V):** To take a brief break
> **Encouragement (EN):** To coach yourself with positive self-talk

Pros and Cons (P&C): To weigh the benefits and costs of a choice

Grounding Yourself (GY): To use OB and DE to come back to the here and now

Radical Acceptance (RA): To acknowledge "what is" to free yourself from suffering

Everyday Acceptance (EA): To accept daily inconveniences that occur in life

Willingness (WI): To remove barriers and do what works in a situation

SOLVED (SO): To apply a values-based system to solving a problem

PLEASED (PL): To use a system of self-care skills

Build Mastery (BM): To do things to help you feel competent and in control

Build Positive Experience (BPE): To seek out events that create positive feelings

Attend to Relationships (A2R): To connect with meaningful people in your life

Mood Momentum (MM): To perform balanced behaviors to maintain positive moods

Opposite to Emotion (O2E): To do the opposite of the action a negative emotion pulls you to perform

ROUTINE (RO): To use a system for developing routines and schedules that help build a satisfying life

TRUST (T): To use a system to learn how to develop trust in relationships

BOUNDARY (BO): To use a system for observing limits and boundaries in your relationships

FAST (F): To use a system for acting in a way that builds your self-respect

GIVE (G): To use a system for acting in a way that builds and maintains relationships

VALIDATION (V): To nonjudgmentally acknowledge someone's experience

DEAR MAN (DM): To use a system for asserting yourself, saying no, or setting a boundary

REASON (RE): To apply a system for shifting thoughts when needed

Source Citations for Modules and Skills

Life Vision: Pederson, 2012

Dialectics module: Pederson, 2012

Mindfulness module: Linehan, 1993b

Wise Mind: Linehan, 1993b

What Skills: Linehan, 1993b

How Skills: Linehan, 1993b

Teflon Mind: Teflon is a registered trademark of DuPont

Distress Tolerance module: Linehan, 1993b

ACCEPTS: Linehan, 1993b

Self-Soothe: Linehan, 1993b; expanded by Pederson, 2012

Urge-Surfing: Similar to Ride the Wave, Moonshine, 2008b

Bridge-Burning: Linehan, unpublished

IMPROVE the Moment: Linehan, 1993b

Pros and Cons: Linehan, 1993b

Grounding Yourself: Pederson, 2012

Radical Acceptance: Linehan, 1993b

Everyday Acceptance: Pederson, 2012

Willingness: Linehan, 1993b

Problem-Solving module: Pederson, 2012

SOLVED: Pederson, 2012

Emotion Regulation module: Linehan, 1993b

PLEASE/PLEASED: Linehan, 1993b; adapted by Pederson, 2012

Build Positive Experience: Linehan, 1993b

Attend to Relationships: Eboni Webb, unpublished

Mood Momentum: Pederson, 2012

Opposite to Emotion: Linehan, 1993b

Building a Satisfying Life module: Pederson, 2012

ROUTINE: Pederson, 2012

Everyday Care: Pederson, 2012

BOUNDARY: Pederson, 2012

Interpersonal Effectiveness module: Linehan, 1993b

FAST: Linehan, 1993b

GIVE: Linehan, 1993b; adapted by Pederson, 2012

VALIDATION: Pederson, 2012

DEAR MAN: Linehan, 1993b

Cognitive Modification module: Pederson, 2012

REASON: Pederson, 2012

Addictions module: Pederson, developed for this book

Social Media module: Pederson, developed for this book

Other Resources

Dialectical Behavior Therapy National Certification and Accreditation Association (DBTNCAA)

This nonprofit organization certifies DBT providers and accredits DBT programs that demonstrate the evidence-based practice of DBT. For more information visit www.dbtncaa.com.

Lane Pederson and Associates, LLC

Lane Pederson and Associates provides customized DBT training and consultation for all types of treatment settings. For more information visit www.DrLanePederson.com.

> For your convenience, purchasers can download and
> print the worksheets, handouts, forms. Go to: go.pesi.com/dbt2

Bibliography

American Psychological Association. (2005). *Report of the 2005 Presidential Task Force on evidence-based practice*. Retrieved June 9, 2016, —from https://www.apa.org/practice/resources/evidence/evidence-based-report.pdf

Clarkin, J. F., Levy, K. N., Lenzenweger, M. F., & Kernberg, O. F. (2007). Evaluating three treatments for borderline personality disorder: A multiwave study. *American Journal of Psychiatry, 164*, 922–928.

Dalai Lama. (2009). *The Dalai Lama's little book of inner peace: The essential life and teachings.* Newburyport, MA: Hampton Roads Publishing.

Dimeff, L. A., & Koerner, K. (2007). *Dialectical behavior therapy in clinical practice: Applications across disorders and settings.* New York, NY: Guildford Press.

Duncan, B. (2015). *On becoming a better therapist, 2nd ed.* Washington, DC: American Psychological Association.

Duncan, B., Miller, S., Wampold, B., & Hubble, M. (2010). *The heart and soul of change: Delivering what works in therapy, 2nd ed.* Washington, DC: American Psychological Association.

Hayes, S. C., Strosahl, K. D., & Houts, A. (Eds.). (1999). *A practical guide to acceptance and commitment therapy.* New York, NY: Springer.

Kübler-Ross, E. (2005). *On grief and grieving: Finding the meaning of grief through the five stages of loss.* New York, NY: Scribner.

Linehan, M. M. (1993a). *Cognitive-behavioral treatment of borderline personality disorder.* New York, NY: Guilford Press.

Linehan, M. M. (1993b). *Skills training manual for treating borderline personality disorder.* New York, NY: Guilford Press.

Linehan, M. M., Korslund, K. W., Harned, M. S., Gallop, R. J., Lungu, A., Neacsiu, A. D., Murray-Gregory, A. M. (2015). Dialectical behavior therapy for high suicide risk in individuals with borderline personality disorder: A randomized clinical trial and component analysis. *JAMA Psychiatry, 72*(5), 475–482.

Marra, T. (2005). *Dialectical behavior therapy in private practice: A practical and comprehensive guide.* Oakland, CA: New Harbinger Press.

McMain, S. F., Links, P. S., Gnam, W. H., Guimond, T., Cardish, R. J., Korman, L., & Streiner, D. L. (2009). A randomized trial of dialectical behavior therapy versus general psychiatric management for borderline personality disorder. *American Journal of Psychiatry, 166*(12), 1283.

Moonshine, C. (2008a). *Acquiring competency & achieving proficiency with dialectical behavior therapy: Vol. 1. —The clinician's guidebook.* Eau Claire, WI: PESI.

Moonshine, C. (2008b). *Acquiring competency & achieving proficiency with dialectical behavior therapy: Vol. 2. —The worksheets.* Eau Claire, WI: PESI.

Nelson, W. (2006). *The tao of Willie: A guide to the happiness in your heart.* New York, NY: Gotham Books.

Pederson, L. (2012). *The expanded dialectical behavior therapy skills training manual: Practical DBT for self-help, and individual and group treatment settings, 1st ed.* Eau Claire, WI: PESI.

Pederson, L. (2015). *Dialectical behavior therapy: A contemporary guide for practitioners.* Chichester, UK: Wiley-Blackwell.

Pederson, L., & Pederson, C. S. (2012). *The expanded dialectical behavior therapy skills training manual: Practical DBT for self-help, and individual and group treatment settings, 1st ed.* Eau Claire, WI: PESI.

Prochaska, J. O., Norcross, J., & DiClemente, C. (2007). *Changing for good: A revolutionary six-stage program for overcoming bad habits and moving your life positively forward.* New York, NY: Harper Collins.

Wampold, B. E. (2001). *The great psychotherapy debate: Models, methods, and findings.* Mahwah, NJ: Lawrence Erlbaum Associates.

Webb, C. A., DeRubeis, R. J., & Barber, J. P. (2010). Therapist adherence/competence and treatment outcome: A meta-analytic review. *Journal of Consulting and Clinical Psychology, 78*(2), 200–211.

Weinberg, I., Ronningstam, E., Goldblatt, M. J., Schechter, M., & Maltsberger, J. T. (2011). Common factors in empirically supported treatments of borderline personality disorder. *Current Psychiatry Reports, 13*, 60–68.